Telling Deaf Lives

Telling Deaf Lives

AGENTS OF CHANGE

Kristin Snoddon, Editor

Gallaudet University Press
Washington, DC

Gallaudet University Press
Washington, DC 20002
http://gupress.gallaudet.edu

Library of Congress Cataloging-in-Publication Data

Telling deaf lives : agents of change/edited by Kristin Snoddon.
    pages cm
    Summary: "The best of the 8th Deaf History International Conference,
members of international Deaf communities around the world relate their
own autobiographies as well as the biographies of historical Deaf
individuals in this engrossing collection"—Provided by publisher.
    Summary: "Stories told by deaf people about deaf people around
the world"—Provided by publisher.
    ISBN 978-1-56368-619-1 (paperback)—ISBN 1-56368-619-8 (paperback)—
ISBN 978-1-56368-620-7 (e-book)
    1. Deaf. 2. Storytelling. I. Snoddon, Kristin, editor.
    HV2353.T45 2014
    362.4'20922—dc23
                        2014014527

    ∞ This paper meets the requirements of ANSI/NISO Z39.48-1992
                    (Permanence of Paper).

Cover photographs (*clockwise from left*): Leonid Kamyshev,
Ekaterina (Katya) Lepeshkin, Daisy Muir, and Samuel Porter.

For Anita Small

Contents

Preface

Kristin Snoddon

My role as editor of *Telling Deaf Lives: Agents of Change* came about through my involvement with the Eighth Deaf History International Conference Program Committee in the year leading up to the conference. The papers for this meeting, which was held July 24–July 29, 2012, in Toronto, Canada, were selected on the basis of their relevance to and compatibility with the conference themes: Deaf pioneers, or individuals who have made an important historical impact; stories from the continents, or group histories; multimedia archives, or historical document preservation; storytelling pedagogy, or historical novels; history of deaf comedy; and the history of Deaf View/Image Art (De'VIA) artists. The committee also sought to ensure the inclusion of Deaf community historians from as wide a range of contexts as possible.

This book's importance derives from its attention to stories told by Deaf people about Deaf people from around the world. The individuals described are often highly accomplished and educated, and they demonstrate great leadership for their time and social position. Such figures instill us with a collective sense of pride in the Deaf community and our tenacity in the face of historical barriers to self-actualization. In celebrating this expression of individual and collective histories, the importance of art and storytelling is highlighted. It is my hope that readers of this book will gain a deeper appreciation of and insight into the lives and historic contributions of Deaf people and will be inspired to undertake further research with an eye to the preservation of Deaf community history on a global scale. As this book demonstrates, the telling of Deaf history is a multimodal, interdisciplinary enterprise that ranges from the digital creation and preservation of sign language story-telling and poetry to the visual arts of painting and photography and to the writing of letters, novels, and carefully researched biographies. This book therefore stands as an invitation, in Joseph Valente's words, "to come forward and tell your stories in whatever way you can and want to tell them."[1]

As a member of the Eighth Deaf History International Conference Program Committee and as editor, I have been privileged to work with the authors and historians whose work is featured in this book. My position as David Peikoff Chair of Deaf Studies at the University of Alberta provided me with the support I needed to carry out my work as editor.

This book is dedicated to Anita Small in recognition of her contributions to the Canadian Cultural Society of the Deaf, which hosted the Eighth Deaf History International Conference.

Note

1. Joseph Valente, "Hearing the Unheard," TEDxPSU. December 6, 2012, http://tedxtalks.ted.com/video/TEDxPSU-Dr-Joseph-Valente-Heari;search%3Atag%3A%22TEDxPSU%22 (accessed February 5, 2014).

FOREWORD

Anita Small

Telling Deaf Lives: Agents of Change is a historical text inspired by presentations at the Eighth Deaf History International Conference in July 2012 in Toronto, Canada. The Canadian Cultural Society of the Deaf hosted the conference. Members of the Deaf[1] community from around the globe were encouraged to record their own autobiographies as well as those of individuals who came before them. The conference featured three keynote presenters, twenty-one plenary sessions, workshops, poster sessions, and three documentaries for a total of twenty-seven presentations. Presenters at the conference represented twelve countries: Australia, Belgium, Canada, England, France, Germany, Japan, the Netherlands, Poland, Russia, Sweden, and the United States. For the first time, the Deaf History International Conference featured a Documentary Awards Program, sponsored by the Ontario Deaf Foundation, to encourage alternate forms of recording biographies, autobiographies, and group histories that are particularly pertinent in the Deaf community given that sign languages are best captured on film.

In this book, the real lives of Deaf people as individuals and as parts of a collective take their rightful place in history through storytelling that reaches a large audience far beyond one conference. The stories are told through a variety of methods, including autobiographies, biographies, visual art, literature (sign language poetry and historical novels), and photography. In these ways, the contributors become agents of change as they preserve Deaf people's contributions and experiences for generations to come.

The book moves from the personal telling of one's history through autobiography to sharing other individuals' histories via biographies and then to sharing collective histories and the products of those histories in terms of evolution of the arts. It concludes with instructions on how to preserve and access these stories and products of history. In this way, readers become engaged in a collective accountability to pass on this rich Deaf experience to future generations. The book is intentionally subtitled *Agents of Change* to convey the message that while the individual pioneers and collective Deaf people studied are "agents of change," so too are the readers as recipients of the knowledge of these individual and collective lives, and they become accountable as potential agents of change to do something with this new knowledge.

The twenty-eight authors included here come from eight countries: Australia, Canada, Japan, Poland, Russia, Sweden, England, and the United States. However, their essays range far beyond these eight countries. For example, Melissa Anderson and Breda Carty's article about the Cosmopolitan Correspondence Club describes a potent nineteenth-century transnational network and sharing of life stories through letter writing that crossed ten countries. This chapter invokes Joseph Murray's notion of the adeptness of the Deaf community at building transnational sharing of life stories, even in the nineteenth century.[2] Furthermore, if one examines *Telling Deaf Lives* as a whole, one finds patterns that disclose transnational themes, as historians recount their lives and those of their communities. This book is designed to highlight some of these themes, thereby connecting the global Deaf community.

As a sociolinguist and ethnographic researcher, I have focused on finding and highlighting interaction patterns as Deaf people take their rightful place in society. I served as program chair for the Eighth Deaf History International Conference in 2012 because I recognized its importance as a vehicle for the international Deaf community to record, analyze, and distribute information about the significant interactions, experiences, and contributions of Deaf people over time. A number of existing scholarly historical texts record the lives of Deaf individuals and groups within single countries, but few cover the international scene.[3] What does this unique collection of *Telling Deaf Lives* tell us and why does it progress as it does?

Autobiographies

In becoming agents of change, we must begin with ourselves. This book therefore begins with a simple and powerful chapter by Ulla-Bell Thorin. It is her firsthand account of growing up Deaf in Sweden and the process of authoring six autobiographies. She was mentored by her mother, who was a prolific author, but was also motivated by everyday occurrences and injustices that she saw in her own educational environment. In her chapter Thorin bears witness to her experiences and shares them with us. By exposing the truths from her lifetime, we are compelled to respond to the present-day educational environment for Deaf children.

This section transitions into Harry Lang's reflections on writing biographies of numerous Deaf Americans in the arts and sciences. Lang's chapter is autobiographical in the sense that it describes his own life journey in recording biographies. Lang's moment of action as a biographer was propelled by a meeting with Dr. Stephen Hawking, who said to him, "It must be difficult to be Deaf."[4] This brief conversation launched Lang on a journey to discover the roles that societal attitudes played in the education and employment of Deaf individuals in the field of science.

Together, these two chapters provide insights into the authors' motivations and worldview and the process of writing autobiographies and biographies as forms of witness to Deaf life experiences and contributions.

Biographies of Deaf Pioneers

This section focuses on individuals who made important historical contributions. It begins with Peter Jackson's chapter about the biographies of five Deaf individuals from seventeenth-century England, all of whom demonstrated unique literacy for their era. Historically, low literacy levels among Deaf individuals have been assumed to exist without due analysis of the educational system that has perpetuated this situation. Jackson's chapter is a refreshing account of high literacy levels among Deaf individuals, serving as a counterpoint to the long-held and misunderstood phenomenon of literacy or the lack thereof in the Deaf community. The chapter by Jannelle Legg includes the biography of a Deaf leader who used the Deaf press as a form of resistance in responding to a US Deaf church's loss of cherished Deaf cultural space. Interestingly, these two chapters highlight the use of written literacy for two distinct purposes. Jackson's goal is to emphasize the literacy of Deaf individuals in the mid-seventeenth century, thus dispelling the myth of a lack of literacy among Deaf people in Britain at this time. His emphasis on instances of literacy is nicely situated next to Legg's chapter, which calls attention to the historical use of literacy for political activism. Edwin A. Hodgson, editor of the *Deaf Mutes' Journal*, used the press as a tool of resistance against the closure of a treasured Deaf cultural space. In the late nineteenth century, Saint Ann's Church for Deaf-Mutes in New York City was to merge with the local hearing church, and the press became the vehicle for Deaf agency and activism. Jackson's and Legg's chapters address different time frames and different parts of the world, but both focus on the use of written literacy and its empowering influence. One can relate this as well to Anderson and Carty's chapter about the Cosmopolitan Correspondence Club in the following section, which highlights the way in which transnational letter writing linked Deaf community members around the world and thus served as a form of empowerment. Again, we see literacy as a tool for agency, one that can enable Deaf people to take charge of their lives and connect to other members of the community.

Newby Ely's chapter in the second section examines the inspiring life and work of Hannah Tagaki Holmes, a Deaf Japanese American activist who, despite multiple hardships, discrimination, and incarceration at two US internment camps, obtained an education and fought for the rights of Deaf people and those with disabilities. The carefully researched piece by Tomasz Świderski highlights the ambitious life of a high-ranking Deaf politician, Joseph George Rogowski, and features his efforts to fulfill his dreams and his sacrifices to improve conditions for Deaf Polish individuals in pre–World War II Poland.

The next three chapters focus on the contributions of Deaf activists, community leaders, and politicians in several countries: Akio Suemori's account of the first Deaf president of a Japanese school for Deaf students; the life of the first Deaf teacher in Ontario, Canada, by Clifton Carbin; and the lives of two Australian Deaf leaders as recounted by Darlene Thornton, Susannah Macready, and Patricia Levitzke-Gray. All three chapters have the goal of ensuring that the contributions of these leaders do not go unnoticed.

The section concludes with a chapter by Christopher Kurz and Albert Hlibok about Laurent Clerc's personal struggles and successes. It includes evidence of Clerc's double consciousness, which influenced his personal perspectives, and new information about his family, work, and interactions with prominent historical figures. This chapter makes an important contribution in that it points to the humanity and complexity of revered historical figures. Issues of identity and Deafhood are increasingly discussed in the transnational Deaf community today, and it is comforting to relate to great historical figures and learn from their personal struggles with identity. In his book *Understanding Deaf Culture: In Search of Deafhood*, Paddy Ladd clearly points out that Deafhood is an "existential state of being-in-the-world" and is "not seen as a finite state but as a process by which Deaf individuals come to actualize their Deaf identity, positing that those individuals construct that identity around several differently ordered sets of priorities and principles, which are affected by various factors such as nation, era and class."[5] Kurz and Hlibok's chapter is illuminating in that it humanizes Clerc, who wrestled with the same stages of identity development and the evolution of Deafhood that Ladd discusses. The chapter encourages readers to consider not only the authors' insights into Clerc's inner existential state of being as a Deaf person in a predominantly hearing world but also the ways in which readers self-identify today. It is particularly interesting to consider the notion of identity and Deafhood as related to a Deaf leader who made a profound impact by contributing to the history of sign language in North America and cofounding the first school for Deaf students in North America.

Deaf Community Collective Histories:
Stories from the Continents

This section shares collective memories from the siege of Leningrad, Russia, by Tatiana Davidenko, who writes about her own Deaf family's experience during this period, and Victor Palenny's chapter, based on the filmed oral (both signed and spoken) stories of elderly Deaf Russians. Palenny's chapter explores community members' strong feelings of identity and belonging to the Deaf world during the tumultuous years of World War II and the period of industrialization that followed.

This section also includes accounts that aim to ensure that the Deaf community is not "written out of history," such as Kim Silva's story of the role of the American School for the Deaf in the famous Amistad affair, which involved the freeing of African slaves wrongly held in the United States. The section ends with a chapter written by Australian authors Anderson and Carty, which describes the transnational nineteenth-century network of Deaf people in the form of a Deaf correspondence club. This final chapter points strongly to Ladd's explanation of the Deafhood dimension referred to earlier in this foreword. Ladd explains that Deafhood is a process of "becoming" through a continuous internal and external dialogue as Deaf individuals contemplate their identity and what being a Deaf person in a Deaf community means to them. Deafhood incorporates collective culture, collective history, collective arts, and collective spiritual issues.[6] The Cosmopolitan Correspondence Club is a prime example of agency in that Deaf individuals from all over the globe sought each other out, thereby broadening their Deaf horizons as they connected with each other to create a transnational shared experience through letter writing.

Deaf Arts Evolution

Tracing the historical development of Deaf arts, this section includes a chapter authored by Theara Yim and Julie Chateauvert of Canada, who describe the stylistic development of sign language poetry through time in relation to the Deaf View/Image Art (De'VIA) movement.[7] A chapter by Tony McGregor examines the rise of Southwestern De'VIA in the

United States. Drew Robarge examines three Deaf American photographers from the nineteenth century and demonstrates how the study of photographers and their work provides insights into Deaf experiences that other sources do not impart.

The section ends with a chapter written jointly by Veronica Bickle of Canada and Jennifer Paul and Bob Paul of the United States, describing their process of creating a historical novel based on the true history of Martha's Vineyard, an island off the coast of Massachusetts, where many Deaf people lived between the seventeenth and the early twentieth centuries. On this island, everyone used sign language, and Deaf people were central to its political and public life. Taken together, these four chapters have in common the use of the arts—poetry, visual art, photography, and literature—as media for sharing Deaf lives and preserving history for future generations.

Preserving and Accessing Deaf History

This final section includes a chapter by Marc-André Bernier of Canada, which highlights archival methodologies and the technical processes of preserving history, including digitization. This section concludes with a chapter written by Diana Moore and Joan Naturale of the United States, which describes how historical treasures can be accessed and provides tips for researching in libraries and archives. This section discusses issues of preservation in light of the rapidly expanding availability of sign language texts in digital format. We must proceed mindfully to preserve Deaf history, ensuring that the stories of contributions, artistic forms, and bearing witness are not lost over time. With the advent of greater and ever-changing technologies in the digital age, we have a responsibility to access these stories, share them, and create new documentation to add to the collective memory. In this way, the collective memory will continue to expand and be passed on to inform the future, and readers themselves will become potential agents of change as they connect to the authors they have read.

In summary, this book provides both an international perspective on Deaf history and insights from autobiographers, biographers, researchers, and historical archivists. It is about the Deaf community taking charge of its own stories and history, compelling readers not only to learn about Deaf history but also to take action by sharing what they have learned and by recording their own Deaf lives and those of the Deaf community around them.

Notes

1. Capital "D" is used throughout this foreword. I do not assume the cultural identity of any particular individual in any particular historical period. Rather, this usage is intended to reflect the view that any Deaf individual, by virtue of having been born Deaf or become so, has a birthright to a Deaf culture and to a sign language.

2. J. Murray, "Taking a Transnational Approach to Deaf History," in *No History, No Future: Proceedings of the 7th DHI International Conference, Stockholm 2009,* edited by T. Hedberg (Orebro, Sweden: Swedish Deaf History Society, 2011), 20–26.

3. See, for example, J. Gannon, *Deaf Heritage: A Narrative History of Deaf America* (Silver Spring, MD: National Association of the Deaf, 1981); J. V. Van Cleve, ed., *Deaf History Unveiled* (Washington, DC: Gallaudet University Press, 1993); H. Lang, *Deaf Persons in the Arts and Sciences: A Biographical Dictionary* (Westport, CT: Greenwood, 1995); C. Carbin, *Deaf Heritage in Canada* (Whitby, ON: McGraw-Hill Ryerson, 1996); P. Jackson and R. Lee, *Deaf Lives: Deaf People in History* (Middlesex: British Deaf History Society, 2001); R. Fischer and H. Lane, *Looking Back: A Reader on the History of Deaf Communities and Their Sign Languages* (Hamburg: Signum, 1993); M. Zaurov, *Overcoming the Past: Determining Its Consequences and Finding Solutions for the Present* (Fulda: Signum, 2009); and T. Hedberg, *No History, No Future: Proceedings of the 7th DHI International Conference, Stockholm 2009* (Orebro: Swedish Deaf History Society, 2011).

4. H. Lang, *Reflections on Biographical Research and Writing,* chapter 2 (this volume).

5. Paddy Ladd, *Understanding Deaf Culture: In Search of Deafhood* (Clevedon: Multilingual Matters, 2003), xviii.

6. Ibid., 170.

7. The term "Deaf View/Image Art" was coined by Deaf artists and explained in the De'VIA Manifesto, created in May 1989 at the Deaf Way arts festival in Washington, DC.

INTRODUCTION

Joseph J. Murray

Every book needs a unifying thread. This book covers a period of time from the mid-seventeenth century to the late twentieth century and includes topics ranging from the global sociopolitical upheaval of the Second World War to the activities of a correspondence club composed of ten individuals. Geographically, the histories presented here relate experiences from the Siberian plateau all the way to a small town in Illinois. They tell the stories of, among others, artists, self-published authors, scientists, members of the Communist Party, and working-class women. The threads that unify these histories are their diversity and their relation to the lives of deaf people.

This collection has been made possible by the creation of a space for such explorations, partially via the establishment of *Deaf History International (DHI)* in 1991.[1] Triennial conferences organized by DHI (and often by Deaf community organizations) attract a wider range of participants than are normally found at academic gatherings. The usual denizens of scholarly meetings—academic historians and graduate students—are in the minority at these conferences, where they are outnumbered by community historians and members of the Deaf community. This book can thus be seen as an artifact of a transnational phenomenon: a widespread interest in the collection, documentation, and dissemination of Deaf history by and for members of the Deaf community.

This book is situated within this movement of community historians and within the DHI tradition, with a mixture of articles by both academic historians and community historians. The chapters reflect the concerns of members of various Deaf communities: They uncover the histories of deaf pioneers, deaf stories as part of larger historical events, and, above all, the lived experiences of deaf people within their societies. These community historians have filled the vacuum left by the relative paucity of professional historians of Deaf history, especially outside US history. The late community historian Jochen Muhs was an internationally renowned presenter who, while best known for his important work unearthing the experiences of deaf Germans in the National Socialist era, also published pamphlets on important nineteenth-century deaf Germans. The work of individuals such as Muhs has been supported by organizations for the study of Deaf history in Great Britain, Sweden, Norway, Denmark, Germany, and other countries. A number of these societies issue publications, whether books or journals, that further document the history of their national Deaf communities. The work of the British Deaf History Society—which has produced a long list of books, a regularly published journal, and an archive—is especially impressive.

Historian Joseph Amato writes, "Local history provides facts, comparisons, and contexts . . . for the abstract reaches of contemporary social sciences and history." The "fidelity" of such community historians is to "details, anecdotes, and particularities."[2] And indeed, the articles in this collection cover "particularities" and "details" of deaf experiences. But taken together, they present readers with a compelling narrative that stands alongside that of academic histories and presents the lives of deaf people as being firmly situated within the societies in which they reside. I have earlier written of the concept of "co-equality," which is the notion that deaf people are simultaneously part of their larger societies even as they create and maintain spaces in which to live as sign-language-using deaf people.[3] This fluidity is present throughout *Telling Deaf Lives*. It is the "details" and "anecdotes" of deaf lives that help us understand what it means to navigate one's difference across various places and times in history. The experience of being deaf is not solely that of being a minority within a larger society but also that of inhabiting deaf-centered spaces, spaces that also replicate discourses found in larger society.

This multiple situating of deaf lives can be seen in Harry Lang's elegantly written reflection on writing biographies of deaf people. Lang borrows the image of a binary star—a solar system with two suns—as a metaphor for the "companion worlds" of deaf and hearing people. His biographies of deaf scientists show the contributions of deaf people in the sciences (at least ten craters on the moon, Mars, and Venus are named after deaf people) and to society at large. As Lang notes, "the experience of deaf people in history holds much power for better understanding our own world," a truism reflected in other chapters in this volume.[4]

Moving from outer space to conceptual spaces of organization and resistance, Jannelle Legg explores the political strategies used by Edwin A. Hodgson during a controversy over the merger of a deaf church, Saint Ann's, with a hearing church in New York City in the 1890s. Legg's meticulous research shows Hodgson as a shrewd advocate who used deaf and hearing spaces to advance the argument for an independent deaf church. As she demonstrates, deaf-centered spaces were not separate self-contained spaces but could rather serve as a "space of resistance" in which deaf arguments could influence larger society.

Deaf people have long had transnational interconnections, and the chapter by Melissa Anderson and Breda Carty shows how deaf people of different nations corresponded across great distances via the formation of the Cosmopolitan Correspondence Club, composed of individuals in Australia, western Europe, and the United States. Deaf women comprised a majority of the members of the correspondence club. Anderson and Carty's work makes an important contribution to ongoing studies of the transnational lives of deaf people. It shows that when we look beyond explicitly political activities such as conferences to a broader array of transnational interactions such as letter writing, a wider range of deaf people can be seen to be transnational actors. The club's members were "observant, aware, socially progressive people who were for the most part allied with established institutions such as schools, churches, and welfare organizations for deaf people," and their correspondence shows an expanded space in which to understand deaf political activities.[5]

A cluster of articles looks at the lives and endeavors of deaf pioneers. Akio Suemori traces the story of Sei-ichirô Matsumura (1849–1891), the first president of the Kanazawa school for the deaf and blind. Suemori uncovers biographical details of Matsumura's life, including that he was deafened at the age of fourteen and was a translator of an American geography textbook. It places Matsumura in the tradition of Japanese scholars oriented toward the West and as an important figure in Japanese Deaf history. Christopher Kurz and Albert Hlibok write of different challenges, namely those faced by Laurent Clerc, cofounder of deaf education in the United States, and interpret Clerc's response to them using twenty-first-century ideas such as audism. Clifton Carbin's contribution is a biography of Samuel Greene, the first deaf teacher at the Ontario Institution for the Education and Instruction of the Deaf and Dumb, who was present at the school's opening in 1870. Carbin's story of how he became interested in Greene's life will be familiar to those who have spent time researching Deaf history. It began with "a huge, impressive 1890 portrait of a man" that hung in the school's auditorium. Such portraits exist in numerous schools, and the discovery that they portray deaf people is often a catalyst for increased historical awareness by local Deaf communities.

Indeed, uncovering and honoring deaf people from the past is an explicit goal of many community historians. Peter Jackson is a prolific author of historical texts published by the British Deaf History Society. His contribution to this volume explores written records about three deaf men in seventeenth-century Britain. Jackson began this research by challenging himself to find the existence of deaf people before the establishment of formal deaf education in the latter half of the eighteenth century. Jackson uses archival records, a will, and other texts to uncover the lives, work, and signing abilities of three deaf men of the period. His compelling synopsis is an excellent example of a well-researched community history. Continuing in this biographical vein, Darlene Thornton, Susannah Macready, and Patricia Levitzke-Gray narrate the influence of two mid-twentieth-century Deaf community leaders in Australia, Fletcher Booth and Dorothy Shaw. They ask two questions about these leaders: "How did they contribute to the Australian Deaf Community?" and "What have they left behind"? Both leaders were active in establishing organizations and publications that fostered deaf political awareness and strengthened the Australian Deaf community. The answers to these questions show how contemporary Deaf communities use history for the maintenance of community norms of working for the benefit of a larger community of deaf people.

Drew Robarge's essay on three US deaf photographers goes beyond thumbnail biographical sketches to explore "deaf cultural sensibilities at the turn of the twentieth century."[6] Robarge relates how being deaf formed a crucial part of these photographers' lives, but historians can find only indeterminate visual evidence of deafness in their photographs. In the collective body of work by these three photographers, only two photographs depict sign language. Theophilus d'Estrella's photographs of students at the California School for the Deaf are representative of this lack of representation—these photographs show no evidence of whether the photographer or the students were deaf. As Robarge notes, although "deaf people might have embraced the invisibility of deafness in these photographers' works, that invisibility hampers researchers who are unable to distinguish between the deaf and the hearing in the creator and the subject."[7] Robarge shows deaf people living within hearing society while making significant contributions to the Deaf community in organizations, artwork, and publications. This interaction between deaf and hearing society is also present in Theara Yim and Julie Chateauvert's piece on ASL poetry. These authors look at the evolution of ASL poetry by analyzing works of prominent ASL poets Clayton Valli and the team of the Flying Words Project, made up of Peter Cook and Kenny Lerner. Valli's work was "explicitly one of validation," showing the legitimacy of ASL poetry vis-à-vis English literature. The Flying Words Project, by contrast, is a project of "radical affirmation" in that it considers deaf cultural identity alongside other cultural identities.

Fittingly, this book looks at the lived experiences of deaf people via oral histories and biographical and autobiographical narratives. A quick look at library collections of deaf works will uncover a large number of biographies and autobiographies. Albert Ballin, in his semifictional autobiography, *The Deaf Mute Howls,* makes clear the reason for this plethora of personal-experience narratives in deaf discourses: "Long, loud and cantankerous is the howl raised by the deaf-mute! . . . He ought to keep it up incessantly until the wrongs inflicted on him will have been righted and done away with forever."[8] Deaf women and men saw the sharing of personal-experience narratives as a political act, as a way to explain to an unknowing society what it means to be deaf.

Victor Palenny's article contains fascinating stories told by deaf people in the twentieth-century Soviet Union, which were gathered via oral history interviews. It is important to note that Palenny's work was done as part of a team of three community historians, showing deaf people collecting the signed histories of other deaf people. Palenny relates that some deaf people worked outside the Communist system to earn extra money on the side, selling postcards or cards with the manual alphabet. These stories are reminiscent of Br'er Rabbit stories in that they portray deaf people winning over hearing oppressors. Exploring similar stories in the British Deaf community, Paddy Ladd calls them examples of a "covert level of social praxis and political activity, the '1001 victories'" composed of small-scale acts of resistance and rebellion.[9]

However, the deaf experience was about not only resistance to power but also collaboration. Palenny shows another side of the deaf experience: the role of deaf people as loyal members of the socialist system. Interviewees who had prominent roles in the government-sanctioned national association of deaf people proudly related the stories of their roles as "constructors of socialism."[10] Tatiana Davidenko also shows the multiple roles played by deaf people. She recounts her deaf family's privations during the World War II siege of Leningrad. Her family's suffering began earlier in Stalin's time, when they lost their bakery and the author's grandfather was sent to a concentration camp. But the main focus is the siege itself. Several members of Davidenko's family died, and those remaining survived by escaping on a "Deaf boat" organized by the Leningrad branch of the VOG, the All-Russian Society of the Deaf. The boat left the city via Lake Ladoga, a route along which thousands had already perished.

Davidenko's story is a chilling account of a famous historical event based on the experiences of one deaf family. She combines research by other historians with her mother's stories, which were told only to her daughter and only late in her mother's life. Davidenko highlights the Russian Deaf community's fear of openly sharing negative experiences due to their oppression during the Stalin era. Equally important to this persecution was the fear of those around them—including deaf people—who sought to adhere to the official line. Both Davidenko and Palenny show the power of oral history in uncovering a range of experiences and illuminating the ways in which deaf people navigate larger society, both resisting and adopting ideologies from the societies in which they lived.

Newby Ely also looks at deaf people's experiences in World War II by writing about the life of Hanna Holmes, a deaf woman of Japanese descent who was incarcerated with her family in a US internment camp during this period. Holmes was a child at the time, and her story is one that exposes the ineptness of the US government in ensuring educational access for her at the camp and the racism she faced outside it. For reasons not given, four schools for deaf people—in Colorado, California, Pennsylvania, and the Kendall School at Gallaudet University—rejected the government's attempts to place her and other deaf children from internment camps into their schools. She moved with her family to Illinois and, facing anti-Japanese hostility at an oral school in Chicago, finally relocated to the Illinois School for the Deaf. Holmes's story is known because she testified before the Congressional Commission on Wartime Relocation and Internment of Civilians, was interviewed by an oral-history project, and gave testimony in a lawsuit to redress the treatment of victims of the wartime relocation. In short, her experiences were uncovered because, as a deaf person, she provided a perspective on a historical event that was different from those of other participants. Thus are deaf stories also of interest to a larger public. Hanna Holmes was discriminated against by the US government and faced prejudice from institutions and individuals because she was of Japanese descent and because she was deaf.

Kim A. Silva's article uses oral-history methods to examine a popular story in the American deaf community that gives a deaf dimension to the Amistad affair. This case involved fifty-three Africans who revolted aboard a slave ship and won back their freedom via a case argued by John Quincy Adams at the US Supreme Court. Laurent Clerc and Thomas Hopkins Gallaudet, pioneers of deaf education in the United States, were called upon to serve as gestural "interpreters" between the Africans and the US authorities when the ship first docked in the United States. The Africans, who were of the Mende people, also visited the

American School for the Deaf (ASD) in Hartford, Connecticut. According to one story, the students were able to easily communicate with the Africans. However, the role of sign language was quickly overtaken by spoken language, with the actual trial interpreted from spoken English into spoken Mende. What is unusual about this article is that it relies heavily on what could be called folklore: stories handed down from one generation to another. Silva uses the methodological criterion of an oral historian: that an oral history must have an "unbroken series of witnesses" in order to be credible. She traces the genealogy of this story back to the nineteenth century through recollections carried from ASD teachers and staff to students, who then took on employment at the school. In addition to broadening our understanding of deaf lives, these articles by Palenny, Davidenko, Ely, and Silva illuminate unknown aspects of larger historical events: the deaf experience in various arenas during and after World War II and during the abolitionist movement.

Telling Deaf Lives also includes autobiographical pieces. Ulla-Bell Thorin is a deaf Swedish woman who has written six books, and among her primary motivations has been "the importance of deaf people telling their own stories in their own words."[11] Five of her six books are autobiographical, and the sixth is a fictional narrative about a deaf woman. Thorin's article is testimony to the struggles and strength of a deaf woman in twentieth-century Sweden. Tony Landon McGregor contributes an artistic autobiography that explores the De'VIA themes in his own artwork. Of particular interest is how his work developed alongside deaf mentors, from a deaf schoolteacher in his youth to informal mentoring by established deaf artists such as Chuck Baird and Betty Miller. Not only artists but also deaf patrons such as curators and critics contributed to McGregor's development. McGregor shows us how membership in the Deaf community can be a boon to individual deaf lives.

All of the contributions in this volume go beyond written archival documents to draw upon an innovative range of sources available in sign language: oral histories collected by professional and community historians, folklore, family memories handed down through the generations, and autobiographical recollections. What these sources highlight is the richness of historical texts in sign language for understanding the varied experiences of deaf people. Fortunately, we have means of accessing these histories. Diana Moore and Joan Naturale show the rich array of written and video sources available to scholars of Deaf history through Gallaudet University and the National Technical Institute for the Deaf (NTID) libraries. However, Marc-André Bernier reminds us that the personal documents of today's deaf people are often in "born-digital" format, which presents its own challenges for the preservation of Deaf history. He also encourages readers to preserve their own histories. Veronica Bickle, Jennifer Paul, and Bob Paul take another perspective on history, sharing their experience with writing historical fiction about deaf people. Their novel, *The Vineyarders*, is situated around the experiences of deaf people on Martha's Vineyard in the late nineteenth century, and the writers clearly elucidate the challenges facing authors of fictionalized accounts of well-known historical figures and events.

These stories narrate a diverse range of deaf lives. While an overarching thread is an intention to relate the experiences of deaf people, another commonality is worth noting. We should not lose sight of the profoundly optimistic orientation of these stories. Uncovering and sharing histories of deaf people are ways of affirming a belief that learning and change are possible and that, by sharing one's stories, one can spark understanding that will better the lives of deaf people and ultimately lead to a more just society. Ballin wrote of the desire to remedy the "wrongs inflicted" on deaf people; these stories continue that tradition. In sharing the histories and narratives of deaf lives, this book ensures that Ballin's howl is not forgotten and that the stories of deaf people continue to be told.

Notes

1. Jack Gannon, "Birth of Deaf History International," *Deaf History International* 1, no. 1 (1993): 1.

2. Joseph Amato, *Rethinking Home: A Case for Writing Local History* (Berkeley: University of California Press, 2002), 3–5.

3. Joseph J. Murray, "Coequality and Transnational Studies: Understanding Deaf Lives," in *Open Your Eyes: Deaf Studies Talking*, ed. H-Dirksen L. Bauman (Minneapolis: University of Minnesota Press, 2007), 100–10.

4. Lang, this volume.

5. Anderson and Carty, this volume.

6. Robarge, this volume.

7. Ibid.

8. Albert V. Ballin, *The Deaf-Mute Howls* (1931; repr., Washington, DC: Gallaudet University Press, 1998), 1.

9. Paddy Ladd, *Understanding Deaf Culture: In Search of Deafhood* (Clevedon, UK: Multilingual Matters, 2003), 329.

10. Palenny, this volume.

11. Thorin, this volume.

PART 1

Autobiographies

On Writing My Story as Deaf History

Ulla-Bell Thorin

As the author of six books, I can point to many motivating factors that first led me to start writing. In this chapter I share with you my reasons for writing and also a few stories from some of my books.

What motivated me to start writing books? First of all, I really enjoy writing, and I think it is a great thing to do. My mother, too, was a writer. Her name was Astrid Pettersson, and she wrote around twenty books in total, some of which I helped her transcribe. Thanks to her, I learned a lot about the creative process of writing and how to go about publishing one's books, and she also helped me develop my written language (figure 1).

When my father died, my doctor encouraged me to start writing down my own stories. Over the course of several years, I gathered notes and contemplated whether my vocabulary was good enough and whether I would have the courage to publish my texts. I am well aware of my shortcomings when it comes to the Swedish language, but still I have had the confidence to write these books on my own rather than having someone else do it for me, and I think that is a very important thing for deaf people.

FIGURE 1. *Ulla-Bell's mother, author Astrid Pettersson.*

This leads to my second motivation for writing: the importance of deaf people telling their own stories in their own words. When you are deaf, you can, of course, sign your stories, but the signs quickly fade away, whereas the written words remain for others to read. In actual fact, very few deaf people have written books. Although the number of deaf authors has been increasing in this century, there were very few during the twentieth century. For a long time I have been wondering why this is the case when so many stories are waiting to be told. One needs to ask who really has the ability and knowledge needed to write about the history of deaf people and their language. I have always felt that deaf people are better suited to tell their own stories and that it is frustrating when hearing people write about deaf people, for deaf people.

I also feel strongly about documenting the life of deaf people from a historical perspective, as our history is something that most people do not know much about. For this reason, my initial thoughts when I started writing centered on the fact that very few deaf people have written with the intent of telling their own individual stories and how they perceived their upbringing. That is why I started to write about my preschool years, my language, and the lack of communication between my family and me when I came home from school for the weekend.

As a young child, I did not have a language until I learned to sign at the age of two. I was very fortunate to live in a place where I had an opportunity to go to a sign language preschool. Other deaf children at

FIGURE 2. *Ulla-Bell Thorin's first novel,* Deprived of Language, *published in 1993.*

this time often had "seven white years": years without a language. My first book, *Deprived of Language* (Thorin 1993), is based on my time at preschool and my life at home with my family during the Second World War (figure 2). During these years I had a truly wonderful teacher named Alma, who communicated with us in sign language. She taught us to read by having us place a card with a word on it next to the corresponding image on the wall. For me personally, this was the best way of learning: by combining sign language with written Swedish (figure 3).

I remember one time when the children from the preschool were invited home to my parents' farm in the rural area south of Gothenburg. During this visit, we were to learn how to make cheese. There were about twenty-five of us helping my father move fifty-liter containers of milk from the barn to the house. We counted the drops of cheese rennet that were poured into the milk, which was boiling on the wood stove. During the entire process, our teacher, Alma, taught us new signs for the concept of cheese making and also for cows and their stomachs. We took the cheese back with us to the school and turned it every day until that year's Christmas party. To this day I can still remember how good it tasted!

The lack of communication between my parents and me made life difficult at times. Once when I came home from school, I knew beforehand that a new baby brother would be waiting for me. When I came

FIGURE 3. *The preschool for deaf children in Gothenburg in the early 1940s.*

home, I immediately ran in to see the little baby sleeping, wrapped in a red blanket. I leaned over and gave him a kiss and thought he looked so beautiful while sleeping. Suddenly my mother was there, pulling me away and shoving me against the wall. She looked scared, angry, and nervous. My head hurt, and I couldn't understand why she was so angry with me. When the weekend was over, I went back to school, where Alma tried to explain to me, using sign language, that my little brother was dead. I had a hard time grasping what she meant, but during the funeral it dawned on me as I watched my father and grandfather bury my brother in a white coffin. I finally understood my mother's tears and the fact that my little brother was never coming back. The fact that the situation could not be explained to me in sign language until several days after this incident with my mother was very upsetting.

My second book, *Deprived of Love* (Thorin 1995), is about a little girl just like me, who must travel far away from home in order to attend a school for deaf children. After preschool, in 1945, I started first grade at the School for the Deaf in Vänersborg, on the west coast of Sweden. I traveled by train and arrived at the school alone, without my parents. Upon my arrival, the principal of the school struck me on the shoulder with his cane to force me to go into the school office and register. Quite a welcome for a seven-year-old girl! After a while, the principal hit me again. I thought this meant that I should leave the office, but I was stopped by yet another blow. The principal was standing behind me with a piece of paper in front of his mouth, talking, in order to find out how well I could hear his voice. I couldn't hear anything, and I was hit again to let me know that I could leave the room. I started to cry, and my shoulder hurt for several days afterward.

During my preschool years, I was very happy and fortunate to have been given a language, and, in a way, these were the happiest five years of my life. Things changed when I came to the School for the Deaf in Vänersborg, where sign language was strictly forbidden. The curriculum was totally centered around lipreading and speaking. It was a shocking experience at first, but I still managed to make some wonderful friends, and, fortunately, we were allowed to use sign language in our spare time, so we could communicate and practice signing then. I spent only one year at the school, as my mother wanted me to attend a different one.

My third book, *Tears of Thorn* (Thorin 1998), is based on the period of my life when I moved to a different school, even farther away from home. This was also a school for deaf children, in Örebro, in the middle of Sweden. Only here, things got even worse. Sign language was forbidden not only during school hours but also in the foster home where I lived. Still, I tried to use it as much as I could. I stayed at that school for seven years and never really liked it.

The principal at the School for the Deaf in Örebro was proficient in sign language and was at times hired as an interpreter in the outside community. I didn't even know he knew any sign language until after I had left school! I was at a lecture that he gave in Växjö, and I was astonished by his use of signs. I went up to him afterward and angrily told him, "I will never forgive you for as long as I live." He simply asked me, "Why?" I replied, "You can sign!" He then told me that he had been afraid of losing his job since sign language was forbidden at the school.

As I mentioned earlier, the seven years at the Örebro school were dominated by speech training, learning lipreading, and hearing tests. With regard to academic education, I wasn't given what I actually needed. I feel that the state deceived parents by taking over the parental role and making deaf students leave home to come to school. When they went home to be with their parents during breaks, the children were then expected to speak perfectly. But in reality, communication never went smoothly since the parents didn't know how to sign (figure 4).

After writing these books about my time at preschool and the schools for deaf children, I took a break from writing about my childhood. That's

FIGURE 4. *Ulla-Bell (right) with her sister and brother.*

when I wrote a book called *My Interpretation of Interpreting*, which in various ways I had been working on for almost thirty years. In it I gathered all of my experiences related to interpreting and interviewed many sign language interpreters. At this time, there were no organizations for interpreters. A lot more can be written about the topic, enough for a sequel. However, at the time I felt that writing this one book was enough for me.

For my fifth book, *Worthy of Respect* (Thorin 2005), I returned to school life. Out of all the books I have written, this is my favorite, and I often give lectures about it. It depicts a school for deaf girls in Växjö, which one could attend after the eight mandatory years in one of the five Swedish schools for deaf students. It tells the story of the girls who went to the school, their teachers, and what they did in their spare time. The school was in operation from 1938 until 1970, after which there were better educational opportunities for young deaf people. I personally thought the school was all right, but in a sense it was also a prison of sorts for the young women. Essentially, they were taught how to be a good housewife and were prepared for married life. During all the years that the school for deaf girls in Växjö was in existence, it had the same principal, Carin Lagerberg-Bergstrand. She was quite hard on us, and I never really liked her.

Over those years, a total of 740 girls enrolled in the school, which had a mandatory two-year program unless you could verify that you had been employed, in which case you could leave after only one year. After a year at the school, most girls found jobs and moved back to their hometowns. You could also attend a third and fourth year at the school, during which the curriculum focused on vocational training. Many of the girls who quit after two years struggled to succeed in the job market due to their lack of skills. Many of the girls felt forced to marry for security and stability. This is why I chose the title *Worthy of Respect* for my book about these young women. I respect and hold in great esteem each and every one of the girls who had the courage to move far away from their families in order to attend that school.

The number of pupils was at a high from 1953 to 1956. It then declined to only seven students in 1970, after which the school was shut down. I personally spent three years at the school, and I wrote *Worthy of Respect* because it represents an era that I don't think many young deaf people in Sweden today know much about.

While at the school for deaf girls, I went home to see my family during breaks, and the communication between my mother and me improved a little, but my parents still did not use sign language. During these breaks, my father and I would often say only two things to each other: "Good day" and "Good-bye." I loved my father very much; he was a good father, and it made me really sad that we could not communicate well. I found it hard to lip-read when he spoke, and he did not articulate very well, either.

My last book to date, *With Your Head Held High* (Thorin 2007), is about a girl who leaves school in Växjö to look for work. She ends up working in a garment factory, unable to get any other work due to her poor grades. At the factory, she falls in love with a hearing foreman. She subsequently gives birth to twins, but the father is not her newfound love. Instead, the children are the result of her having been raped by the priest for deaf people, for whom she had previously worked as a housekeeper.

While writing this sixth book I suffered a stroke, which affected my vision. Since then I have taken a long break from writing, but the urge to write has made me start on my seventh book. The title of the book is still a secret, but it is going to be about sign language. Wise from experience, I am not sure whether I have the courage to publish this book. The marketing aspect of book publishing is very demanding, and I feel that I am not good at it. Maybe this is why my books have not always been as successful as I have hoped.

While publishing my books over the years, at times I have struggled with my self-confidence and my Swedish. I have fought hard to write and publish the books, and in the end I am proud that I have managed to do so in spite of poor marketing. Unfortunately, my books are not available in English. As much as I have wanted them to be, it has proven more difficult than I imagined. I am, however, still very happy and proud of the fact that some of my books are available to buy and to be borrowed from libraries.

When I started writing, I used a manual typewriter while transcribing some of my mother's books. I then bought my own typewriter, which wore out. My second typewriter weighed almost ten kilograms. I later got a clumsy, old computer. Things have really changed, and nowadays I have a modern, flat-screen computer, but it is far from my best friend. In fact, I sometimes hate it. I would still prefer a good old electric typewriter!

My books were published by different publishers. The same deaf publisher published the first two books. The publisher of the third book was also deaf, whereas the remaining books have hearing publishers. Nowadays I have a hard time trusting publishing companies since they seem to pop up everywhere like mushrooms. It is also difficult to know which ones are reliable and have reasonable costs and a good attitude toward deaf people.

Writing will probably never make me rich, but I am still happy that I have managed to publish six books, and doing so has always been my main objective. I hope that my books will provide valuable insight into the lives of deaf people at a time when circumstances were very different from those confronting deaf people today.

References

Thorin, Ulla-Bell. *Berövad Kärlek.* Växjö, Sweden: Förlaget Hony, 1994.

———. *Berövat Språk.* Växjö, Sweden: Förlaget Hony, 1993.

———. *Med Högburet Huvud.* Gothenburg, Sweden: B4 Press, 2007.

———. *Tolktrubbel.* Harplinge, Sweden: Neas Förlag, 2003.

———. *Törnetårar.* Malmö, Sweden: Döviana, 1998.

———. *Värda Respekt.* Harplinge, Sweden: Neas Förlag, 2005.

Reflections on Biographical Research and Writing

Harry G. Lang

Over the past few decades of research in the field of Deaf history, biographical writing has evolved into a powerful genre that has helped us reconstruct our past, understand our place as deaf[1] people today, and shape our future. This essay briefly summarizes my journey of discovery as a deaf biographer over a period of thirty years and describes how biography has developed my worldview, interpreted pragmatically as a framework of ideas and beliefs used to interact with the world. Biographies and autobiographies in Deaf history have demonstrated a wide range of approaches, emphases, and purposes. There are historical, literary, reference, and even fictional biographies. Biographers may also have particular interests that include sociopolitical constructs such as audism, marginalization, and the promotion of multiculturalism. Alternately, they may be interested in the enhancement of self-efficacy in a younger deaf readership—the belief that being deaf should not be a barrier to success in any field of endeavor.

---

1. The term "deaf" refers to both deaf and hard of hearing individuals.

Biographical research can also shed new light on the experience of deaf people in history and may lead to the integration of knowledge into a worldview—a personal construct that may be different for each biographer. The extent to which biographical research may actually influence a writer's own personality has not been adequately investigated. In a sense, this summary of such a worldview is autobiographical by nature—it is based on personal experiences in the realm of research and writing.

My interest in biography began when I was a teenager studying at the Western Pennsylvania School for the Deaf (WPSD) in Pittsburgh. I had my heart set on becoming a scientist, but I had never read about any deaf person in science. Fifty years ago my worldview regarding deafness was very limited by the scarcity of Deaf studies resources. My teachers, like the local librarians, knew of no material related to deaf scientists, and no one knew of a living deaf scientist whom I might contact. Consequently, I began studying physics in college with considerable uncertainty.

After graduating from college, I continued to teach physics at the National Technical Institute for the Deaf at the Rochester Institute of Technology. Then, in 1984, as president of an organization called the Science Association for Persons with Disabilities, I had the special honor to meet the British theoretical physicist Dr. Stephen Hawking (figure 1). The chance exchange we had in Boston one day was the impetus for my biographical writing. As a physicist myself, I admired Dr. Hawking's perseverance as a scientist paralyzed by disease and respected all that

FIGURE 1. *Dr. Stephen Hawking (seated) and Dr. Harry Lang (right) at a meeting of the American Association for the Advancement of Science in 1984. In the center is an ASL interpreter. Hawking's assistant is in the upper left.*

he had accomplished. During our meeting I was taken aback when he looked at me and said, through my ASL interpreter, "It must be difficult to be deaf." This brief conversation made me start wondering about the roles such attitudes have played in influencing the education and employment of deaf men and women in science.

Soon after this personal encounter I embarked on a nearly three-decade-long quest to examine the experience of deaf people in history. At first I focused on the fields of science, technology, engineering, mathematics, medicine, and invention. One by one I discovered several thousand deaf men and women who had different ages of onset, a variety of etiologies, lived during different periods in history, communicated in many diverse ways, and yet found remarkable strategies to overcome communication and attitudinal challenges to contribute meaningfully to their fields.

In my first book, *Silence of the Spheres: The Deaf Experience in the History of Science* (1994), I used biography to emphasize that there has been a continuous and impressive presence of deaf people in the history of one discipline—science. But over the years I followed other paths in conducting research and writing biographies. *Deaf Persons in the Arts and Sciences: A Biographical Dictionary* (Lang and Meath-Lang 1995) contains 151 biographical sketches and focuses on the contributions of deaf people in a variety of disciplines. In *A Phone of Our Own: The Deaf Insurrection against Ma Bell* (Lang 2000), biographical tidbits about many individuals blend into a single story about service to a community with a goal—the ninety-year battle for telephone access.

During this journey there were also various skirmishes with book publishers. I learned many lessons about the precautions that need to be taken when one is depending on secondary sources; the dangers of using the World Wide Web as a resource; and the challenges of writing full-length biographies of living deaf legends Robert R. Davila (Lang, Cohen, and Fischgrund 2007) and Robert F. Panara (Lang, 2007a). These dangers were summarized in a paper titled "Reflections on Biographical Research and Writing" (Lang, 2007b).

While I was working on *Silence of the Spheres,* one story about a young deaf astronomer named John Goodricke introduced a metaphor that had a profound influence on my subsequent books. In the late eighteenth century Goodricke had observed what would later be called a "binary star" system (figure 2). Born deaf (or possibly deafened in early

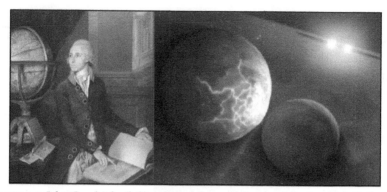

FIGURE 2. *John Goodricke (left) was one of several thousand deaf and hard of hearing women and men in the history of science who were discovered through research. Photograph courtesy of Wikimedia Commons. At right is an artist's conception of a binary star system, two worlds that share material and energy, which became a metaphor for my worldview. Photograph courtesy of NASA/JPL-Caltech.*

infancy), this young man had studied at the Braidwood Academy in Edinburgh. He was only a teenager when he discovered variable stars, and for this work he was awarded the Copley Medal in 1783.

The metaphor that became an element of my worldview focused on the notion of how deaf men and women in history lived to various degrees in two worlds, sharing their time and energy between these worlds as they pursued their scientific work. As I wrote in 1994:

> I look one last time tonight into the vast expanse of space. Far out there is Beta Lyrae—two worlds orbiting one another. To me there is something wonderful about binary stars. Two worlds which share energy. Yet, usually one star in the pair is larger and brighter and it overwhelms the retina of human vision. To the unaided eye, these two stars appear as one. In the darkness, as the breeze blows softly, I think about the worlds of hearing and deaf persons. Different worlds. Companion worlds. To the unaided student of the history of science these worlds, too, appear as one. (Lang 1994, xiii–xiv)

It became a goal, then, not only to distinguish these worlds but also to show the struggle and strategies deaf people used to share energy between the different spheres where they participated. This notion, including the astronomical metaphor, kept surfacing. For example, when researching the deaf physicist Robert H. Weitbrecht, I found a letter he had written to his codeveloper of the TTY modem, James C. Marsters. "I was a pretty lonely star gazer," he wrote, "moving in the void between the galaxy of the hearing people and the galaxy of the deaf people" (Lang 2000, 148).

A second element of the worldview developed from biographical research was derived from the realization of how much we take for granted with regard to the roles deaf people played in developing the things we enjoy in life. It was Vinton Cerf, now known as the "Father of the Internet," who wrote a 1978 article in the *American Annals of the Deaf* regarding "a new communication tool" that he called "The Electronic Mailbox" (Cerf 1978). Because of the protocol he developed, we now use email on a daily basis. Similarly, Thomas Alva Edison improved the light bulb, which allows people today to read and communicate at night much more easily than our predecessors did with candles. Thanks to this deaf inventor, we also have motion picture films. And each time I watch a rocket blast into space, I think of the pioneer Konstantin E. Tsiolkovsky, the "Father of Astronautics." This Russian felt "isolated, humiliated—an outcast," yet he attributed the increased power of concentration to his deafness. It helped him, he wrote, "to withdraw deep within myself, to pursue great goals" (Lang 1994; Lang and Meath-Lang 1995).

In March 2012, during my first year of retirement after forty-one years of teaching, I took, for the first time, a photograph of the moon. Most people would recognize the lunar craters in this photograph as having been formed by either volcanic activity or meteorites striking the moon's surface. But biographical research has for me given new meaning to this picture. At least ten of these craters on the moon, Venus, and Mars are named for deaf men and women who made significant contributions throughout history (figure 3). As an example, "Crater Edinger" on Venus was named for Tilly Edinger, a woman who hid from the Nazis in a museum for many months. Her brother was killed in a concentration camp, and she was fortunate to escape Germany during the Holocaust. Deafened as a teenager, she went on to become one of the foremost experts on horse fossils, a subject she had become fascinated with while reading by candlelight in the darkened museum. Each of the craters named for deaf people represents a unique life story. So, too, does the minor planet named for John Goodricke, the comet named for the deaf Norwegian Olaf Hassel, and thousands of stars that were discovered and/or classified by deaf astronomers.

FIGURE 3. *Through biographical research it was found that at least ten of the craters on Earth's moon, as well as on Venus and Mars, were named in honor of deaf people for their contributions to science and the humanities.*

But this worldview, which includes a sense of pride in the accomplishments of these women and men in history, is by no means limited to astronomy. As a scientist, I found the natural world to be rich with such stories. When I look out at my gardens, I think about how many plants have been named for deaf people in honor of their work in botany and horticulture. *Lesquerella,* for example, a genus of flowering plants in the family Brassicaceae, is named in honor of Leo Lesquereux, the Swiss American "father of North American paleobotany" (Lyons, Morey, and Wagner 1995). *Hughesia reginae* is a plant genus named in honor of Regina Olsen Hughes, a deaf botanical illustrator. There are many more.

In entomology, which is the study of insects, the remarkable adventures of many deaf men and women can be found. They, too, were honored for their work in this science. *Cassida alpina* Bremi-Wolf, named for Johann Jacob Bremi-Wolf, was one of many insects he studied and classified. His sketchbook included fifty-four sheets of colored drawings of butterflies, beetles, caterpillars, and other insects, most with handwritten legends. Additionally, he wrote poetry. "I'm deaf!" Bremi-Wolf exclaimed in one of his poems, "Yet, I will not grieve. I know from whence fate comes. God deemed it well to take from me this sense and knows what good will come from it" (Lang and Santiago-Blay 2012).

There is the exciting story of a deaf man who helped the eminent Charles Darwin during the famous voyage of the *HMS Beagle.* Syms Covington was a cabin boy on the ship. Hard of hearing when he first met Darwin, he lost much more of his hearing from firing rifles while collecting specimens for Darwin. They became lifelong friends, and Darwin even bought him an ear trumpet.

Deaf people have discovered chemical elements. A deaf person determined the source of typhus fever, saving tens of thousands of lives. Deaf people have won Nobel Prizes and discovered important scientific principles, and they have played equally important roles in the history of the humanities.

I am often asked whether the people I have studied were "really deaf." The question is a very contemporary one, and there are no economical answers. Deaf people in history, as today, represent a huge range of degrees of deafness, ages of onset, causes of deafness, types of schooling, and relationship to communities. There are many ways to be deaf, and, collectively, these people are part of our heritage.

As examined through biographical research, the experience of deaf people in history holds much power for better understanding our own world. As an example, we have all read about the conflicts arising from the oralists' efforts to ban the use of sign language. This "war of methods" has gone on for centuries and still rages today. However, during my research for the book *A Phone of Our Own*, I learned that it was three oral deaf men who developed the modem, which finally brought telephone access to the Deaf world. Importantly, they knew they could not disseminate this technology on their own. It was during a convention of oralists in 1964 that Robert Weitbrecht, James C. Marsters, and Andrew Saks invited National Association of the Deaf (NAD) president Robert Sanderson and vice president Jess Smith to a demonstration of the visual telephone-teletypewriter system, or TTY. An organization was then established with a signing president (Smith) and an oral vice president (H. Latham Breunig) to develop a national deaf network to promote deaf people's access to the telephone. This was the first significant step toward the broad telecommunications access we now enjoy with our pagers, email, and videophones.

Sanderson wrote a letter to me about how sad it was that the oral and the signing communities could not work together in education as they had in telecommunications. This story provides a powerful message about respecting differences in language and culture and effecting real change in society as a result.

Through biographical research we also learn many things that broaden our thinking about deaf people as human beings. Edmund Booth is a deaf icon. In the nineteenth century he was regarded as one of the best signers in the United States and as the "honored Nestor" of the American Deaf community (Lang 2004). Yet he had sought a cure for his deafness. So, too, did the revered Laurent Clerc contemplate the possibility of a cure. Others, like Laura Redden, a distinguished poet and journalist, saw value in taking speech lessons after many years of never using her voice. They were human.

Biographical research also teaches us that we deaf people have a "dark side" to our history, as in the case of the historian and writer Heinrich von Treitschke, who became deaf at a young age. His anti-Semitic writings later fell into the hands of Adolph Hitler, who found them inspiring (Lang and Meath-Lang 1995). These and many other facts discovered through biographical research help us reflect intelligently on our deaf predecessors.

As an educator, I also experimented for almost thirty years with signing biographies. For this I used the theater-in-education approach (TIE), which was introduced to me by my wife, Bonnie Meath-Lang. Using a fictional "time machine," I "brought back" both hearing and deaf characters from history and interviewed them in front of various audiences, including graduate classes in a course titled "History of Deaf Educational Thought and Practice," professional development workshops in university settings, and the Convention of American Instructors of the Deaf. The characters that I interviewed included, for example, Edward Miner Gallaudet, Sophia Fowler Gallaudet, Alexander Graham Bell, Anne Sullivan Macy, Laurent Clerc, and Edmund Booth (figure 4). The approach required extensive reading by the actors, who needed to be prepared for a variety of questions.

There are many other forms of theater in education. As an educator, I chose this format and found great value in comparing the art of acting with the art of writing. In formal theater, too, we see how artists, writers, actors, and directors interpret the lives of deaf individuals through sign language as a means of appreciating our culture and heritage. During the three hundredth anniversary of the Abbé de l'Épée in 2012, I was happy to see that commemorative performances took place around the world.

FIGURE 4. *Theater in Education: Laurent Clerc, portrayed by Patrick Graybill, a deaf actor, describes his experiences as a student at the Royal Institution for the Deaf in Paris to "time machine" scientist Harry G. Lang.*

Conclusion

Through biography we reconstruct our pasts, continue our heritage, and construct our future. As an educator, as I presented in schools for deaf children around the country, I quickly saw the positive impact of sharing biographies. Teachers asked the children what they had learned from my presentations, and in their written reactions I saw surprise and inspiration.

I also presented to parents, and the workshop evaluations showed that the biographies were influencing them as they guided their children in their education. "Those deaf predecessors . . . send a message of encouragement and inspiration to all of us," wrote one parent. "As a mother of a child that is deaf, I felt hope and pride for my son. I had a sense of validation and promise that my son, Aaron, could truly do anything he wanted."

Biographies can also serve as agents of change. A deaf woman once wrote to me that she was not accepted by a university because the officials did not believe she was capable of doing science. She showed them my book *Silence of the Spheres*, which features many deaf women in the history of science. The graduate committee changed its decision and accepted her as a student in the master's degree program in neuroscience. She later completed a doctorate at the same university.

There is an enduring value in biography. From my own worldview, the characters I have researched have shown the courage and spirit to find ways to go over, under, and around barriers in attitudes and communication. As Thomas Carlyle has written, our "history" is "the essence of innumerable biographies." These life stories provide an aid to interpreting our current life experiences and have the potential to be agents of change by enhancing the lives of future generations of deaf people.

References

Cerf, Vinton. "The Electronic Mailbox: A New Communication Tool for the Hearing Impaired." *American Annals of the Deaf* 123 (1978): 768–72.

Lang, Harry G. *Edmund Booth, Deaf Pioneer.* Washington, DC: Gallaudet University Press, 2004.

———. *A Phone of Our Own: The Deaf Insurrection against Ma Bell.* Washington, DC: Gallaudet University Press, 2000.

———. "Reflections on Biographical Research and Writing." *Sign Language Studies* 7(2) (2007a): 141–51.

———. *Silence of the Spheres: The Deaf Experience in the History of Science.* Westport, CT: Bergin and Garvey, 1994.

———. *Teaching from the Heart and Soul: The Life and Work of Robert F. Panara.* Washington, DC: Gallaudet University Press, 2007b.

Harry G. Lang, Oscar Cohen, and Joseph Fischgrund. *Moments of Truth: The Journey of Robert R. Davila, Deaf Educator.* Rochester, NY: RIT Cary Graphic Arts Press, 2007. Also published in Spanish in 2011 as *Momentos decisivos: La historia de un líder sordo.*

Lang, Harry G., and Bonnie Meath-Lang. *Deaf Persons in the Arts and Sciences: A Biographical Dictionary.* Westport, CT: Greenwood, 1995.

Lang, Harry G., and Jorge A. Santiago-Blay. "Contributions of Deaf People to Entomology: A Hidden Legacy." *Terrestrial Arthropod Reviews* 5 (2012): 223–68.

Lyons, Paul C., Elsie Darrah Morey, and Robert H. Wagner. *Historical Perspective of Early Twentieth-Century Carboniferous Paleobotany in North America: In Memory of William Culp Darrah.* Boulder, CO: Geological Society of America, 1995, vii.

PART 2

Biographies of Deaf Pioneers

Finding the Connections: Educated Deaf People in England in the Mid-Seventeenth Century

Peter Jackson

I chose this topic because of my fascination with stories of deaf educa-tion, as formal deaf education did not start in Britain, France, or Germany until the mid-to-late eighteenth century. I never believed that there were no deaf persons without any form of education who lived in Britain prior to the start of Braidwood's Academy in Edinburgh. At that time, famous British academics like Dr. John Wallis also conducted widespread studies of chirology (the study of sign language) and all things linked to deafness.

The starting point for my research was John Bulwer's *Philocophus, or, the Deafe and Dumbe Mans Friend,* published in 1648, which men-tions the names of twenty-five deaf people who could lip-read, read, and write. The key name mentioned in Bulwer's book was Sir Edward Gostwicke (1620–1671), to whom the book is dedicated. Gostwicke also had a brother, William. Bulwer states that the Gostwicke brothers were excellent lip-readers and were able to write. Other people who were living at the time

Sir Edward Gostwicke

and kept diaries (such as Samuel Pepys) noted that the Gostwickes communicated very well by "signes" (the use of sign language was commonly spelled in Old English in this form). However, I was unable to find any trace of documents allegedly written by the Gostwicke brothers anywhere in the various British archives, including the National Archives.

So, their ability to read and write could not be proven, and research about the Gostwicke brothers was reluctantly shelved. But this research did uncover interesting facts about other deaf people whose ability to read and write could be proven.

In the years 1650–1660 most people in Europe did not go to school and could not read and write. Only about one in every hundred persons living at that time was literate. Priests or sons of rich people who went

Sir John Gaudy

to the university and became lawyers or had any form of employment that required them to read and write were the exceptions. Therefore, Deaf people from the 1650s who could be proven to be literate were unique. I was able to find three such individuals living between 1650 and 1670, and these I researched in depth. Fortunately, the British National Archives and other archives near where these individuals had resided contained considerable material about them. These three Deaf people were Sir John Gaudy (1639–1708) and his younger brother Framlingham (1642–1673), who lived in the English county of Norfolk, and Alexander Popham (1648–1707), who grew up in the English county of Berkshire but lived most of the latter part of his life in the county of Gloucestershire.

The Gaudy Brothers

Sir John and Framlingham Gaudy were part of the extended Gawdy family of lawyers, parliamentarians, and physicians that left thousands of documents to be preserved in the British National Archives. These documents tell of the day-to-day routines of family members, thus enabling a fascinating picture to be painted of family life in rural England in the seventeenth century. Sir John and Framlingham, as well as their sister and descendants, preferred to spell their last name as "Gaudy" to distance themselves from other branches of the Gawdy family who fought in the English Civil War of 1641–1645 between those who supported Parliament (known as Parliamentarians) and those who supported the king (known as Royalists). Those who supported the king lost most of their wealth and estates at the war's end, but the Gaudys retained most of theirs.

The Gawdy documents in the National Archives contain several references to how the Gaudy brothers, along with their hearing sister, learned to read and write from the local parish priest, John Cressner, who was also a teacher. Together with the priest's two sons and another boy who was the son of a tenant farmer on the Gaudy estate, the Gaudy children formed a "class" of children who were all roughly the same age within the priest's own house. Additionally, the priest managed to acquire a book (called a "most remarkable book" by the Gaudy children's uncle), which he used to teach sign language to both the deaf and the hearing children. The children learned sign language so well that the youngest Cressner boy, Henry, who later became the parish priest when his father died, also became Sir John's interpreter and scribe, helping to manage the Gaudy estate.

When John and Framlingham were respectively aged sixteen and fifteen, they were sent to study painting at Sir Peter Lely's art school, where they were mentored by one of Lely's tutors, George Freeman. Freeman was said in Bulwer's *Philocophus* to have two deaf daughters who could read and write. The two girls, who were at least ten years older than the Gaudy boys, used sign language with their father. It therefore seemed logical that the two boys should board with the Freeman family while at art school, thereby exposing them to a signing environment.

After the death of his father in 1669, John acceded to the baronetcy and painted only for amusement, but proof that he could read and write comes from the fact that he fought and won two court cases in London's Chancery Court and also left three letters among the family documents in the National Archives.

Framlingham was more of a social person than Sir John (as he was now known). Whereas the latter preferred to stay at home in rural Norfolk, Framlingham preferred to live in London, where he would get together with his Deaf and nondeaf friends. He was much loved by the people who knew him. Only when he contracted a severe attack of smallpox, which was prevalent in the seventeenth century, did Framlingham return home to Norfolk after spending six years in London. He never properly recovered from the smallpox and never married. People who wrote about Framlingham mention several times that he used to carry pencil and paper with him to help him to communicate with hearing people that he encountered. These writings are probably the first references to the way deaf people use pen and paper as a means of communication.

Framlingham Gaudy left one of the greatest legacies to Deaf history: His will, dated May 2, 1672, written in excellent English and beautiful cursive script, is the earliest known will confirmed to have been written by a Deaf person. We know that Framlingham wrote it because it is authenticated on the back by a notary public as being in the handwriting of Framlingham Gaudy.

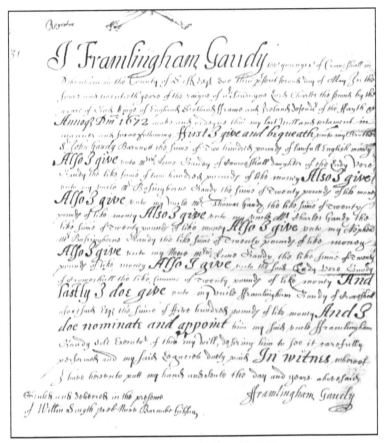

The will of Framlingham Gaudy

Alexander Popham

The third individual researched was Alexander Popham, who was born to Colonel Edward Popham, one of Oliver Cromwell's generals-at-sea. (Cromwell did not use the term "admiral," considering this to be a Royalist title.) Alexander's father died when Alexander was only three years old, and the family, consisting of his mother and five-year-old sister, Letitia, moved to live with Edward Popham's brother at the vast country estate of Littlecote House in Berkshire. By then the family knew that Alexander was deaf. Alexander's uncle was Colonel Alexander Popham, a wealthy Parliamentarian. Colonel Popham had eight children and employed governesses who encouraged the children to play at reading, writing, and learning about

The authentication of the Gaudy will

things in general; thus by the time Alexander was about ten or eleven years old, he was said to be expert "in the use of the pencil."

It has also been recorded that Alexander developed his own form of sign language around this time, which he used with his family and servants on the estate. His family, however, felt it was important that he learn to talk because, when he became an adult, he would come into possession of his dead father's numerous properties and estates, which he would need to manage.

The family therefore engaged a doctor of divinity, William Holder, to teach Alexander to speak. Holder took advantage of Alexander's ability to read, write, and sign to teach him how to enunciate certain syllables and words, as the following excerpt illustrates: "Write down on paper a P and B, and make signes to him to endeavour to produce [them]."

However, Alexander was not with Holder for long because in 1659 Holder took up a new post as a canon at Ely Cathedral, which meant he had to leave the area. After a gap of about eighteen months, the family succeeded in getting a new teacher for Alexander. This was another doctor of divinity, John Wallis, who found that Alexander had "forgotten much of what he had been taught [by Holder]." Like Holder, Wallis took advantage of the boy's ability to read and write, but his methods were very different. What Wallis did was to write numerous pages in a small octavo-sized pocketbook in fine

William Holder   *John Wallis*

handwriting, covering many different subjects in detailed lists of vocabulary for items such as parts of the body (back, breast, belly) and grammatical phrases and sentences such as "a sheep hath wool on his back."

Speech training was not forgotten, and to ensure that Popham would remember how to pronounce certain words, Wallis created several pages on phonetics, thus becoming the first person to use symbols to represent speech sounds in the English language. (It was not until 1867 that Alexander Melville Bell introduced a system of more precise notation for writing down speech sounds.)

A page in a different handwriting appears at the end of Wallis's notebook. It appears to be the writing of a schoolboy, and it may well be that Alexander wanted to make his own mark in the notebook. His signature on that page is very similar to signatures attributed to him in estate documents and deeds as a middle-aged man, after he had left Littlecote and was living in Gloucestershire. Documents in local archives show that he was adept at managing his estates and handling accounts and leaseholds of water mills, land, and buildings. These documents demonstrate that it might be accurate to define Alexander Popham as the first Deaf businessman.

Lessons from Their Lives and Particularly Their Education

Because of their upbringing, the Gaudy brothers and Alexander Popham were able to acquire a social standing unheard of for deaf persons of their time. As children, the Gaudys and Popham were able to practice

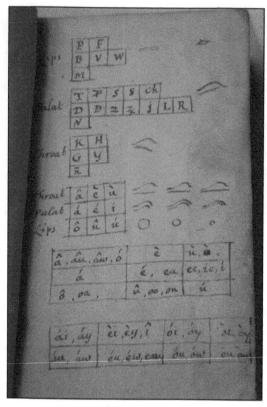

Wallis's written phonetics system

reading and writing in a supportive environment consisting mainly of close family members and, in the Gaudy brothers' case, their teacher's children, who were very similar to them in age.

Comparisons

Gaudy Brothers	Alexander Popham
Taught in a sign language environment	Taught through speech
Were able to read and write well but had poor math skills (they were almost always in financial difficulty)	Excellent literacy and math skills (he kept his estates in good financial order)
Could not speak at all	Allegedly able to speak
Used interpreters (family members and a scribe), especially in court	No evidence of using communication support

The stories of these three people have been made into two books, *The Gawdy Manuscripts* (Jackson 2004) and *Alexander Popham's Notebook* (Jackson 2012).

References

Arnold, Thomas. *Education of Deaf Mutes.* London: Wertheimer Lea, 1888.

Bulwer, John. *Philocophus, or, the Deafe and Dumbe Mans Friend.* London, 1648.

Dobson, Austin, ed. *The Diary of John Evelyn.* London: Macmillan, 1906.

Jackson, Peter. *A Pictorial History of Deaf Britain.* Winsford Cheshire, UK: Deafprint Winsford, 2001.

_____. *The Gawdy Manuscripts.* Feltham, England: BDHS Publications, 2004.

_____. *Alexander Popham's Notebook.* Feltham, England: BDHS Publications, 2012.

Popham, Frederick W. *A West Country Family: The Pophams from 1150.* Published privately in a limited edition, 1976.

Wheatley, H. B., ed. *The Diary of Samuel Pepys.* London: Bell, 1949.

Manuscript Sources

British Library, Add. Mss 27395–7

_____, Add. Mss 36989–90

_____, Egerton Mss 2716–2722

Church of St. Lawrence, Bourton-on-the-Hill: *Parish Register and Ledger*

Gloucestershire Records Office: D2957/52/3

_____: D2957/302/56

_____: D2957/302/59

_____: D2957/302/60

Historical Mss Commission, *The Family of Gawdy.* London, 1885

Norfolk Record Office: MC98

_____: NRA 7825

Nottingham University Archives: PW2HY.110/1

Original notebook belonging to Alexander Popham, 1662

Public Record Office: Chancery Proceedings, Bridges Division 1613–1714, no. 108

Somerset Record Office: DD/PO, POT (Popham Papers)

Suffolk Record Office: *Pupils List, King Edward Grammar School 1550–1700*

Writing Resistance: Edwin A. Hodgson and the Controversy at St. Ann's Church

Jannelle Legg

In 1897 a visible and volatile crisis occurred at St. Ann's Church for Deaf-Mutes in New York City. Following the sale of St. Ann's church buildings, the parishioners struggled with a rapidly diminishing congregation and limited options for relocation.[1] For two years the church was temporarily housed in the Church of St. John the Evangelist. Around that time a proposed merger with St. Matthew's Church, a struggling parish with a hearing congregation, incited a passionate and public outcry from deaf members of the congregation, led by Edwin A. Hodgson, editor of the influential *Deaf Mutes' Journal (DMJ)*. Though attempts to block the consolidation of St. Ann's Church failed, the controversial merger reflects far more than contentious parish unification. Closer examination reveals this to be an important social and political moment for the deaf community, where the struggle for autonomy is public and concerted, largely carried out and legitimized by a narrative of resistance in the pages of the deaf press.

Hodgson was well known throughout the national and international deaf communities. Though he was born in Manchester, England, on February 28,

1854, in his youth his family relocated to Canada. Following "an attack of cerebro-spinal meningitis" at the age of eighteen, Hodgson became deaf. He abandoned his plans of becoming a lawyer and obtained an apprenticeship in the field of printing and typography.[2] After Hodgson relocated to New York City, a chance encounter with a deaf man in a composing room led Hodgson to meet Dr. Isaac L. Peet, principal of the Fanwood School, and in short order he was offered a position teaching printing. Under his control, the printing department at the New York Institution for the Deaf was greatly expanded, and Hodgson became well known for producing "first-class workmen."[3]

An active member of St. Ann's Church, Hodgson served as a layman under Rev. Thomas Gallaudet and was a member of St. Ann's Vestry for a number of years.[4] In matters of the church, "Mr. Hodgson's counsel, always given calmly and gently, was as indispensable to the progress of the work as are the walls to a house."[5] As a writer, Hodgson was well known for the fearlessness with which he composed his editorial column.[6] In 1898 James E. Gallaher described him as "a clear and forcible writer, not afraid to express his opinions and to stand by them, and yet always according those who may differ with him the courtesy due them."[7] His involvement in many deaf organizations, and particularly his prominent role as editor, not only characterized but also defined the direction of deaf activism in the early twentieth century.[8]

He and other deaf writers of this time utilized the press to collaborate, inform the public, and challenge the paternalism and oralism that limited the autonomy of the deaf community in the United States.[9] The written medium enabled Hodgson to bridge the language barrier between nonsigning hearing people and signing deaf people and to disseminate information widely.[10] Given that the *DMJ* was extensively circulated and available to both deaf and hearing readers, Hodgson's writing on this topic provided a counterdiscourse to proponents of the merger and a means of representation for a community that understood too well the tragic loss they faced when St. Ann's was merged with St. Matthew's.[11] In publicizing this controversy and directly opposing the church leaders, Hodgson and other deaf individuals risked the loss of the very social and cultural center they sought to defend.

Throughout St. Ann's history, the church received frequent, albeit relatively innocuous, attention in the *DMJ* as Hodgson and local contributors posted summaries of parties, disclosed information about upcoming meetings, and distributed announcements related to church business.[12] For a full account of the importance of the merger we can turn to Hodgson's dramatic editorial writing between the years 1894 and 1897.[13] An examination of texts from this period indicates that Hodgson used writing as a form of resistance, taking to the pages of the *DMJ* to highlight his discontent, promote alternative solutions to a merger, and keep his audience abreast of the changing events. In a broader view, however, the coverage of this controversy framed these events in terms of deaf agency and space. Over the course of four years, increased attention was paid to issues of autonomy, representation, and space as Hodgson's opposition developed and his resolve deepened.

For more than forty years St. Ann's Church had operated with a dual mission. Each week, two congregations, one deaf, the other hearing, divided their time between the chapel and the church rooms.[14] This arrangement served for years to buttress a system of vocational and social support between the two groups.[15] As the controversy grew, the narrative that undercut Hodgson's writing increasingly focused on the divided congregation, drawing a greater distinction between deaf and hearing people with more concise strokes. This was further complicated by Hodgson's own social networks, which involved hearing people, specifically Rev. Dr. Thomas Gallaudet and John H. Comer. "The hearing have hundreds of churches, but the deaf have only one. They will soon be obliged to seek temporary quarters, and will have no permanent place of worship until the hearing representatives, who know nothing about their needs, get ready to provide one."[16] With increasing emphasis, Hodgson called for full autonomy for the deaf members of the church, with a separate church structure and a board composed of deaf members of the congregation.

From the first announcement in 1894 of the sale of the church buildings, Hodgson's editorial column outlined a plan for a new church for deaf congregants.[17] In the initial descriptions of the church, his writing did not include a direct appeal for funds or assertions about the church structure.[18] Instead, he made clear recommendations for accommodations that would be better suited to deaf congregants in terms of location and arrangement and even mentioned the construction of additional buildings.[19] These requests were not unreasonable, as there was a history of renovating St. Ann's church buildings to make the space more accessible to signing deaf congregants.[20] Representation did not appear as a theme in Hodgson's writing at this time. At this stage, the search committee responsible for soliciting a new location for the church included a deaf representative and several deaf members of the vestry. Hodgson was confident that the deaf members would receive "the consideration to which they [were] surely entitled."[21]

After a failed attempt to build on lots in upper Manhattan, the spring of 1895 was marked by a rapid escalation in Hodgson's coverage and prose. He called for separate church buildings that were adapted specifically to the requirements of the deaf congregants.[22] As events, including an attempted merger with another church, unfolded, the lack of equal representation in the vestry became a very important feature of Hodgson's writing.[23] In one editorial he asserted, "In the councils of the consolidated church, the deaf have no representation at all proportionate to the needs and demands of their mission."[24] Throughout this period he highlighted that, beyond the few deaf vestrymen, those who were members "knew absolutely nothing about the deaf congregation."[25] Hodgson warned his readers that these church leaders would continue to take action without the input of the deaf community. He reiterated that, although the hearing congregants had a multitude of churches at their disposal, for members of the deaf community, St. Ann's was the sole option: "[W]e protest against sacrificing the spiritual welfare of the deaf in order to suit the convenience of the hearing congregation. There are plenty of churches with which hearing people can affiliate, but there is only one for deaf-mutes."[26] This argument, which appeared throughout the controversy, indicated the disparity between the deaf and the hearing congregants and also the significant loss of access to social space that threatened the deaf community. Despite his initial critique, in mid-April 1895 Hodgson's editorial writing took a conciliatory step back. Where he had directly called for a division between the deaf and the hearing congregations, Hodgson shifted his attention to maintaining the church's dual mission, while also achieving a level of autonomy and obtaining distinctive deaf spaces within a new church structure.[27]

By the fall of 1895 attendance at church services and social organizations had begun to decline. Without directly criticizing the church or its leaders, Hodgson again called for the establishment of a distinct and separate space for the deaf congregants. This time, he claimed the church funds belonged to the deaf congregants:

> The deaf-mutes of this city are in urgent need of such a building. They contributed much to St. Ann's and it is their peculiar condition that has enlisted the sympathy of wealthy people and thus secured many donations to St. Ann's. They are, therefore, entitled to first considera-tion, for while hearing people can become members of any number of other churches the deaf-mutes are dependent upon the one where sign language is used in preaching . . . Build the parish house at once, and save the deaf-mutes from temptation and disaster![28]

A tentative repose continued in his coverage until the fall of 1896, when Hodgson's column erupted yet again after he learned that, despite assur-ances to the contrary, church leaders had continued to discuss options for relocation without open communication with the church's deaf members:

> [I]t seems the religious welfare of deaf-mutes is neglected, because the church *for deaf-mutes* is also for hearing persons. Promises were given over a year ago that active work to procure a new house of worship would be begun at once, and that the deaf-mutes affiliated with "St. Ann's Church for Deaf-Mutes" would be kept informed. . . . Lately, we have been told that the efforts to build on the site selected . . . have been abandoned; that plans have been discussed by the *hearing* vestrymen;—but secrecy has been observed towards the deaf-mutes. "St. Ann's Church *for Deaf-Mutes*" has a vestry composed of hearing persons who control everything—the three deaf-mutes on the vestry being in the minority by about three to one. The hearing vestrymen are undoubtedly good and generous Christians. But they know noth-ing about deaf-mutes, they never are seen among deaf-mutes and not one deaf-mute of St. Ann's congregation even knows their names. "St. Ann's Church for Deaf Mutes" has prospered from the labors of its ministry to a very great extent, but it has been helped far more (from a financial point of view) by its *name*—"St. Ann's Church for Deaf-Mutes." . . . Therefore it is right and just for the deaf-mutes to receive first consideration in the planning of the new church edifice.[29]

Hodgson openly renewed his disdain for the lack of representation and emphasized that these actions denied the deaf congregants agency within the church that carried their name.

In April 1897 Bishop Henry C. Potter and the vestry of St. Ann's Church began a series of meetings with the vestry of St. Matthew's Church to discuss the possibility of a merger. Renewing his protest about the lack of representation of the deaf congregants and criticizing the physical space, Hodgson outright demanded that a large portion of the financial holdings of St. Ann's be directed to the deaf congregants for their own use:[30] "The deaf-mutes of New York are indignant and angry at the attempt to deprive them of the funds which rightly belong to the church work among deaf-mutes."[31] His editorial concisely exhorted the leaders of St. Ann's to take action against the merger and lamented that the lack of representation had functionally limited the deaf community from actionable dissent: "Any one can see that the work and accumulation of money for forty years in the name of deaf-mutes are to be wrecked at one fell swoop, and the deaf-mutes are to be stranded high and dry without a dollar they can call their own."[32] Finally, he openly castigated the church leaders for using the deaf congregants as an object of pity to obtain funds and then divert these funds for the leaders' own benefit:[33] "St. Ann's Church for Deaf-Mutes has thrived on donations and legacies. . . . And with pity and charity in their hearts, good people gave liberally. . . . How indignant these donors must feel to-day, if they know that effort is being made to divert the accumulated funds of 'ST. ANN'S CHURCH FOR DEAF-MUTES' to alien purposes."[34]

The division between the hearing and the deaf congregants, which Hodgson had highlighted in his writing, was complicated by a partnership with John H. Comer, a hearing member of the vestry and strong opponent of the church consolidation. Comer, a senior warden of the church, had publicly denounced the merger and in protest attempted to resign his position as a member of the vestry.[35] The collaboration between these men was fostered by Hodgson's writing on the subject, and through correspondence the pair combined their efforts to contest the consolidation.[36] Though the motivations driving their individual opposition differed, Hodgson and Comer worked closely to prevent the consolidation, sharing information and providing each other with support as events unfolded.[37]

By the beginning of the summer, the tension surrounding the controversy had reached a breaking point, as evidenced by tumultuous meetings held on June 18, 1897. Two distinct accounts of these events exist. The first, published in the *New York Times (NYT)*, featured a salacious headline and a description of the events that largely faulted the deaf congregants. The article, titled "Nearly a Riot in Church; Opposition to the Consolidation of St. Ann's and St. Matthew's Leads to Blows; One Man Thrown Down Stairs," described a "crowd of mutes wildly gesticulating" and a "small sized riot" that ensued after a supporter of the merger "smothered the lamps lighting the room [and] a deaf person struck that individual and was then captured by the group and thrown down the stairs."[38] The second account, published in the *DMJ* by Hodgson and Theo Lounsbary and disclosed in a private letter from Comer to Hodgson, told a vastly different story.[39] While the *NYT* version of events indicated that the "faction in opposition to the consolidation" was at fault, Hodgson's column emphasized the lack of justice in the overall process of the merger and highlighted a systematic disregard by hearing people for the deaf congregants. "In defiance of all parliamentary law, and utterly ignoring what is right and just, a number of men in the rear of the hall were counted so as to defeat the solid vote of the deaf gentlemen present, the ladies not being the allowed the privileges of voting. The Chairman of the meeting hurriedly announced that the agreement had been approved, jammed it in his coat pocket and hastened from the hall."[40] Hodgson challenged the report in the *NYT* and declared that the size of the opposition to the merger was larger than indicated. "After the meeting, the deaf members—in fact, all the deaf gentlemen and ladies present—organized and voted solidly and unanimously against the 'agreement' which Dr. Krans told a reporter had been approved with practically no opposition."[41] This marked a significant event in the controversy and, more broadly, has direct implications for the role of the press in disseminating information and providing a counternarrative of deaf discourse.

The fall of 1897 brought renewed attempts to challenge the merger, but these proved unsuccessful. On October 27 the Supreme Court Order of Consolidation was signed by Judge Truax. Though Hodgson followed these events closely, little was known about their progression until the merger was announced.[42] As the facts became clear, Hodgson provided a full accounting of the consolidation for his readers, emphasizing that even though they had succeeded in guaranteeing a separate space for the deaf congregants of St. Ann's, they had done so at the cost of their church funds and drastically limited autonomy and representation in the church structure.[43] Hodgson wrote dejectedly, "The fight to prevent the 'consolidation' of St. Ann's Church for Deaf-Mutes with St. Matthew's Church has ended with defeat for the deaf-mutes who, almost to a man, protested and pleaded against the absorption of their church and transfer of its funds to St. Matthew's Church."[44] In short order, the new St. Matthew's carried out the agreement, and a chapel was quickly constructed on 148th Street.[45]

At the conclusion of the controversy, one deaf writer declared that the deaf community would not "live long enough to ever forget the loss of their church."[46] Though this remains a valuable example of deaf resistance and historical claims for autonomy and deaf spaces, the story of these events has been largely absent from the deaf historical record. The reasons for this resistance are myriad and complex; however, it is important to identify St. Ann's Church for members of the New York deaf community as a social and cultural institution. While churches serve as houses for religious worship, enabling the expression of faith and community by members of the congregation, they also serve a number of other social functions. In this case, St. Ann's Church provided an array of social and welfare services for its congregants, including financial aid, employment assistance, legal and interpreting services, housing, and educational opportunities.[47] Beyond this, the physical spaces available to deaf community members provided an opportunity to develop agency and organization through the number of deaf clubs and associations that operated out of St. Ann's.

As the escalation of Hodgson's writing demonstrates, the dual congregation of St. Ann's struggled to align the needs and aspirations of the deaf congregants with the patriarchal church structure. The increasing division between both deaf and hearing congregants demonstrated an increasingly organized and politically active American deaf community struggling to redefine its position in terms of autonomy and representation. In the span of three years, the narrative Hodgson utilized shifted from a tacit acceptance of the dynamics at St. Ann's to an assertion that the deaf congregants had a right to control both the church funds that they had donated and a distinct space for themselves. As Hodgson's writing strongly opposed the merger, his framing of these events in terms of a loss of agency and space was disseminated across the United States to the *DMJ*'s readers.

These efforts are significant in the role they played in creating an informed audience. The readers of the *DMJ* and similar deaf newspapers utilized these texts to stay current on issues relevant to their community.[48] In the United States the deaf press featured selected articles of interest from the mainstream press, generating a deaf-centered forum that would be published and reprinted elsewhere.[49] The St. Ann's controversy demonstrates how effective this web of information could be in creating an informed narrative of resistance. The coverage of this controversy in the *DMJ* elicited responses of support from distant members of the deaf community and gained increasing attention in another paper in the network of private and deaf school newspapers known as the Little Paper Family.[50]

Significantly, the attention garnered extended beyond the deaf community. As evidenced by the collaboration between Hodgson and Comer, the resistance written about in the *DMJ* created a counter-discourse to the coverage that appeared in the *New York Times*. Though it is noteworthy that this collaboration crossed hearing/deaf boundaries, it indicates that, in moments of controversy, the press may be used to draw a distinction between deaf and hearing discourses and further illustrates the distribution of power in the deaf community. Further consideration of the controversy suggests that, within the deaf community itself, the esteem Hodgson garnered as editor of a prestigious publication lent legitimacy to his arguments and editorials, and it appears that the press can act to legitimize opinions to the point of eliciting a direct response from church leaders, though, in this case, it was ineffective in preventing the merger.[51]

An important aspect of Hodgson's resistance was his role as editor of a nationally circulated newspaper. Each week Hodgson had a platform from which to circulate information, promote his personal opinions, and direct his readers' attention to certain issues. This platform created a public space for discussing the issues confronting the American deaf community in which deaf perspectives and writing were given primacy. Whether presenting direct or veiled critiques, the columns of the deaf press enabled Hodgson and other deaf writers to publicly collaborate and to challenge coercive power relations.

Even though this episode has largely been lost to history, Hodgson's actions indicate that he understood the value of using these newspapers as his pulpit, exhorting deaf people and the public at large to act. Despite his failed efforts to stave off the merger, these events reflect a number of larger issues that deaf people grappled with at the time. Deaf church members' autonomy was wrested away without any input from them, and the community suffered another defeat in the loss of their physical space and control of their finances. Hodgson was uniquely able to insert himself into a dialogue on the issues of representation, space, and autonomy, and though he was unsuccessful, this episode also demonstrates the importance of harnessing the pages of the deaf press to create a space for resistance.

Notes

1. For additional analysis see Jannelle Legg, " 'Not Consolidation but Absorption': A Historical Examination of the Controversy at St. Ann's Church for the Deaf" (master's thesis, Gallaudet University, 2011).

2. Guilbert C. Braddock, "Edwin Hodgson," *Fanwood Journal* 2, no. 1 (October 1933): 5–7; William Robert Roe, *Peeps into the Deaf World* (London: Bemrose and Sons, 1917); Raymond Lee, *Deaf Lives: Deaf People in History,* ed. Raymond Lee and Peter Webster Jackson (Middlesex: British Deaf History Society Publications, 2001); Lawrence R. Newman, *Sands of Time: NAD Presidents 1880–2003* (Silver Spring, MD: National Association of the Deaf, 2006).

3. Roe, *Peeps into the Deaf World,* 352–54.

4. Newman, *Sands of Time,* 31.

5. Braddock, "Edwin Hodgson."

6. T. Alan Hurwitz, "Education; Other Deaf Educational Leaders," in *Gallaudet Encyclopedia of Deaf People and Deafness,* 1st ed., ed. John V. Van Cleve (New York: McGraw-Hill Professional, 1987), 364.

7. James Ernst Gallaher, *Representative Deaf Persons of the United States of America: Containing Portraits and Character Sketches of Prominent Deaf Persons (commonly Called "Deaf Mutes") Who Are Engaged in the Higher Pursuits of Life* (Chicago: Gallaher, 1898), 162.

8. For further biographical information about Hodgson consult ibid., 159–62; Roe, *Peeps into the Deaf World,* 352–54; Jack R. Gannon, *Deaf Heritage: A Narrative History*

of Deaf America, ed. Jane Butler and Laura-Jean Gilbert (Silver Spring, MD: National Association of the Deaf, 1981), 62, 65; Hurwitz, "Education; Other Deaf Educational Leaders," 364; Lee, *Deaf Lives,* 98–99; Newman, *Sands of Time,* 23–44.

9. For further examination of this facet of deaf history see Christopher Krentz, *Writing Deafness: The Hearing Line in Nineteenth-Century American Literature* (Chapel Hill: University of North Carolina Press, 2007); John V. Van Cleve and Barry A. Crouch, *A Place of Their Own: Creating the Deaf Community in America* (Washington, DC: Gallaudet University Press, 1989); Susan Burch, *Signs of Resistance: American Deaf Cultural History, 1900 to World War II* (New York: NYU Press, 2004); "The Silent Worker Newspaper and the Building of a Deaf Community: 1890–1929," in *Deaf History Unveiled: Interpretations from the New Scholarship,* ed. John V. Van Cleve (Washington, DC: Gallaudet University Press, 1999), 172–97.

10. Christopher Krentz expands on this at length in his texts: Christopher Krentz, *A Mighty Change: An Anthology of Deaf American Writing, 1816–1864* (Washington, DC: Gallaudet University Press, 2000), xx, xxi; Krentz, *Writing Deafness.*

11. The *DMJ* is further described in "Edwin Allan Hodgson, M.A.," *Silent Worker* 7, no. 3 (November 1894): 1–2; and Newman, *Sands of Time,* 25. For more information about the American deaf press, see Beth Haller, "The Little Papers: Newspapers at the Nineteenth-Century Schools for Deaf Persons," *Journalism History* 19, no. 2 (1993): 43.

12. These articles provide a bit of insight into church structures and proceedings and enable us to flesh out the convergence of events that led to the controversy. Several examples of these articles include Henry C. Rider, "St. Ann's Church for Deaf-Mutes," *DMJ* 5, no. 1 (January 6, 1876): 2; Edwin A. Hodgson, "Editor's Column," *DMJ* 15, no. 29 (July 22, 1886): 2; Montague Tigg: "New York; Society Doings and Other Happenings; Personal and Not Personal," *DMJ* 15, no. 41 (October 14, 1886): 3; "Services for Deaf-Mutes," *DMJ* 21, no. 41 (October 13, 1892): 2; "Special Notice to Deaf-Mutes," *DMJ* 21, no. 43 (October 27, 1892): 4; "Manhattan Literary Ass'n," *DMJ* 21, no. 43 (October 27, 1892): 4.

13. Legg, " 'Not Consolidation but Absorption.' "

14. Beginning in 1874, the church had two additional ministers for each congregation: the Reverend Edward Krans for the hearing and the Reverend John Chamberlain for the deaf. Thomas Gallaudet, "History," Sacramental Register 3 (St. Ann's Church, 1873–1887), 6, Box 45, File 1, Archives of the Episcopal Diocese of New York.

15. Gallaudet wrote that his goal was to join families together in one church house for mutual support. Thomas Gallaudet, "A Sketch of My Life," unpublished autobiographical manuscript (Washington, DC, n.d.), 10, Thomas Gallaudet Papers, Gallaudet University Archives.

16. Hodgson, "Editor's Column," *DMJ* 24, no. 12 (March 21, 1895): 2.

17. Hodgson, "Editor's Column," *DMJ* 22, no. 44 (November 1, 1894): 2; "In the Real Estate Field," *New York Times* (October 31, 1894), New York Times Archive 1851–1980.

18. Hodgson, "Editor's Column," *DMJ* 23, no. 48 (November 29, 1894), 2. It is possible that Hodgson and the other deaf congregants did not directly consider representation because representation was a facet of Episcopal church structures. For further discussion of the Episcopal Church system see Legg, " 'Not Consolidation but Absorption.' "

19. Hodgson, "Editor's Column," *DMJ* 23, no. 48 (November 29, 1894), 2.

20. Tigg, "New York," October 14, 1886.

21. W. O. Fitzgerald was a member of the five-person search committee, and the vestry members included H. J. Haight, A. A. Barnes, and William Fitzgerald. Ted,

"New York," *DMJ* 23, no. 45 (November 8, 1894): 3; Hodgson, "Editor's Column," *DMJ* 23, no. 48 (November 29, 1894).

22. Hodgson, "Editor's Column," *DMJ* 24, no. 9 (February 28, 1895): 2; Hodgson, "Editor's Column," *DMJ* 26, no. 10 (March 7, 1895): 2; Hodgson, "Editor's Column," *DMJ* 24, no. 11 (March 14, 1895): 2; Hodgson, "Editor's Column," *DMJ* 24, no. 12 (March 21, 1895); Hodgson, "Editor's Column," *DMJ* 24, no. 13 (March 28, 1895): 2.

23. Hodgson, "Editor's Column," *DMJ* 23, no. 48 (November 29, 1894); Hodgson, "Editor's Column," *DMJ* 24, no. 11 (March 14, 1895); Hodgson, "Editor's Column," *DMJ* 24, no. 12 (March 21, 1895); Hodgson, "Editor's Column," *DMJ* 24, no. 13 (March 28, 1895).

24. Hodgson, "Editor's Column," *DMJ* 24, no. 13 (March 28, 1895).

25. Hodgson, "Editor's Column," *DMJ* 24, no. 12 (March 21, 1895): 2.

26. Hodgson, "Editor's Column," *DMJ* 26, no. 10 (March 7, 1895); Hodgson, "Editor's Column," *DMJ* 24, no. 11 (March 14, 1895).

27. Hodgson, "Editor's Column," *DMJ* 24, no. 13 (March 28, 1895); Hodgson, "Editor's Column," *DMJ* 24, no. 14 (April 4, 1895): 2; Hodgson, "Editor's Column," *DMJ* 24, no. 17 (April 25, 1895): 3; Hodgson, "Editor's Column," *DMJ* 24, no. 21 (May 23, 1895): 2.

28. Hodgson, "Editor's Column," *DMJ* 24, no. 39 (September 26, 1895): 2.

29. Hodgson, "Editor's Column," *DMJ* 25, no. 35 (August 27, 1896): 2.

30. Hodgson, "Editor's Column: St. Ann's Church for Deaf-Mutes," *DMJ* 26, no. 14 (April 8, 1897): 2.

31. Ibid.

32. Hodgson, "Editor's Column," *DMJ* 26, no. 16 (April 22, 1897): 2.

33. Ibid.

34. Ibid.

35. John H. Comer, "Correspondence: Comer to the Rector and Vestry of St. Ann's, March 30, 1887," Correspondence, March 30, 1897, Box 44, File 12, Archives of the Episcopal Diocese of New York; "Church Merging Blocked," *New York Times* (May 7, 1897), New York Times Archive 1851–1980, http://query.nytimes.com/search/query?srchst=p.

36. John H. Comer, "Correspondence: Comer to Hodgson, April 12, 1897," Correspondence, April 12, 1897, Box 44, File 12, Archives of the Episcopal Diocese of New York; Hodgson, "Editor's Column," *DMJ* 26, no. 19 (May 13, 1897): 2.

37. Legg, " 'Not Consolidation but Absorption.' "

38. "Nearly a Riot in Church," *New York Times* (June 19, 1897), New York Times Archive 1851–1980.

39. Hodgson, "Editor's Column," *DMJ* 26, no. 25 (June 24, 1897): 2; "Ted," "New York: St. Ann's–St. Matthew's Consolidation Matter," *DMJ* 26, no. 25 (June 24, 1897): 2; John H. Comer, "Correspondence: Comer to Hodgson, June 22, 1897," Correspondence, June 22, 1897, Box 44, File 12, Archives of the Episcopal Diocese of New York.

40. "Nearly a Riot in Church"; Hodgson, "Editor's Column," *DMJ* 26, no. 25 (June 24, 1897).

41. Hodgson, "Editor's Column," *DMJ* 26, no. 25 (June 24, 1897).

42. Hodgson, "Editor's Column," *DMJ* 26, no. 42 (October 21, 1897): 2; Hodgson, "Editor's Column," *DMJ* 26, no. 45 (October 28, 1897): 2.

43. Hodgson, "Editor's Column," *DMJ* 26, no. 46 (November 18, 1897): 2.

44. Ibid.

45. Hodgson, "Editor's Column," *DMJ* 27, no. 46 (November 17, 1898): 2; Alexander L. Pach, "Greater New York," *Silent Worker* 11, no. 4 (December 1898): 54–56.

46. Robert E. Maynard, "Greater New York," *Silent Worker* 10, no. 6 (February 1898): 92.

47. For further examination of the role of religious institutions see Otto Benjamin Berg and Henry L. Buzzard, *A Missionary Chronicle: Being a History of the Ministry to the Deaf in the Episcopal Church, 1850–1980* (Hollywood, MD: St. Mary's Press, 1984); Legg, " 'Not Consolidation but Absorption' "; Burch, *Signs of Resistance*, 44–52; Kent R. Olney, "The Chicago Mission for the Deaf," in *The Deaf History Reader*, ed. John Vickrey Van Cleve (Washington, DC: Gallaudet University Press, 2007), 174–208; Van Cleve and Crouch, *Place of Their Own*, 1–8; Douglas C. Baynton, *Forbidden Signs: American Culture and the Campaign against Sign Language* (Chicago: University of Chicago Press, 1996); Harlan Lane, *When the Mind Hears: A History of the Deaf* (New York: Vintage, 1984); Otto Benjamin Berg and Henry L. Buzzard, *Thomas Gallaudet, Apostle to the Deaf* (New York: St. Ann's Church for the Deaf, 1989); Gannon, *Deaf Heritage*.

48. Krentz, *Mighty Change*, xxi.

49. Haller, "Little Papers"; Van Cleve and Crouch, *Place of Their Own*; Krentz, *Mighty Change*, xxi.

50. Olaf Hanson, "Correspondence: Olaf Hanson to Hodgson, July 1, 1897," Correspondence, July 1, 1897, Box 44, File 10, Archives of the Episcopal Diocese of New York; C. M. Nelson, "Correspondence: C. M. Nelson to Hodgson, July 20, 1897," Correspondence, July 20, 1897, Box 44, File 10, Archives of the Episcopal Diocese of New York; "A Quad," "Our New York Letter," *Silent Worker* 7, no. 7 (March 1895): 10.

51. Hodgson, "Editor's Column," *DMJ* 24, no. 39 (September 26, 1895); Hodgson, "Editor's Column," *DMJ* 26, no. 14 (April 8, 1897); Edward H. Krans, "Rev. Dr. Krans Writes about St. Ann's," *DMJ* 24, no. 19 (May 9, 1895): 4.

Hannah Holmes: A Case of Japanese American Deaf Incarceration

Newby Ely

Hannah Tomiko Takagi Holmes (1927–1996), a Deaf Japanese American, endured decades of adversity marked by multiple forms of discrimination, wartime incarceration, and cancer. Nevertheless, she fought endlessly for equality and justice for Deaf people, Asian Americans, and women. Citing relevant examples, this chapter examines the important historical impact of Hannah as a Deaf pioneer.

I chose to study Hannah because, after I had reviewed the wartime files of approximately sixty Deaf and hard of hearing Japanese Americans who were incarcerated in US concentration camps, Hannah stood out as one of the most distinguished. An important indicator is the relatively high number of Google entries on Hannah, while there are nearly none on the rest of these victims.

Early Childhood

Hannah was born into a Japanese American family in Elk Grove, a rural town near Sacramento, California. Her parents had emigrated to the United States from Hiroshima, Japan, via Hawaii. They were fruit farmers.[1] Hannah's deafness was discovered at age three or four, when her father noticed that she had not begun talking. So Hannah was taken to a doctor, who confirmed her deafness. Her parents spoke only Japanese. They often asked Ruth, Hannah's older sister, to interpret for them with Hannah. It was often a challenge for Ruth, as a young girl, to translate from Japanese to English.[2] Hannah's first school was a hearing school in Elk Grove, California. Her first teacher had a lot of patience with her. Although she was one of Hannah's best teachers, she did not have enough time to spend with Hannah because she had to balance her teaching time among all of her students. Therefore, she arranged to send Hannah to the California School for the Deaf in Berkeley,[3] where Hannah enrolled in 1935. The following years proved to be an awakening for her because she could finally converse with people in sign language. Her academic performance was deemed to be adequate.[4] She discovered her talent for art in an art class taught by a Deaf teacher.[5] Hannah's childhood innocence, which was soon to be shattered, is evident in a passage from her school newsletter of January 1942:

> Blackouts or no blackouts, life goes on as usual in the Girls' Primary Hall. The girls just cannot let such a little thing as a blackout interfere with their many and varied activities! There are many more exciting things happening to claim their interest. Only the other day Hannah Takagi came running into the house to tell us that out on the playground there was a great monster with horns and a great, red tongue hanging from his mouth. Dubiously, we investigated, and sure enough, there he was, not a monster, but a beautiful deer. He was surrounded by a mob of wildly excited youngsters and did not know where to turn. Finally he dashed away and was later rounded up by the police.[6]

On December 7, 1941, Japan had launched a surprise attack on the US naval bases at Pearl Harbor, Hawaii. The two following months were fueled by intense pressure by politicians on the West Coast, who demanded restrictive action against Japanese American residents. On

February 19, 1942, President Franklin Delano Roosevelt signed Executive Order 9066, which authorized the War Department to designate military areas, from which any or all persons could be excluded. This enabled the military authorities to designate the West Coast as a restricted zone and to force approximately one hundred and twenty thousand Japanese Americans to leave their homes. One month later President Roosevelt signed Executive Order 9102, creating a wartime civilian agency, the War Relocation Authority (WRA), to oversee the detention of Japanese Americans. It was the new agency's responsibility to build concentration camps and to provide food, clothes, employment, education, and other services within the camps. The WRA was also authorized to grant leave clearance for Japanese Americans wishing to resettle in nonrestricted areas for education or employment, providing that the FBI and other security agencies had also cleared these individuals.

Incarceration

One week after Executive Order 9066 was issued,[7] Hannah's father removed her without explanation from the California School for the Deaf, leaving her feeling confused. She later learned the reason for her father's actions from her sister Ruth. Her family was relocating to an asparagus farm in Clarksberg, near Sacramento. At this farm, a group of hearing Japanese men mocked Hannah, angering her father. As a result, the family moved again, this time to a potato farm in Stockton. Here several Filipino workers threatened to kill the Japanese American workers. Because of this, Hannah had to stay inside the family's barracks for safety. With only newspapers to read to keep her busy, Hannah felt like a prisoner. After this, her family was forced to return to their home in Elk Grove to pack for the move to the Manzanar concentration camp. Each family member was allowed to take only one piece of luggage.

Shortly after the arrival at Manzanar in May 1942, Hannah encountered discrimination from the hearing Japanese children there, who made fun of her deafness. She observed them "looking at her, pointing at her, and whispering behind their hands. She knew they were talking about her. She did not make any friends among them because they did not know how to communicate with her."[8]

In the fall of 1942 four schools for Deaf students rejected the WRA's requests to enroll Hannah and other Deaf Japanese American children. These were the California School for the Deaf, the Colorado School for the Deaf, the Kendall Green School (at Gallaudet College), and the Pennsylvania School for the Deaf.[9]

At the camp Hannah attended some flower-making classes for a while. But the teacher of the class later asked her not to come to the class anymore because it was overcrowded. Consequently, Hannah became discouraged.[10] According to her sister Ruth, Hannah "began feeling left out and unhappy at times because she could not go to school" like the hearing Japanese Americans in the camp.[11] In January 1943 the camp's health department arranged for a Miss E. Thomas to teach Hannah for an hour twice weekly, with emphasis on speech and lipreading. On Saturdays, Hannah and Miss Thomas attended a typing class. But so few hours of class time did not suffice for Hannah. She wanted part-time work like sewing just to keep busy.[12] In her 1981 testimony for the Commission on Wartime Relocation and Internment of Civilians in Los Angeles, Hannah criticized Miss Thomas's teaching. When Hannah asked Miss Thomas for help, the latter said she was "just too busy." Hannah stated that she, and not Miss Thomas, taught herself to type.[13] Hannah also had trouble understanding Miss Thomas in class.[14]

An undated memo from E. B. Dykes, the Manzanar Elementary School principal, states that Hannah was not graded in the camp hospital's special class because of her deafness. The principal also stated that she did not make any progress. He added that her parents did not appreciate her difficulties or the school's services.[15] In her 1981 testimony to the Commission on Wartime Relocation and Internment of Civilians, Hannah challenged Dykes's comments.[16] After further investigation, it was learned that Dykes did not become principal until January 1945. In May 1943, however, Hannah had already transferred to the Tule Lake concentration camp, where Dykes was a science teacher at the high school.[17] Therefore, Dykes's memo lacks credibility.

In 1943 the WRA granted Hannah's family's request to transfer Hannah to the Tule Lake concentration camp, where they had heard that a special school for children with handicaps was going to be established.[18] Hannah and her family took the bus from Manzanar to Tule Lake, changing buses in Reno, Nevada. They were not permitted to eat lunch at a café in Reno because a sign reading "No Japs served" was posted there.[19]

In an interview, Nancy Ikeda, another incarcerated Deaf Nikkei (or Japanese emigrant), recollected that in the 1980s Hannah expressed anger about being interned. Nancy and Hannah had met at Tule Lake, where Hannah jokingly scolded Nancy for stealing something.[20] When Tule Lake established the special school for children with handicaps, one of the teachers invited Hannah and the other students to name the facility. Hannah's proposal to name the school after Helen Keller, whom Hannah had read about, was unanimously accepted. The teacher then asked Hannah to write a letter to Helen Keller. One or two months later Hannah received a letter in response:

> Let them [the students] only remember this . . . their courage in conquering obstacles will be a lamp throwing its bright rays far into other lives besides their own . . . War, change, sorrow cannot take from us anything really noble, gracious and helpful in our lives . . . With best wishes for the children in their studies and victory over limitation, and warmest thanks for writing to me, I am affectionately your friend, Helen Keller.[21]

The letter was published in the Tule Lake camp newspaper with an editor's note listing Hannah as the "spokesman" for the students.[22] As she later related, Hannah felt that Helen Keller was her only friend during her stay at Tule Lake.[23]

Relocation to Chicago

When Hannah's father obtained a job in Chicago and applied for his family to be relocated with him, the WRA granted Hannah and her parents leave from the Tule Lake camp.[24] The WRA's Chicago office then arranged for Hannah to be enrolled at the Alexander Graham Bell Elementary School in Chicago.[25] Here she encountered adversity on several fronts. Some of her white classmates, who had brothers and fathers fighting against Japan on the Pacific front, expressed their anti-Japanese feelings toward Hannah, as did a white teacher. In addition, sign language was expressly forbidden at the school, which frustrated Hannah.[26] Encouraged by another student, Hannah applied for a job at Zenith Factory in Chicago. However, upon seeing her Japanese family

Hannah Holmes

name on her job application, the factory rejected her, although it had already employed several other students from the school.[27]

Hannah was still determined not to give up her educational pursuits. In September 1944 she enrolled at the Illinois School for the Deaf (ISD) in Jacksonville.[28] According to Hannah, the older students were not friendly with her, but the younger students were.[29] She encountered a hostile housemother who referred to her as a "Jap." In response, she summoned up enough courage to write to Superintendent Daniel T. Cloud, asking for this situation to be resolved. She initially feared that she would be expelled in retaliation. Shortly afterward, Hannah was surprised to see the housemother no longer on the ISD campus.[30]

During the wartime years the school dormitories and dining hall were racially segregated, although the classes were integrated. Despite Hannah's experiences of discrimination, former ISD students Alice Vespa and Russell Raines recalled no apparent hostility toward Japanese Americans at the school.[31] During this time Hannah wrote several articles for the monthly school newsletter. In one article she quoted a favorite poem from an untitled book that had been printed in 1865: "Help the weak if you are strong."[32] She also wrote that books help us forget about an unhappy, poor, or sad life.[33] Hannah graduated from the school in 1948.

The Postschool Years

From 1948 to 1953 Hannah held several jobs in Chicago. In 1953 she returned to California for the first time since 1942. For a period of time she lived in her brother Paul's home in Los Angeles,[34] and there, around

1954, Hannah met Dwight Edwin Holmes, a white Deaf man, at a Deaf club.[35] Her family, however, did not approve of Dwight because he was not of Japanese descent. In 1959, because she knew that her family would not approve of her marriage, Hannah married Dwight in a private ceremony in Las Vegas.[36] Their marriage lasted nearly forty years.

With the aid of her niece Carol Ann Friedman, who took class notes and interpreted for her in class, Hannah earned a teacher's certificate at the University of California–Los Angeles (UCLA).[37] She then became a teacher's aide at a vocational school, teaching hearing Vietnamese refugees.[38] Despite the language barrier, they communicated by writing back and forth.[39] Horrified by the school's blatant lack of concern and support for the refugees, Hannah filed a discrimination complaint against the school on their behalf. She later remarked that she felt much better by fighting back in pursuit of equality for Asians, Deaf people, and women.[40] However, the vocational school closed, forcing Hannah to retire from her job.[41]

Bearing Witness

Hannah was the only Deaf person among the 153 persons who testified before the Commission on Wartime Relocation and Internment of Civilians, an official group created by the US Congress, in Los Angeles on August 4–6, 1981. Its objective was to investigate matters regarding the wartime camps and to make recommendations for reparation. Hannah had been invited to testify because the commission and the general public were apparently not familiar with the experiences of interned Japanese Americans who were Deaf or had a disability.[42] Her testimony focused on the adverse impact of incarceration on education for these individuals. Drawing on her own experiences and those of other Deaf Japanese Americans, she gave testimony on the following points:

1. During wartime, Japanese American children on the West Coast were excluded from every public institution for children who were Deaf or had a disability.
2. The War Relocation Authority neglected the educational needs of such children, some of whom never recovered from the incarceration's interruption of their education.

3. Although hearing Japanese Americans received an education in the camps, their counterparts who were Deaf or had a disability had no such opportunity at Manzanar.

4. At the Tule Lake concentration camp, children who were Deaf or had a disability were lumped together in the Helen Keller School, where sign language was not allowed.

5. Monetary compensation should be provided to these Japanese Americans for their wrongful incarceration.[43]

Three months later Hannah discovered that she, under a different name, was being portrayed as a character in a play called *Christmas at Camp*. Her testimony for the commission had inspired the playwright Don McWilly to model a Deaf character after her. Hannah's character was the first cast member listed in the playbill. The play ran for three weeks at an Asian American theater in Los Angeles called East-West Players. Alerted by her lawyer, Gerald Sato, she attended a performance with complimentary tickets. She became very emotional and happy. Afterward she thanked the playwright warmly.[44]

Hannah was also the only Deaf victim of wartime incarceration to be interviewed by the Oral History Project at California State University.[45] It is likely that her testimony to the commission led to her being invited to participate in these two interviews, which resulted in more than one hundred pages of typed transcripts. Her input provided rare insight into what incarceration in concentration camps was like for Deaf Japanese Americans. From my interviews with other people, including Hannah's husband and other Deaf Japanese Americans who had been interned, it appears that Hannah never shared her camp experiences with anyone else, not even with other Deaf people who had been in the same camp at the same time as Hannah.

Earlier, in May 1979, William Hohri had formed the National Council for Japanese American Redress.[46] In March 1983 the National Council filed a lawsuit against the federal government on behalf of approximately one hundred and twenty thousand Japanese Americans for their wartime incarceration, seeking monetary reparations. Of the twenty-one plaintiffs, Hannah was the only person who was Deaf or had a disability. She was listed as the second plaintiff in the lawsuit after William Hohri.[47]

Hannah announced the lawsuit's filing at a press conference in Los Angeles.[48] Again, her 1981 testimony for the Commission on Wartime Relocation and Internment of Civilians likely led to her involvement in this lawsuit.

In an interview, Ronald Hirano recalled Hannah showing him several articles and photos about the lawsuit that were featured in the 1980s in *Rafu Shimpo*, a Los Angeles–based Japanese American newspaper. Hannah displayed enthusiastic dedication to her work with the National Council.[49] William Hohri later told Hannah's sister Ruth that Hannah had made critical contributions to the redress movement.[50] However, in 1988 the US Supreme Court dismissed the lawsuit. Nevertheless, the US Congress passed an act authorizing monetary reparations to the surviving Japanese Americans who had been incarcerated in the camps. President Reagan signed this act on August 10, 1988. The federal government also issued an official apology to Japanese Americans for their wrongful confinement. This was unique because, to date, the federal government still has not apologized for the forced relocation of American Indians or the enslavement of African Americans.

In 1986 Roger W. Axford published an anthology of twelve Japanese Americans' oral history narratives related to their wartime incarceration. Hannah was the only storyteller who was Deaf or had a disability to be included in this compilation. Her narrative's title is catchy: "Meet the Deaf Plaintiff."

In 1995 a production company selected Hannah as the subject of one episode of the Deaf Women's History Series titled *A Neglected Cultural Legacy: Life Stories of Deaf Women*. These producers wanted to interview her about her life, but she was too ill. Her sister Ruth Takagi Miyauchi, however, took her place, drawing on her recollections of growing up with Hannah.

In April 1988 Hannah presented her doll and quilt to the Manzanar National Historic Site's museum.[51] These two artifacts were her labor of love, focusing on the spirit of Japanese Americans incarcerated in the ten US concentration camps, including Manzanar. They are on permanent display at the museum.

Hannah battled cancer for nearly twenty years. As a registered nurse, her niece Carol Ann Friedman provided medical assistance to Hannah until her death.[52] Dwight Holmes had purchased two plots in a cemetery before Hannah died. However, to respect Hannah's wishes, Dwight and Hannah's brother Paul had her cremated, later scattering her ashes at the site of the Manzanar camp.[53]

Conclusion

This chapter has provided chronological examples of Hannah's important historical impact. This is not the definite or final work on Hannah's life, however, because of the limited access to certain data such as Hannah's photo and document collection. It is to be hoped that these sources will be made accessible for a future full-length biography and a video documentary. At this point, one still can be inspired by the examples cited here of how Hannah endured decades of bitter adversity, refusing to give up and fighting to achieve equality and justice for Asians, Deaf people, and women. This is highlighted by her role in the redress movement, which won the government's apology for the wrongful incarceration of Japanese Americans. In the end, perhaps Helen Keller's letter had provided Hannah with a moral compass to continue her fight.

Notes

1. Individual Record, form WRA 26 [Tomokichi Takagi], Evacuee Case File, Record Group 210, National Archives, Washington, DC.

2. Ruth Miyauchi, interview by Caroline L. Preston, in *A Neglected Cultural Legacy: Life Stories of Deaf Women* [Northridge, CA: PepNet Resource Center, 1999]. Video recording.

3. Hannah Takagi Holmes, interview by Arthur A. Hansen, February 8, 1982, transcript.

4. Mary W. Robinson, supervising teacher, California School for the Deaf [Hannah Takagi's] *Final School Report,* September 24, 1942, [Hannah Takagi] Evacuee Case File, Record Group 210, National Archives, Washington, DC.

5. Holmes interview by Hansen.

6. Amelia Luken, "Girls' Primary News," *California News* 57, no. 5 (1942): 66.

7. Robinson, *Final School Report.*

8. Holmes interview by Hansen.

9. Letter from Elwood A. Stevenson, superintendent of the California School for the Deaf, to Ruth Takagi, September 11, 1942; letter from Dr. Al. Brown, superintendent of the Colorado School for the Deaf, to Ruth Takagi, October 7, 1942; letter from Dr. Morris Wistar Wood, superintendent of the Pennsylvania School for the Deaf,

November 6, 1942; and letter from Dr. Percival Hall, Gallaudet College, to the War Relocation Authority, November 7, 1942, [Hannah Takagi] Evacuee Case File, Record Group 210, National Archives, Washington, DC.

10. Untitled welfare report, August 29, 1942, to February 29, 1943, [Hannah Takagi] Evacuee Case File, Record Group 210, National Archives, Washington, DC.

11. Ibid.

12. Ibid.

13. Commission on Wartime Relocation and Internment of Civilians, Los Angeles, testimony of Hannah Takagi Holmes, August 8, 1981.

14. Memo to Dr. Genevieve W. Carter, February 9, 1943, [Hannah Takagi] Evacuee Case File, Record Group 210, National Archives, Washington, DC.

15. Eldridge B. Dykes, undated memo, [Hannah Takagi] Evacuee Case File, Record Group 210, National Archives, Washington, DC.

16. Commission on Wartime Relocation and Internment of Civilians, Los Angeles, testimony of Hannah Takagi Holmes, August 8, 1981.

17. *Our World, 1943–1944*, Manzanar High School yearbook, UCLA, Special Collections, Charles E. Young Research Library, Los Angeles.

18. War Relocation Authority Application for Leave Clearance, WRA Form 126, [Tomokichi Takagi] Evacuee Case File, Record Group 210, National Archives, Washington, DC.

19. Holmes interview by Hansen.

20. Nancy Ikeda Baldwin, in discussion with the author, June 12, 2012. She also shared her incarceration experiences with me.

21. Helen Keller, letter to Hannah Takagi, August 2, 1943.

22. "Helen Keller Sends Message to Handicapped Student Here," *Daily Tulean Dispatch* (Tule Lake, CA), August 13, 1943.

23. Holmes interview by Hansen.

24. War Relocation Authority Application for Leave Clearance, WRA Form 126, [Tomokichi Takagi] Evacuee Case File, Record Group 210, National Archives, Washington, DC.

25. [Hannah Takagi] Registration Card, Board of Education, City of Chicago, courtesy of Chicago Public Schools, Department of Compliance, Former Student Records, June 19, 2012. Her enrollment was from September 22, 1943, to September 5, 1944.

26. Holmes interview by Hansen.

27. Holmes, Hannah Takagi, "Meet the Deaf Plaintiff—An Adult Educator!" In *Too Long Silent: Japanese Americans Speak Out*, edited by Roger W. Axford, 36–39 [Lincoln, NE: Media Publishing and Marketing, 1986].

28. [Hannah Takagi] Registration Card, Board of Education, City of Chicago, courtesy of Chicago Public Schools, Department of Compliance, Former Student Records, June 19, 2012.

29. Marene Clark-Mattern, email to the author, May 5, 2012.

30. Axford, *Too Long Silent*, 38.

31. Alice Vespa, in discussion with the author, September 15, 2012; Russell Raines, in discussion with the author, September 15, 2012.

32. Hannah Takagi, "My Favorite Little Poem," *Illinois Advance* 80, no. 2 (1946).

33. Hannah Takagi, "If We Had No Books," *North Wing* 5, no. 3 (1944).

34. Carol Ann Friedman, in discussion with the author, September 14, 2012.

35. Dwight Edwin Holmes, in discussion with the author, July 17, 2012.

36. Friedman discussion.

37. Ibid.

38. Axford, *Too Long Silent,* 39.

39. Dwight Edwin Holmes discussion.

40. Axford, *Too Long Silent,* 39.

41. Friedman discussion.

42. Commission on Wartime Relocation and Internment of Civilians, Los Angeles, testimony of Hannah Takagi Holmes, August 8, 1981.

43. Ibid.

44. Holmes interview by Hansen.

45. Dr. Arthur Hansen, email to the author, July 15, 2012.

46. Kitayama, Glen, "National Council for Japanese American Redress (NCJAR)," in *Encyclopedia of Japanese American History: An A-to-Z Reference from 1868 to the Present,* updated ed. [New York: Facts on File, 2009].

47. Bulk Access to Govdocs, 847 F.2d 779, William Hohri; Hannah Takagi Holmes et al., Plaintiffs-Appellants, v. The United States of America, Defendant-Appellee. No. 87-1635. http://www.justice.gov/osg/briefs/1986/sg860392.txt.

48. Associated Press, "Japanese-Americans Sue the U.S. over Internment," *Spokane Chronicle* [Spokane, WA], March 17, 1983.

49. Ronald Hirano, in discussion with the author, May 15, 2012.

50. Ruth Miyauchi, interview by Preston, *Neglected Cultural Legacy.*

51. Manzanar Historic Site, Doll and Quilt, National Park Service, US Department of Interior, 1988, http://www.nps.gov/history/museum/exhibits/manz/exb/Remembering/Pilgrimage/MANZ2596_doll.html.

52. Friedman discussion.

53. Dwight Edwin Holmes discussion.

Józef Jerzy Rogowski: A Unique Figure in Polish Deaf History

Tomasz Adam Świderski

The history of Deaf people in Poland is a brand-new field of research. In fact, in-depth studies in the field did not begin until 2008. Before that, the history of Deaf people had been raised sporadically, for example, during anniversary celebrations or in short articles. I was the first to research the topic thoroughly. I have studied numerous forgotten sources, covered with the dust of time. In my research I discovered many stories of Deaf community activists. Thanks to this work, the figure of Józef Jerzy Rogowski was rediscovered.

Rogowski was one of the most outstanding Deaf community activists of the pre–World War II period. As a child, he was determined to become a role model for Deaf people even though those who were closest to him did not believe he could do so. Nonetheless, because of his relentless efforts to fulfill his dream, he managed to procure a position in the Magistrat, the local government office for the capital city of Warsaw. At the turn of the twentieth century, for a Deaf person to get such a job equated to entering the social elite and proved how effective faith in one's abilities can be. A self-taught person, Rogowski, from his earliest years, was eager to develop his knowledge and vocabulary. Thanks to his educational achievements, he was able to improve the living conditions of Deaf people, and he dedicated his life to serving them. The essential traits of hard work and persistence helped shape an appropriate attitude for working with the Deaf community. Rogowski's name should be well known, as he is an excellent role model for generations of Deaf people not only in Poland but also worldwide.

Childhood

Józef Jerzy Rogowski was born on March 12, 1871, on the estate of Repla, near Grodno. He was the son of Piotr Rogowski and Pelagia Rogowska, née Leinhardt. His father was a land steward, a position that was usually granted only for several years, and because of that, the family often had to move.

In 1879, when Józef was eight, he began studying at the Institute for the Deaf-Mute and Blind in Warsaw. At this time oralism was not officially sanctioned. An in-house school statute adopting oralism was enacted in 1906. At the time Józef was attending the institute, the position of schoolmaster was held by Jan Papłoński,[1] a hearing educator who is well known in the history of surdopedagogy (a branch of pedagogy concerned with teaching people with hearing impairments). Papłoński favored the use of sign language as the first language of Deaf children. He claimed that speech should be an additional element that would facilitate the lives of Deaf children. Every year Józef received school awards for his achievements. He wrote: "We had to study hard because the schoolmaster did not like lazy pupils and often controlled our school progress."[2] In Józef's day, people attached great significance to education. Classes were held both mornings and afternoons. In due time Józef completed his studies at the institute: "At the age of 14, with a graduation certificate and an award—a book with a red cover."[3] One of the book awards from 1881, when Józef was ten years old, has been preserved; its inscription says that Józef received it for outstanding diligence, school progress, and good conduct.

After graduation, Józef came back to the Białystok region, where his parents were then employed as land stewards on Baron Kruzensztern's

The name sign of Józef Rogowski. Photo by Michał Jaromin.

estate.[4] During his stay, he helped his mother sew clothing for his younger brothers and took up sculpting. It was during this time that he read a book by the Polish writer Kraszewski and wrote about his impressions: "I will never forget this good novel."[5] Later he read works by other famous Polish writers, including Adam Mickiewicz and Henryk Sienkiewicz. Undoubtedly, Józef's love of reading helped him improve his command of the Polish language.

Józef also helped his father with office work such as calculating the weekly reports of workers' daily wages. There and then, he began to love this type of work and started dreaming about a career as a clerk. When Józef was still at school, Eustachy Rosnowski, a former student, visited one of his old teachers. Rosnowski worked as a clerk in a currency-exchange bureau at the government bank in Warsaw. Since he had managed to achieve his goals, he served as a role model for Rogowski, who wrote about meeting Rosnowski: "A nice title tempted me and a thought crossed my mind that I should follow in his footsteps. I decided to choose this occupation."[6] However, Józef's father did not support his son's goals, as he did not believe his son could ever land such a job. He advised him to instead become a tailor—a job that seemed more achievable for a Deaf person. However, Rogowski could not imagine working as a tailor because, as he wrote, "after sewing for a long time, I felt an unpleasant pain in my neck."[7] Around this time he wrote letters about his career aspirations to his old teacher, Mr. Witkowski, and to the Rev. Prelate Teofil Jagodziński.[8] Both of these men politely advised him not to try to get a clerking job as there were many hearing graduates applying for such positions, and in those days it was difficult for Deaf people to find professional employment.

When he was at home, Rogowski studied a lot on his own. He was assisted by his older brother, who was a student in Petersburg. Rogowski studied foreign languages: Russian, German, and French. He explained to his surprised father that "the lesson is never wasted, learning foreign languages is never a waste of time and maybe one day I will go abroad."[9] Having no prospects at home, he decided to go back to Warsaw to look for a job.

Back in Warsaw: The First Search for Work

Around 1889[10] Rogowski returned to Warsaw. Initially he worked in a sculpting workshop, but he did not abandon his dream of becoming a clerk. He said: "But the dream of a government post still tormented me. One of my dear friends[11] used to say that those who look for a job by storm [or with daring] can always find it." Encouraged by this friend, in 1894 he summoned up the courage to visit the governor, Pavel Shuvalov.[12] He stood in a crowd of applicants with an application form in his hand, waiting for his turn. Count Shuvalov started questioning each applicant, and when it was Rogowski's turn, the Count read his application and wrote in one margin that he should go to the main office. "It was a glimmer of hope, but I was afraid to go there,"[13] wrote Rogowski about his first unsuccessful attempt to get a clerical job.

He did, however, get a job in the private office of an engineer,[14] but it was only temporary. Rogowski was hoping for a permanent position, so he was directed to the senior engineer[15] for the city of Warsaw in the Magistrat's office. After a long struggle, he began working at a registrar's office, where he kept records of commissioned and completed work. He also started working as a graphic designer, copying site plans. He had been employed in this capacity for two years when the governor forwarded his application to the incumbent mayor of Warsaw, Nikolai Bibikov. At first the mayor had some doubts as to whether a deaf person could effectively work as a clerk. Then he learned that one Deaf person was an employee of the national bank[16] and another worked for the Credit-Landed Society[17] and that they were very highly regarded. After confirming these facts, the mayor agreed to appoint Rogowski as a grade-crossing attendant. Rogowski started working on October 1, 1896, which was a memorable date for him since this was the first step toward achieving his dream. He wrote: "The job was minor, but I know that a lot of people with secondary and even higher education had fought for it. I remember one young engineer who had been forced to stick with this job until a more suitable vacancy arose."[18] Rogowski was satisfied merely by the thought that he had managed to get a job. He had been chosen from a large group of applicants. His supervisor liked him for his reliability and experience, and Rogowski held the position for twenty years, which made him an object of envy among his coworkers.[19] A year after the outbreak of World War I, he was forced to evacuate with the Russian authorities. Initially he stayed near Vilnius and later went to Russia. In his memoirs Rogowski wrote that when he arrived in Kiev, he had to handle the official correspondence from Moscow, the current seat of Warsaw's Magistrat. In Kiev, Rogowski found a job in building strategic roads for the war effort.

Rogowski returned to Warsaw in 1918 and was employed as a measurement technician, or office clerk, in the Magistrat. He emphasized

Józef Jerzy Rogowski

that, because of his perseverance and patience, he was happy in his job. In his writings he advised other Deaf people as follows: "I wholeheartedly recommend these virtues to all my companions in the disability."[20] On November 17, 1918, at noon, Rogowski married Maria Wiktoria Łopieńska, a Deaf woman.[21] The wedding service was held in Saint Alexander's parish, and the mass was said by the Rev. Stefan Kuczyński, chaplain of the Institute for the Deaf-Mute and Blind. The couple was childless.

Rogowski's Work for the Deaf Community

"Providence," the Christian Deaf-Mute Society

On May 5, 1883, the Institute for the Deaf-Mute and Blind Alumni Association (Towarzystwo Głuchoniemych Byłych Wychowanków i Wychowanic Warszawskiego Instytutu Głuchoniemych i Ociemniałych) was founded. It was the second Deaf society in the former Polish territory and the first under Russian rule. (Poland was then divided into Russian, Austrian, and Prussian partitions, and Warsaw belonged to the Russian partition.) At that time, Rogowski, who was twelve years old, was a student in the fifth grade and could watch the first organizational meeting, which was attended by the elite of the Deaf community, who held higher-status jobs. Rogowski recalled this meeting in the following words: "I felt strangely moved seeing those strangers, so tall that I felt like a dwarf compared to them and I had to look up to see the faces of these giants."[22] Undoubtedly, the meeting made an impression on the little boy and influenced his future work for the Deaf community. Rogowski became a member of the society in 1889, when he was eighteen.[23] He became a member of its board in 1901,[24] the earliest date found in the sources. He was reappointed as a board member during a society meeting in 1904[25] and again in 1907.[26] In the documentation from 1908, his function is listed as secretary[27] of the board. After the death of Józef Maksymilian Sułowski, chairman and treasurer of the society, during a meeting on March 7, 1909, Rogowski was appointed secretary and treasurer[28] in place of the deceased.[29]

The society frequently organized balls for Deaf persons, to which it invited journalists from local newspapers. Articles about these events were filled with admiration, as at that time it was believed that

Deaf people were unable to dance because they could not hear. One newspaper article[30] reported that Rogowski and A. de Flasillier served as the masters of ceremony. Apparently, then, after three years Rogowski had settled into the Warsaw Deaf community.

Records of similar events also appear in newspapers from 1894, which report that Rogowski, who was one of the masters of ceremony, danced traditional Polish dances.[31] He was also one of the originators of masquerade balls for members of the Deaf-Mute Society. One such event took place on February 16, 1901, and was photographed.[32] On March 8, 1908, the society organized a lottery for Deaf persons. The lottery took place in the Deaf tavern on Piwna Str. 11 in Warsaw. Rogowski was one of its organizers. The money collected was given to the poorest Deaf people.[33]

During the twenty-fifth anniversary celebration of the Warsaw Deaf-Mute Society on November 25, 1908, Rogowski gave a talk on the topic of establishing a home for elderly Deaf people. Afterward, donations were collected for this undertaking. Thanks to Rogowski's words, a sum of around 155 rubles was raised. This amount did not cover all of the costs but was a milestone in the process of creating such a necessary institution.[34] The initiative was still ongoing in 1909.[35]

Participants of the 1919 general meeting of the society passed a resolution that changed its name to the Christian Deaf-Mute Society. (For unknown reasons, a separate association for Deaf Jewish people had been formed in 1916.) The "Providence" part was most probably added in 1923 or 1924.[36] Later that year, the society's bylaws were changed to allow current members to hold the position of chairman. In the past, that office had automatically been assigned to the headmaster of the Institute for the Deaf-Mute and Blind, and Deaf individuals could serve only as board members. After the bylaws were changed, the headmaster served only as guardian, and members could be appointed as chair. Rogowski was appointed for this post. He became the first deaf chairman in the history of the province of Mazovia and held the office until 1933. However, Rogowski did not serve as chair from 1924 to 1930, as during this period he was chairman of the Polish Association of Deaf-Mute Societies (discussed later).

The Institute for the Deaf-Mute and Blind offered evening courses for Deaf people who could not read or write and those who wanted to improve their education. Rogowski voluntarily served as lecturer for these courses. He was joined in this endeavor by Kazimierz Włostowski.[37] Apart from these two men, the classes were given by the institute's teachers, who were hearing and followed an oralist approach.[38]

The Polish Association of Deaf-Mute Societies

Before the establishment of the Polish Association of Deaf-Mute Societies, there had been about twenty deaf societies in the territory of the Second Polish Republic. These groups had a limited field of action, usually restricted to one city. Deaf persons faced many problems and had many interests that had to be protected. For example, only one in five Deaf children received a formal education. As a result, illiteracy among Deaf people was a serious problem, especially in rural areas. Moreover, Deaf people were frequently exploited by both their families and strangers and were treated as a cheap workforce in farming. In response, activists from the different societies proposed that one common association of Deaf people should be created to safeguard their interests.[39]

From the twenty-first to the thirty-first day of December 1923, the Christian Deaf-Mute Society celebrated its fortieth anniversary in Warsaw. At this time, the idea of establishing the Polish Association of Deaf-Mute Societies was put forward. Leading activists from the largest societies in the Second Polish Republic—Gdańsk, Toruń, Bydgoszcz, Łódź, Warsaw—took part in the anniversary celebrations. This was an opportunity to discuss the issue. Rogowski himself was likely the originator of the idea to establish a new organization, as he was appointed its chairman. Agreeing to assume this office, Rogowski appointed a committee of three people to draw up bylaws for the association. He chose Józef Jaworski,[40] Eugeniusz Stankowski, and Kazimierz Włostowski for this committee. Rogowski was also elected chairman of the meeting of Deaf-Mute Society representatives, which took place on August 15–16, 1924. The convention was held to discuss matters connected with establishing the association. Rogowski, as one of the initiators, raised the issue of standardizing Polish Sign Language (which had been influenced by the period of partitions, which resulted in different sign languages being used in different areas of the country) and publishing a newspaper for Deaf persons.

After the second convention on January 1, 1925, efforts were made to approve the bylaws of the Polish Association of Deaf-Mute Societies. On June 17, 1925, the Ministry of Labor and Social Welfare issued a letter asking the association to send one member to make amendments in the bylaws. Rogowski agreed to do so. He wrote, "A curious incident took place there. The chairman was shocked to see that I had come with a notebook and a pencil and said that it would be hard to communicate using these. But once he had learned that the statutes were created by me, he asked me to sit closer to him! We talked for almost three hours."[41] The bylaws were legalized by the ministry on August 11, 1925. During the general meeting of the association, Rogowski was appointed chairman; Kazimierz Kraszewski (grandson of Józef Ignacy Kraszewski, a well-known Polish writer), treasurer; and Józef Jaworski, secretary.[42] Establishing the association was an important achievement for the Deaf community in the Second Polish Republic. Letters sent from the organization to the Ministry of Education drew the authorities' attention to the lack of schools for Deaf children in most cities. As a result, such schools were founded in Cracow, Vilnius, and Rybnik. All of this demonstrates that Rogowski, a knowledgeable man, put a great deal of emphasis on the education of Deaf children.

The issue of establishing a home for elderly Deaf people was also raised by the association. Moreover, in 1926, several conferences were organized to address the cultural and educational problems of Deaf persons. At these conferences Rogowski gave speeches encouraging charitable work.[43] Rogowski acted as chairman until 1930, at which time he began serving as treasurer, an office he held until about 1932 or 1933.[44]

Warsaw Sport Club for the Deaf-Mute

Little information is available about Rogowski's work to promote sports among Deaf people. It is known that he was chairman of the Warsaw Sport Club for the Deaf-Mute [Warszawski Klub Sportowy Głuchoniemych] in 1924 and that he held this office for a year. He might have renounced this position in order to assume the duties of chairman of the Polish Association of Deaf-Mute Societies. Due to lack of information, however, I do not discuss Rogowski's involvement in

Deaf sports organizations any further.[45] However, his service to the club was not forgotten. In 1932 Rogowski became an honorary member of the committee formed on the occasion of the tenth anniversary of the Warsaw Sport Club.[46]

Rogowski as Delegate to International Conventions of Deaf People

From the first to the fourth day of August 1912, the International Congress of the Deaf-Mutes was organized in Paris. This process was combined with celebrations of the two-hundredth birthday of the Abbé Charles-Michel de l'Épée. An invitation to this event was sent to three members of the Warsaw Deaf-Mute Society: Józef Rogowski, Maria Łopieńska (Rogowski's future wife), and Zygmunt Wojciechowski. Rogowski was overjoyed at receiving an invitation. He wrote, "I cannot miss such a rare opportunity to take part in the congress."[47] He wrote an appeal to the Warsaw newspapers for funding to attend the congress, but no one responded. Rogowski received one hundred rubles from the society's fund, but this amount did not cover the travel costs. He nonetheless wrote, "Having confidence in myself and counting on some savings, I set out to the country of great culture and civilization. I hoped that I would come back with more experience and a handful of good advice useful to our community."[48] Together with his friends Tadeusz Tłuchowski and Jakub Wajtzblum,[49] he went to Berlin by train. They stopped in Częstochowa to pray in the sanctuary. Rogowski had a gift for the organizers of the congress: a silver plate[50] with an inscription engraved by Zygmunt Wojciechowski, a Deaf craftsman.[51] The inscription, in Polish and French, read as follows: "The Warsaw Deaf-Mute Society pays tribute to Rev. de l'Épée, the first Enlightener of the Deaf on the occasion of his 200th birth anniversary. 4-August-1912." The plate had a mahogany frame decorated with four small rosettes made of silver, which had been made by Antoni Lamentowicz. An interesting anecdote is connected to the plate. Rogowski recalled that "A Prussian customs officer wanted to take away the plate to impose a customs duty on it. Tłuchowski made a violent gesture, trying to explain in sign language that the plate was a gift for 'Paris.' Astonished, the customs officer gave it back."[52] On July 29, 1912, Rogowski visited a hostel for elderly Deaf people in Berlin. He also visited a local Deaf society and met its members, with whom he shared work-related experiences.

Rogowski and Tłuchowski then set out from Berlin to Paris, arriving on July 30, 1912 (Wajtzblum joined them at the German-Belgium border). The congress addressed the issues of education, career opportunities, national and international collaboration, sign language and its value, Deaf societies, religious works, pastoral care, monasteries, legal duties, provisions for old age, religion, and schools and universities.

During his stay in Paris, Rogowski had an opportunity to meet and to share calling cards with the elite of the international Deaf community, including Eugen Sutermeister[53] and Henri Gaillard.[54] He also visited the National Institute for the Deaf in Paris and the palace of Versailles. The ceremony paying tribute to the Abbé de l'Épée in front of the cathedral was filmed.[55] Rogowski, Tłuchowski, and Wajtzblum attended a banquet in the France Hotel near Versailles.[56]

On their way home, Rogowski and Tłuchowski discussed "the high level of education and culture among the Deaf in other countries."[57] Rogowski summarized the discussion by saying, "All comparisons that we made showed how far behind these countries we were. We were filled with compassion for our Deaf back in Warsaw, who were deprived not only of the newest educational resources but also the indispensable cultural life. These countries are an example to follow."[58]

The congress in Paris was not the last international event that Rogowski attended. He also participated in the All-Russian Convention of the Deaf-Mutes, which was held in Moscow in 1917.[59] He went to the convention directly from Kiev, where he was staying due to the compulsory evacuation of Warsaw during World War I (during this time of the partition of Poland, Warsaw was under Russian rule).[60] He was the only Deaf representative from Poland. In Moscow, after receiving twenty-one votes, he was elected a member of the editorial committee.[61] It is significant that Rogowski won so much recognition during the convention that he was chosen for the committee. It is likely that, because of his solemnity, skills, and poise, he gained the respect of Deaf representatives from the many countries represented. At the convention Rogowski gave a lecture about, among other subjects, a religious approach to raising Deaf children.

In 1928 the International Deaf-Mute Convention was organized in the Czech Republic capital of Prague. The convention was attended by a larger group of Polish Deaf leaders: Wiesław Dobrowolski,[62] Roman Petrykiewicz,[63] Bogumił Liban,[64] Józef Bäcker,[65] H. Łabęcki,[66] and Józef Rogowski as a representative of the Polish Association of Deaf-Mute Societies. Rogowski can also be seen in a photograph[67] taken at the International Convention of the Deaf-Mutes in Liege, Belgium, dated 1930.

Rogowski's Publications

In 1914 Rogowski published under his own imprint a booklet titled "The International Deaf-Mute Congress in Paris, 1–4 August 1912: A Report Presented at the Deaf-Mute Meeting on 6 October 1912." The profit from selling the booklet was earmarked for the cultural goals of the Deaf-Mute Society to promote a positive Deaf identity. The pamphlet was a detailed and vivid description of Rogowski's journey to Paris and his stay at the congress.

From 1927 to 1928 Rogowski was a member of the editorial council of the *Deaf-Mute World (Świat Głuchoniemych)* monthly magazine, which published several of his articles on different aspects of the Deaf societies' work.[68] Some of the articles had an autobiographical character.[69] During his work for the Polish Association of Deaf-Mute Societies, Rogowski published a newsletter called the *Announcement of the Polish Association of the Deaf-Mute Societies.* He also published an interesting article titled "Summer Holidays"[70] about his vacation trips. Moreover, in 1909 Rogowski also wrote the funeral speech for Józef Maksymilian Sułowski, whose service to the Deaf community he extolled.[71]

Rogowski's Sudden Death

At seven o'clock on January 25, 1933, Rogowski fainted in his house on Żurawia 29/12 Street. Although an ambulance came immediately, Rogowski died. The cause of death was an aortic aneurysm. His obituary was published in the next morning's newspaper, *Express Poranny War-szawski.*[72] He was buried in Powązki Cemetery. His grave (number 315) is in the PPRK section, next to the cemetery wall and near the fifth gate. His wife, Maria, died in 1957, and she was also buried there.

Conclusions

Having read the biography of Józef Rogowski, one can say without hesitation that Rogowski was an outstanding Deaf activist. His public service to the Deaf community through the Warsaw Deaf Society (later known as the Christian Deaf-Mute Society "Providence") and the Warsaw Sport Club for the Deaf-Mute was of great benefit to Deaf people from Mazovia. His work in the Polish Association of Deaf-Mute Societies led to increased attention from the government with regard to the problems confronting Deaf people in the Second Polish Republic. His participation in international congresses shows his willingness to learn more about the situation of Deaf people in different countries, his efforts to improve the education of Deaf children, and his readiness to look for solutions to their problems. In his public work, Rogowski used the knowledge he acquired while attending these events.

Rogowski's wisdom is reflected in his articles about the Deaf community, which now have historical value. His works also attest to his interest in the everyday problems of Deaf people. Undoubtedly Rogowski can well serve as an exemplary role model for current and future generations of the Deaf community not only because of his work but also because of his ambition, which drove him to achieve his childhood dreams. His efforts to encourage solidarity among Deaf people set a commendable example for others to follow.

Notes

1. Jan Papłoński (1819–1885), schoolmaster of the Institute for the Deaf-Mute and Blind in Warsaw from 1864 to 1885.

2. J. Rogowski, "Życiorys Jana Papłońskiego [Jan Papłoński's biography]," *Nasze Pisemko. Gazetka szkolna głuchoniemych* (May 1932): 2.

3. J. Rogowski, *Przewodnik Głuchoniemych* (March 1933): 1.

4. This was probably Aleksander Kruzensztern (1807–1888), chairman of the diplomatic office of the viceroy of the Kingdom of Poland and a senator.

5. J. Rogowski, "Jak dostałem się na służbę rządową," *Świat Głuchoniemych* (April 1927): 2.

6. Ibid.

7. Ibid.

8. Rev. Teofil Jagodziński (1833–1907), catechist at the Institute for the Deaf-Mute and Blind from 1858 and schoolmaster at the institute from 1885 to 1887. Coauthor of *Słownik mimiczny dla osób głuchoniemych [Sign Language Dictionary for the Deaf-Mute]* published in 1879, which is considered the first sign language dictionary in Poland.

9. Ibid.

10. That year, Rogowski became a member of the Deaf-Mute Society of the Alumni of the Institute for the Deaf-Mute and Blind. It is the presumed date of his arrival in Warsaw. Having heard about the society, he probably became a member soon after his arrival.

11. Unfortunately, the friend's identity remains unknown. Rogowski never mentioned the person's name in writing.

12. Pavel Andreyevich Shuvalov (1830–1908), count, Russian politician and diplomat, governor-general of Warsaw from December 13, 1894, to December 12, 1896.

13. J. Rogowski, "Jak dostałem się," 3.

14. His identity remains unknown.

15. Rogowski did not mention the engineer's name.

16. This was probably Eustachy Rosnowski, graduate of the Institute for the Deaf-Mute and Blind in Warsaw.

17. This was probably Mieczysław Pętkowski, clerk in the administration branch of the Credit-Landed Society in Warsaw.

18. J. Rogowski, "Jak dostałem się," 3.

19. Ibid.

20. Ibid.

21. Diocese Archive in Warsaw, records of married couples in Saint Aleksander's parish, 282/1918.

22. J. Rogowski, "Z pamiętnika Głuchoniemego [From the diary of the Deaf-Mute]." In *Pięćdziesięciolecie Chrześcijańskiego Towarzystwa Głuchoniemych "Opatrzność" w Warszawie* [25th Anniversary of the Christian Deaf-Mute Society "Providence"] (Warsaw, 1934), 27.

23. Ibid.

24. "Zabawa głuchoniemych [Party for the Deaf-Mute]," *Kurier Warszawski* (February 17, 1901).

25. "Warszawskie Towarzystwo Głuchoniemych [Warsaw Deaf-Mute Society]," *Kurier Warszawski* (December 19, 1904).

26. "Posiedzenia u głuchoniemych [Meeting of the Deaf-Mute]," *Kurier Warszawski* (December 30, 1907).

27. "Komitet Towarzystwa Głuchoniemych w Warszawie [The Committee of the Deaf-Mute Society in Warsaw]," *Goniec Poranny* (April 8, 1908); *Archiwum Zarządu Głównego Polskiego Związku Głuchych (AZGPZG)* [Archive of the Polish Deaf Society Board; hereafter cited as *AZGPZG*], Pismo Komitetu *Warszawskiego Towarzystwa Głuchoniemych z 19 października 1908 r.* In Kronika Sułowskiego, 163.

28. Needs further research.

29. "The Deaf-Mute Society," *Kurier Warszawski* (March 8, 1909).

30. "U głuchoniemych [Visiting the Deaf-Mute]," *Kurier Poranny* (February 8, 1892).

31. "Bal głuchoniemych [The Ball for the Deaf-Mute]," *Kurier Poranny* (February 9, 1896); "Zabawa u głuchoniemych," *Kurier Warszawski* (February 9, 1896); "Na balu głuchoniemych," *Kurier Poranny* (January 1, 1894); "U głuchoniemych," *Kurier Poranny* (February 15, 1899); "Bal głuchoniemych," *Kurier Poranny* (February 6, 1902); "U głuchoniemych," *Kurier Warszawski* (February 24, 1903); "'Sylwester' u głuchoniemych," *Kurier Warszawski* (January 2, 1908).

32. "Zabawa głuchoniemych [Party for the Deaf-Mute]," *Kurier Poranny* (February 17, 1901).

33. "Podziękowanie [Gratitude]," *Kurier Warszawski* (April 5, 1908).

34. "25-lecie Towarzystwa Głuchoniemych [25th anniversary of the Deaf-Mute Society]," *Kurier Warszawski* (November 26, 1908); "Schronisko dla głuchoniemych [Shelter for the Deaf-Mute]," *Kurier Warszawski* (December 13, 1908).

35. "Z Towarzystwa Głuchoniemych [From the Deaf-Mute Society]," *Dziennik* (January 25, 1909).

36. No sources were found that explicitly give the date on which "Divine Providence" was added. Needs further research.

37. Kazimierz Włostowski (1903–1991), born deaf, one of the most active Deaf community activists in Poland. Cofounder of the Lodz Sport Club for the Deaf-Mute, the Warsaw Sport Club for the Deaf-Mute, chairman of the Christian Deaf-Mute Self-Help Society in Lodz (1934–1935), member of the Polish Association of the Deaf-Mute Societies (1930–1931), and author of numerous articles on the problems of Deaf communities. Włostowski also took part in the Warsaw uprising and was held in a POW camp in Sandbostel.

38. Komunikat 2-gi Polskiego Związku Towarzystw Głuchoniemych [The Second Announcement of the Polish Association of the Deaf-Mute Societies], Warsaw (1932), 15.

39. B. Szczepankowski, Zarys historii stowarzyszeń głuchoniemych 1876–1946 [An Outline History of Deaf-Mute Societies from 1876 to 1946], Warsaw (1996), 33–34.

40. Józef Kościesza Jaworski (1863–?), Deaf painter and photographer; student of the Academy of Fine Arts in Cracow; and chairman of the first Galician Deaf-Mute Society "Hope" in Lviv (1913–1917) and of the Christian Deaf-Mute Society "Providence" (1924–1930).

41. J. Rogowski, "Polski Związek Towarzystw Głuchoniemych. Szkic historyczny [Polish Association of the Deaf-Mute Societies. Historical outline]," *Świat Głuchoniemych* (February 1927), 4.

42. Ibid., 2–5.

43. J. Rogowski, "Polski Związek Towarzystw Głuchoniemych (Dokończenie) [Polish Association of Deaf-Mute Societies. Ending]," Świat Głuchoniemych (March 1927), 6–7.

44. In 1932 his official position was treasurer, but it is not known whether he held the office until his death (Komunikat 2-gi Polskiego Związku Towarzystw Głuchoniemych, Warszawa (1932), 1).

45. Despite my requests, the board of the Polish Deaf-Mute Sport Club and the Warsaw Sport Club for the Deaf-Mute denied access to their archives.

46. *AZGPZG*, Kronika Sułowskiego, 213.

47. J. Rogowski, *Międzynarodowy Kongres Głuchoniemych w Paryżu d.1–4 sierpnia 1912r. Sprawozdanie przedstawione na Zjeździe Koleżeńskim Głuchoniemych dnia 6 października 1912 r. [International Congress of the Deaf-Mute in Paris, August 1–4, 1912. A report presented on the Deaf-Mute Convention on October 5, 1912]*, Warsaw (1913), 4.

48. Ibid., 5.

49. Jakub Wajtzblum, a Deaf man of Jewish origin, owner of the "Snycerpol" work-shop in Warsaw, board member of the Jewish Deaf-Mute Society "Spójnia" in Warsaw, and student at the Institute for the Deaf-Mute and Blind in Warsaw. Wajtzblum perished at the Majdanek concentration camp in May 1943.

50. Rogowski wrote that the plate was donated to the museum of the Deaf-Mute Institute in Paris. In 2009, during my stay in Paris, I attempted to find the plate, but the current authorities of the institute did not know anything about it. The museum was closed due to renovation.

51. Zygmunt Wojciechowski, board member of the Warsaw Deaf-Mute Society. An engraver by trade. Before World War I Wojciechowski had his own engraving workshop in Warsaw, on Podwale 14/5 Str.

52. J. Rogowski, *Międzynarodowy Kongres Głuchoniemych*, 6.

53. Eugen Sutermeister (1862–1931), a deaf engraver, founder of the Swiss Deaf-Mute Society (1911), first evangelical preacher for Deaf people, and editor of the *Schweizerische Taubstummenzeitung* from 1907 to 1931. In J. Hruby, *Velký ilustrovaný Průvodce neslyšících a nedoslýchavých po jej ich vlastním osudu* (Prague: Federace Rodicu a pratel sluchove postizenych, 1999), 237.

54. Henri Gillard (1866–1939), a deaf Frenchman, "the consul of the Deaf," editor of *La Revue des Sourds-Muets*, and writer. In J. Hruby, *Velký ilustrovaný Průvodce neslyšících a nedoslýchavých po jej ich vlastním osudu* [Prague: Federace Rodicu a pratel sluchove postizenych, 1999], 238.

55. The film was screened at the Siła theater on Marszałkowska 118 Str. during the Deaf-Mute meeting in Warsaw on October 6, 1912. It has not been preserved.

56. J. Rogowski, *Międzynarodowy Kongres*, 1–22.

57. Ibid., 22.

58. Ibid.

59. J. Rogowski, *Jak dostałem się*, 3.

60. W. Kowalew, *U Istokowi obszczestwa: Perwaja wserossijskaja organizacja gluho-nemyh (1917–1920)*. In materials from *Wtorogo Moskowskogo simpoziuma po istorii głuhih* [Moscow: Izdannje osuszczestwleno za sczet sredstw MGO WOG, Komiteta socjalnoj zaszczity g. Moskwy, ROOI "Pomoszcznik," 1999], 53–54.

61. The committee consisted of the following members: A. S. Grizanow, Józef Petrowicz Rogowski, Aleksandr Siergiejewicz Dawidow, Gawrił Georgijewicz Aleksiejew, and E. A. Smirnowa.

62. Wiesław Dobrowolski (1899–1969), who took part in the October Revolution, worked for Deaf groups for many years. He was a member of the publishing committees of many local newspapers, such as *Świat Głuchoniemych*, *Sport i Wychowanie fizyczne głuchoniemych*, and *Kalendarz Głuchoniemych*. After WWII he served as secretary of the Polish Deaf Association.

63. Leon Roman Petrykiewicz (1901–1986), a Deaf man who was a pre-WWII activist in the Deaf community in Lviv, took part in the defense of the city. He was a board member of the Lviv Sport Club for the Deaf-Mute and the Lesser-Poland Deaf-Mute Society "Hope" in Lviv. After WWII he served as chairman of the executive board of the Polish Deaf Society in Warsaw (1955–1967).

64. Bogumił Liban, chairman of the Jewish Deaf-Mute Society "Przyjaźń" in Cracow.

65. Józef Bäcker (1899–1983) was one of the most outstanding activists of the Deaf community in Lviv. He was a board member of the Lviv Sport Club for the Deaf-Mute,

the Lesser-Poland Deaf-Mute Society in Lviv, and the Polish Sport Club for the Deaf-Mute. After WWII he served as chairman of the Polish Deaf Society in Wroclaw.

66. H. Łabecki, "Międzynarodowy Zjazd Głuchoniemych w Pradze Czeskiej [International Deaf-Mute Convention in Prague]," *Świat Głuchoniemych* 8–9 (1928), 4.

67. Archives of the Polish Deaf Society in Poznan, Władysław Krzyżkowiak's chronicle, no pagination.

68. J. Rogowski, "Polski Związek Towarzystw Głuchoniemych. Szkic historyczny," *Świat Głuchoniemych* (February 1927), 2–5.; J. Rogowski, "Polski Związek Towarzystw Głuchoniemych (Dokończenie)," *Świat Głuchoniemych* (March 1927), 6–7; J. Rogowski, "Noc Sylwestrowa," *Świat Głuchoniemych* (January 1928), 2; J. Rogowski, "Hołd głuchoniemych Polski dla Ojca Świętego [Polish Deaf Paying Tribute to the Pope]," *Świat Głuchoniemych* (November–December 1929), 5.

69. J. Rogowski, "Jak dostałem się," 2–3.

70. J. Rogowski, "Z wywczasów letnich," *Komunikat Polskiego Związku Towarzystw Głuchoniemych* (March 1932), 19–23.

71. *AZGPZG, Kronika*, k.261.

72. "Nagły zgon prezesa Instytutu Głuchoniemych" [Sudden death of the chairman of the Institute for the Deaf-Mute and Blind], *Express Poranny Warszawski* (January 26, 1933).

Matsumura Sei-ichirô: The First Deaf President of a Japanese School for Deaf People

Akio Suemori

According to several biographies (Nishi-Tonami District Office 1909; Ishizaki 1955; Fukumitsu Town Office 1971; Kitano 1979), Matsumura Sei-ichirô (1849–1891) was the first president of the Kanazawa school for the deaf and blind (SDB) (see figure 1), which means he was the first deaf president of a SDB in Japan. Indeed, only three deaf presidents of a SDB in Japan have been identified up to the present time: Matsumura of the Kanazawa SDB, Tsujimoto Shigeru (1893–1979) of the Yakumo SDB, and Koiwai Zehio (1894–1981) of the Matsumoto SDB. Such historical facts strongly indicate that Matsumura was an outstanding deaf person and should be considered an important part of Japanese deaf history.

However, Matsumura resigned as president of the Kanazawa SDB in 1881, the same year the school was founded (table 1). In addition, the school completely closed in 1887 because of financial problems and the difficulty of recruiting sufficient numbers of deaf students (table 1).

FIGURE 1. *Matsumura Sei-ichirô.*

Accordingly, some historians of special education evaluate his managerial effectiveness as poor, as he had limited abilities to solve financial problems, and he often asked his relatives for loans (Kitano 1979). Nevertheless, few historical documents describing the financial problems of the Kanazawa SDB have been discovered, and thus it has not definitively been established how Matsumura managed the Kanazawa SDB.

TABLE 1. Chronological Table of the Kanazawa School for the Deaf and Blind, *Bankoku Chishi Kaitei*, and Matsumura

Years	Kanazawa School for the Deaf and Blind	*Bankoku Chishi Kaitei*	Matsumura
1875 (Meiji 7)		The book was translated and compiled.	
1876 (Meiji 8)			
1877 (Meiji 9)			living in Tokyo
1878 (Meiji 10)			
1878 (Meiji 11)		The first edition was published.	
1879 (Meiji 12)			living in Kanazawa
1880 (Meiji 13)	The school was founded.		

(continued)

TABLE 1. (*Continued*)

Years	Kanazawa School for the Deaf and Blind	*Bankoku Chishi Kaitei*	Matsumura
1881 (Meiji 14)		The second edition was published.	
1882 (Meiji 15)	transfer of management to *Kanazawa kyôiku sha*	The third edition (first version) was published.	
1883 (Meiji 16)	The school was closed. *Kanazawa kyôiku sha* was dissolved.		
1884 (Meiji 17)			
1885 (Meiji 18)			
1886 (Meiji 19)		The fourth edition was published.	living in Fukumitsu
1887 (Meiji 20)	Assets and liabilities were disposed.	The fifth edition was published.	
1888 (Meiji 21)			living in Kanazawa
1889 (Meiji 22)			
1890 (Meiji 23)			
1891 (Meiji 24)			died (44 years old)

Bankoku Chishi Kaitei

Alternatively, some sources state that Matsumura published the geographic text *Bankoku Chishi Kaitei (BCK) (A Guide to World Geography)*. The *BCK* was mainly a translation of *Mitchell's Primary Geography*, which had been published in the United States in 1851 (Mitchell 1851). Therefore, Matsumura clearly belongs to the group of Japanese scholars of Western studies who introduced European and/or American works to Japan during the early

Meiji period (Ishizaki 1955). However, no bibliographic studies on the *BCK* were reported. Apparently little or no research has been done on how Matsumura as a scholar of Western studies contributed to the Kanazawa SDB and the education of deaf children in the early Meiji period in Japan. These issues led me to bibliographically investigate the *BCK*.

In this essay I present a bibliographic analysis of the various editions of the *BCK*, reevaluate Matsumura's activities from that viewpoint, and suggest the possibility of a relationship between the publishing of the various editions of the *BCK* and support of the Kanazawa SDB.

A Bibliographic Analysis of the Book
Different Editions

The *BCK* was republished in several different editions and was finally approved by the Ministry of Education in 1887 as a textbook to be used in hearing elementary schools (Ishizaki 1955). However, various editions of the *BCK* have not yet been bibliographically analyzed. To do this, I first tried to collect copies of different editions of the *BCK* from the National Diet Library and other university libraries (Suemori 2011). As table 2 shows, the bibliographical classification of the copies indicates that at least five different editions were printed. The titles of those that were published from 1878 to 1887 are as follows: *BCK* in 1878, *Kôtei BCK* (revised *BCK*) in 1881, *Zôho kôtei BCK* (revised and enlarged *BCK*) in 1882, *Sakutei BCK* (compiled *BCK*) in 1886, and *Shinsen BCK* (newly compiled *BCK*) in 1887. As figures 2 through 6 illustrate, an analysis of the cover styles of the five editions indicates that the editions can be divided into two groups. One group comprises two editions (published in 1878 and 1881), and the other consists of three editions (published in 1882, 1886, and 1887). This chapter presents the first bibliographical analysis of the *BCK*.

The First Edition

Previous biographies and papers have reported that the *BCK* was translated and first published in 1875 (Nishi-Tonami District Office 1909; Ishizaki 1955). However, the oldest edition of the *BCK* found during my

TABLE 2. Editions and Versions of *Bankoku Chishi Kaitei*

Groups	Editions and Versions	Titles (in Japanese)	Descriptions	Reviewers and a Translator	Libraries
α	first edition (1878) (Meiji 11)	*Bankoku Chishi Kaitei*	offered on August 23, 1878; printed in September 1878	reviewed by Fujita Toshikatsu; translated by Matsumura Sei-ichirô	National Diet Library
α	second edition (1881) (Meiji 14)	*Kôtei Bankoku Chishi Kaitei*	accepted on February 24, 1881	reviewed by Fujita Toshikatsu; translated and revised by Matsumura Sei-ichirô	National Diet Library
β	first version, third edition (1882) (Meiji 15)	*Zôho kôtei Bankoku Chishi Kaitei*	accepted on February 22, 1879 (error); revised in March 1882	reviewed by Fujita Toshikatsu; translated and revised by Matsumura Sei-ichirô	University of Nagoya
β	second version, third edition (1882) (Meiji 15)	*Zôho kôtei Bankoku Chishi Kaitei*	literary permit received on February 22, 1881 (error); revised in March 1882; revised edition approved on April 9, 1882; revised edition printed and made available on April 10, 1882; revised title was made available on April 20, 1882	reviewed by Fujita Toshikatsu; translated and revised by Matsumura Sei-ichirô	Tsukuba University; Hitotsubashi University

β	third version, third edition (1882) (Meiji 15)	*Zōho Kōtei Bankoku Chishi Kaitei*	literary permit received on February 22, 1881 (error); revised in March 1882; revised edition approved on April 9, 1882; revised edition printed and made available on April 10, 1882; revised title was made available on April 20, 1882	reviewed by Fujita Toshikatsu; translated and revised by Matsumura Sei-ichirō	author
β	fourth edition (1886) (Meiji 19)	*Sakutei Bankoku Chishi Kaitei*	literary permit received on February 24, 1881; title revised on February 24, 1886; revised and printed on March 8, 1886	reviewed by Arai Ikuno-suke; translated and revised by Matsumura Sei-ichirō	National Diet Library, Tōsho Bunko
β	fifth edition (1887) (Meiji 20)	*Shinsen Bankoku Chishi Kaitei*	literary permit received on February 24, 1881; printed in March 1886; title revised on May 13, 1887; officially approved on June 13, 1887	reviewed by Arai Ikunosuke; translated and revised by Matsumura Sei-ichirō	Tokushima University, Gifu University

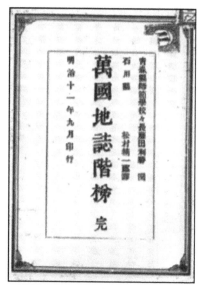

FIGURE 2. *An inside cover of the first edition of the* BCK, *published in 1878.*

FIGURE 3. *An inside cover of the second edition,* Kôtei BCK, *published in 1881.*

FIGURE 4. *An inside cover of the first version of the third edition,* Zôho kôtei BCK, *published in 1882.*

FIGURE 5. *An inside cover of the fourth edition,* Sakutei BCK, *published in 1886.*

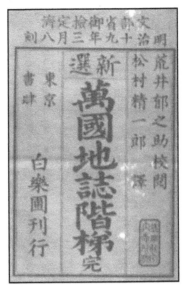

FIGURE 6. *An inside cover of the fifth edition,* Shinsen BCK, *published in 1887.*

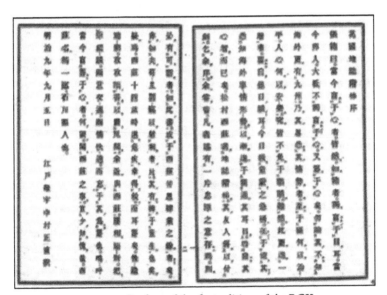

FIGURE 7. *Preface of the first edition of the* BCK.

research was printed in 1878. The colophon of this edition notes that the Tokyo Metropolitan Office was assigned the right to sell the book in August 1878 (table 2). As figure 7 shows, the preface of the *BCK,* dated September 5, 1876, was written by Professor Nakamura, who was one of Matsumura's teachers (Kitano 1979). This date unquestionably indicates

FIGURE 8. *A bill attached to the fourth edition, published in 1886.*

that the first edition was published sometime after 1876. As figure 8 shows, a bill attached to the colophon of the fourth edition, printed in 1886, which was owned by a publishing company, Tôhô Bunsho, was discovered during my research (table 2). This bill states that the *BCK* had been in publication since 1879. The analysis led me to hypothesize that the first edition was compiled by 1875, printed in 1878, and finally sold in 1879.

In addition, my analysis has uncovered some errors in previous biographies and other writing about the *BCK*. For example, the information that the *Shinsen BCK* was published in 1875 has appeared in a previous source (Kitano 1979); however, my research indicates unequivocally that the *Shinsen BCK* was published in 1887. Such errors have arisen due to the citation of these historical sources without sufficient examination of the original documents and further secondary citations.

The *BCK* and the Kanazawa SDB's Financial Problem

The Dawn of Education for Deaf People in Japan

It is generally believed that the first school for deaf and blind students (SDB) was established in 1878 by Furukawa Tashirô (1845–1907) in Kyoto after the Meiji Restoration (1867–1877). It was at first a private school and later became a public school. However, there is no universally accepted theory as to when the teaching of reading and writing to deaf children was first carried out in Japan (Nakano and Katô 1967). In the following year, the second SDB was founded in Osaka. However, it unfortunately went from being a public school to a private school within a year because the Osaka prefectural assembly rejected the budget for the Osaka SDB (ibid.).

In Tokyo in 1880 Professor Nakamura Masanao and other supporters initiated the third SDB, which became the predecessor of the present national schools for deaf and blind children in Japan (ibid.). In 1881 Matsumura Sei-ichirô founded a semigovernmental SDB (i.e., a private school supported by a subsidy from Ishikawa Prefecture), in Kanazawa, Ishikawa Prefecture (table 1) (Ishikawa Prefecture 1909, 1974). It was not until twenty-three years later, in 1900, that a new SDB was established in Ishikawa Prefecture (Committee of the Conference on 13th Education for the Deaf 2001).

This period, during which four SDB were established in Kyoto, Osaka, Tokyo, and Kanazawa, was considered the first wave of the establishment of SDBs in the history of special education in Japan (figure 9). However, because economic slackening from the 1880s to the 1900s led to fewer SDBs, the second wave of the founding of SDBs nationwide occurred after the turn of the century, which eventuated in the developmental division of an SDB into two schools during the 1930s: One is a school for deaf children, and the other is a school for

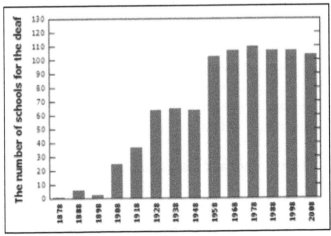

FIGURE 9. A chronogram of the number of schools for deaf children in Japan.

blind youngsters. The first wave of SDB foundation should be analyzed from a viewpoint of financial problems.

The Book Revision and the Colophons

Owners of bookshops were recorded in each colophon of the different editions, and this provided useful information about the sales network for the BCK. In the first edition, printed in 1878, only ten storekeepers in the Tokyo metropolitan area and in Akita, Miyagi, Yamagata, and Fukushima prefectures in Tôhoku were listed. However, in the second edition, printed in 1881, twenty-seven storekeepers in those prefectures and in Aomori Prefecture were discovered. In addition, in the third edition, printed in 1882, the colophon styles were divided into three versions based on the recorded storekeepers. For example, storekeepers in Aichi Prefecture were newly recognized in a colophon of the first version of this edition, indicating that the BCK was purchased in the Tôkai region, in addition to the Tokyo metropolitan area and the Tôhoku region.

While the second edition of the BCK was published in 1881, the third edition was substantially revised and first sold in Aichi Prefecture and the surrounding area of the Tôhoku region in 1882. Coincidentally, in 1882 the Kanazawa SDB was transferred to another organization, Kanazawa Kyôiku Sha, because of financial trouble. This simultaneous occurrence strongly suggests that the third edition, printed in 1882, was an attempt to raise financial support for the Kanazawa SDB.

In addition, as figure 8 shows, the bill with the fourth edition also indicates that the first three editions of the BCK sold sixty thousand copies and that Matsumura and Ejima had a plan to publish a new Japanese geography text. This discovery suggests that Matsumura intended to use the royalties from the sale of the BCK and the proposed new geography text for financial support for the Kanazawa SDB.

Matsumura and Education for Deaf People

It has been learned that, even from the end of the Edo period to the early Meiji period, administrators and teachers in SDBs received information about special education from Europe or China (Nakano and Katô 1967).

The preface of the BCK indicated that Matsumura was taught by Professor Nakamura, who was one of the founding contributors of the Tokyo SDB and was thoroughly versed in educational methods for deaf children through his familiarity with special education in Europe and the United States. Therefore, Matsumura seemed to be well acquainted with educational techniques for teaching deaf children that were in use at this time.

In addition, newspaper stories and private letters during the 1870s and 1880s indicate that Matsumura communicated with the founding contributors of the Tokyo SDB, Professor Ôuchi Seiran (1845–1918) and Tsuda Sen (1837–1908), and that they also supported the founding of the Kanazawa SDB. These sources suggest that scholars of Western studies contributed to the founding of the Kanazawa SDB. Therefore, Matsumura's contributions should be reevaluated in light of his role as a scholar of Western studies in the early Meiji period, and he should also be considered a deaf pioneer.

Interestingly, the preface of the *BCK* also indicated that Matsumura was born in Toyama Prefecture, became deaf at the age of fourteen, and communicated with Professor Nakamura in Nakamura's private school in Tokyo in writing. However, from 1880 to 1881 Matsumura visited the Kyoto, Osaka, and Tokyo SDBs, where old Japanese sign language was used, before he founded the Kanazawa SDB. Thus, I hypothesize that Matsumura would have known of the existence of sign language and that deaf students of the Kanazawa SDB would have used old Japanese sign language.

In this essay I have reevaluated Matsumura from the viewpoint of a bibliographic analysis of the *BCK* and the financial problems of the Kanazawa SDB, leading me to a hypothesis about the relationship of revised editions of the *BCK* and the Kanazawa SDB's monetary difficulties. To corroborate my hypothesis, I was required to look for new historical documents such as the account books of the Kanazawa SDB of those days.

References

Committee of the Conference on 13th Education for the Deaf. "Dawn of the Education of the Deaf in Ishikawa Prefecture and Japan during 19th-Century Japan." *Rô kyôiku no asu wo motomete* 13 (2001). In Japanese.

Fukumitsu Town Office. *Fukumitsu chô shi* [A history of Fukumitsu town]. Toyama: Fukumitsu Town Office, 1971. In Japanese.

Ishikawa Prefecture. *Môa gakkô* [Schools for the deaf and blind]. Ishikawa ken kyôiku yôran [A survey of education in Ishikawa Prefecture] (1909): 26–27. In Japanese.

Ishikawa Prefecture. *Ishikawa ken kyôiku shi* [A history of education in Ishikawa prefecture]. Ishikawa: Ishikawa prefecture, 1974. In Japanese.

Ishizaki, T. *Rô gakusha Matsumura Seisô sensei* [A deaf scholar, Seisô Matsumura]. *Ecchû shidan* 5 (1955): 42–47. In Japanese.

Kitano, Y. *Shiritsu Kanazawa môa in ni kansuru kôsatsu* [Analysis of the private school, Kanazawa school for the deaf and blind]. *Tokushu kyôiku gaku Kenkyû* 17 (1979): 1–8. In Japanese.

Mitchell, S. *Mitchell's New School Geography,* 1872.

———. *Mitchell's Primary Geography,* 1851.

———. *Mitchell's School Geography,* 1st ed. 1845.

———. *Mitchell's School Geography,* 2nd ed. 1860.

Nakano, Y., and Y. Katô. *Waga kuni tokushu kyôiku no seiritsu* [A history of special education in Japan]. Tôkyô: Tôhô Shobô, 1967. In Japanese.

Nishi-Tonami District Office. *Toyama ken Nishi-Tonami gun kiyô* [The outline of Nishi-Tonami District, Toyama Prefecture]. Toyama: Nishi-Tonami District Office, 1909. In Japanese.

Suemori, A. "Bankoku Chishi Kaitei no shoshi gaku teki kôsatsu" [A bibliographic study of *Bankoku Chishi Kaitei*]. In *Proceedings of the 14th Japanese Deaf History Conference.* 2011. In Japanese.

Remembering a Legacy: Samuel Thomas Greene

Clifton F. Carbin

A famous British historian and journalist once wrote, "History is not another name for the past, as many people imply. It is the name for stories about the past."[1] This chapter contains a few selections from the story of Samuel Thomas Greene (1843–1890), a Deaf teacher and community leader. Through the decades his noteworthy contributions to Deaf history nearly disappeared into obscurity until a movement to honor his memory came about in the 1980s and 1990s.

For nearly a century the eyes of residential students at the provincial school for the Deaf in Belleville, Ontario, Canada, were drawn to a huge, impressive 1890 portrait of a man, which was previously hung high on a wall in the auditorium. For years, both the identity of this gentleman and the reason for his portrait were unknown. He was simply forgotten after the school adopted the oral philosophy in 1906, gradually eliminating the use of sign language in the classrooms and by Deaf employees. The staff and teachers assumed the portrait was that of a politician or philanthropist who had contributed to the school. There were no stories about him to tell to the students.

1. Attributed to Alan John Percivale Taylor (1906–1990).

Details about the mysterious man in the portrait began to emerge in the 1970s after I stumbled across some information in the *American Annals of the Deaf and Dumb* (1847–1886) and its successor, the *American Annals of the Deaf* (1886–present). The subject of the painting was identified as Samuel Thomas Greene, the first Deaf teacher at the Ontario Institution for the Education and Instruction of the Deaf and Dumb (now the Sir James Whitney School for the Deaf) when it opened on October 20, 1870, in Belleville. Further discoveries about Sam's life, his accomplishments, and his importance to the history of the Deaf community led to the publication of a biography in 2005.

Childhood and School Days

Sam's childhood began in the secluded wilderness of Maine. On June 11, 1843, he was born Deaf to a family of seven children in North Waterford. The youngest of the children, he had an older sister, Sarah, who was also Deaf. Because the family lived far away from any village, church, or schoolhouse, Sam received some education at home on the farm until the age of twelve. His parents then sent him to the American Asylum for the Education and Instruction of the Deaf and Dumb (now the American School for the Deaf) in Hartford, Connecticut, which his sister had previously attended from 1846 to 1851. On September 18, 1855, Sam was officially enrolled to begin his formal education.

During his stay at the American Asylum, Sam progressed well in both his studies and extracurricular student activities. One of his instructors was the famous Laurent Clerc (1785–1869), a Deaf Frenchman who came to the United States and played a pivotal role with the American-born Thomas Hopkins Gallaudet (1787–1851) in founding the Hartford institution in 1817. Sam eventually entered the "Gallaudet High Class," a class of crème-de-la-crème scholars who often continued their education after graduation. From 1864 to 1866, while still a student, he was given an opportunity to teach a younger class. Exhibiting a keen interest in the school's extracurricular activities, Sam served as librarian (1863), treasurer (1864), president (1864), and secretary (1865) of the Athenaeum of the American Asylum, an elite, student-run literary and debating society. He was also a foreman of a student fire brigade. During the American

Civil War (1861–1865), Sam was made captain of the school's noncombat military company of students, known as the "Gallaudet Guard."

In 1866 Sam, then twenty-three years old, ended his student days at the American Asylum and decided to further his education at the National Deaf-Mute College (now Gallaudet University) in Washington, DC, where he was admitted in September that year.

Sam was too much in love with college life. He struggled to balance his academic studies with campus activities. He participated in the literary society, called the College Reading Club, and was team captain of the college's first athletic initiative, known as the Kendall Base-Ball Club. Sam was well liked by his professors and fellow students, and some lively stories about him became legendary around campus. A few examples include his catching a ball with one hand while pirouetting on one toe, carrying ladies across flooded brooks, and a frightening experience that once happened to him in the dark:

> During one evening adventure, Sam left the college and went to Baltimore, Maryland, to visit a hearing friend. When he arrived at the doorstep of his friend's residence at nearly midnight, he forcefully pulled a rope to ring the bell several times. The loud ringing angered the residents. His friend, who quickly picked up a loaded revolver and opened the upper bedroom window, shouted down, asking for the name and business of the nocturnal caller. But Sam continued ringing the bell, as he could neither hear his friend nor see him in the darkness. Suddenly Sam felt the vibrations from a loud warning shot. He immediately "made rapid strides for the street, and with excited gesticulation succeeded in revealing his identity and saving himself from his friend's revolver." Sam often told his deaf friends about his experience and advised them to be careful of the danger when creating a disturbance. Most certainly his dire warning would have been accompanied by humorous actions and with twinkling eyes. (Carbin 2005, 56)

Professional Career

On June 30, 1870, Sam, who turned twenty-seven that month, graduated from the college with a Bachelor of Arts degree. Prior to that day, he had been offered teaching positions at three US institutions for Deaf students. He opted for his alma mater in Hartford.

However, in early September Sam received a surprise invitation to teach in Canada. He was highly recommended by Dr. Edward M. Gallaudet, then president of the National Deaf-Mute College, for a position at the Ontario Institution for the Education and Instruction of the Deaf and Dumb in Belleville, which was scheduled to open the following month as a new, permanent, government-funded school in the province. After much consideration, he accepted the position and arranged for his journey to Ontario.

To the delight of a large crowd of dignitaries, functionaries, school staff, and visitors, the Ontario Institution officially opened on October 20, 1870. Sam, who was the only Deaf teacher, was introduced along with the inaugural teaching staff, which consisted of Wesley "Willie" J. Palmer (principal), Daniel R. Coleman, and John Barrett McGann (school founder), and McGann's oldest daughter, Mrs. J. J. G. Terrill (née Euphemia McGann). Sam gave the audience a demonstration of the sign language (which became widely known as American Sign Language in the 1960s) by depicting the various passions of love, hatred, bravery, cowardice, hope, and scorn.

For the next twenty years of his tenure at the Ontario Institution, Sam used his experiences as a student at the American Asylum as the source of most of his ideas for classroom practices and extracurricular activities. He devoted his teaching career to classes that were usually made up of pupils of various ages who had entered the school with few or no language skills. He recognized the need to help these students build a strong foundation for learning skills throughout their stay. Because the school embraced the American system of manual education, Sam was also assigned to train its new staff in sign language. For student activities, he started a fire brigade of older boys, a small literary group known as the Dufferin Literary Society, and a hymn-signing choir for the female students. He often entertained students who could not go home for the Christmas holidays.

Sam became the first graduate of the National Deaf-Mute College to marry. On August 15, 1871, he married Caroline "Cassie" Campbell Howard, a hearing woman and a member of Belleville's famous Wallbridge family, noted for its wealth and business enterprises. Sam and Cassie had five hearing children: one son and four daughters, none of whom embarked on a teaching career like their father.

Community Activities

In additional to his educational work, Sam contributed significantly to the social activities of the Ontario Deaf community. He was the originator of several associations and publications. For example, in 1886 he cofounded and became the first president of the Ontario Deaf-Mute Association (now the Ontario Association of the Deaf). He also cocreated an eight-page, semimonthly publication titled the *Canadian Silent Observer* in 1888. Sam traveled to many parts of the province and south of the border, where he gave outstanding presentations in sign language.

Sam loved boating and the outdoors. Sadly, his extraordinary life abruptly ended in February 1890 after he was thrown off his homemade iceboat with sails on the frozen Bay of Quinte near the Ontario Institution. He hit his head on the ice with considerable force and remained unconscious for two weeks before dying at home. Both the school community and the Deaf community in general were devastated. The funeral took place at the school, and his remains were buried in section "P" of the Belleville cemetery.

Honoring Memory

A few months after Sam's passing, his friends and colleagues decided to honor him with a suitable marker in the Belleville cemetery. A committee was set up to raise funds, and contributions were received from the school staff, the Deaf community, and the general public. In October 1890 a monument in the form of a twelve-foot-tall circular column of red Scotch granite was unveiled. At the base of the marker, Sam's surname was distinctively displayed in bas-relief characters of the manual alphabet. In the summer of the same year, during the Third Biennial Convention of the Ontario Deaf-Mute Association in Toronto, a large portrait in oils of Sam was unveiled and later given as a gift to the school.

It was painted by one of Sam's closest Deaf friends, Ambrose W. Mason, soon after Sam's death.

Over the years, Sam's name and legacy slowly faded from the school's history. The students no longer visited his monument in the Belleville cemetery, and his portrait simply became part of the wall décor. This was partly due to the lack of Deaf employees at the school, who would have kept his memory alive by telling stories. By the 1970s, due to my research findings, Sam's name had resurfaced, and in the 1980s and 1990s the Deaf community of Ontario gradually came to know of his accomplishments.

In 1993 one of the school's residences was renamed "Greene Hall." On July 1, 1995, during the school's 125th-anniversary reunion week-end, a plaque to commemorate Sam's achievements in the education of Deaf students was unveiled by the Ontario Heritage Foundation, an agency of the Ontario Ministry of Culture, Tourism, and Recreation. Funds were eventually raised by the school and the Deaf community to replace the base of Sam's century-old grave marker because his finger-spelled surname had badly deteriorated. A dedication ceremony for the replacement grave marker took place on June 11, 1997, the date of Sam's 154th birthday. In 1999 one of the streets of the school campus became "Greene Drive." Each year, festivities take place with skits and stories about him presented by students and alumni. The Ontario Association of the Deaf commissioned me, as one of the school's well-known gradu-ates and author of a previous historical book, to write a biography about Sam, which was completed and published in 2005.

Sam is no longer a forgotten legend. His memory will continue to grow prouder and stronger within both the school community and the Deaf community for generations to come.

References

Carbin, Clifton F. 1996. "Samuel Thomas Greene, Ontario's First Deaf Teacher." In *Deaf Heritage in Canada: A Distinctive, Diverse, and Enduring Culture*, 105–106. Whitby, ON: McGraw-Hill Ryerson.

———. 2005. *Samuel Thomas Greene: A Legend in the Nineteenth Century Deaf Community*. Belleville, ON: Essence/Epic.

Written into History: The Lives of Australian Deaf Leaders

Darlene Thornton, Susannah Macready, and Patricia Levitzke-Gray

This essay attempts to redress the imbalance of the focus on non-Deaf people and their participation and achievements within Australian Deaf history. Out of numerous candidates, two Deaf individuals were selected who are excellent Deaf role models for younger generations. Fletcher S. Booth and Dorothy Shaw, born in different eras, were strong and vocal leaders in the New South Wales and Australian Deaf communities from the 1870s to the 1990s.

Fletcher Samuel Booth (1870–1956)

Fletcher Samuel Booth, the eldest son of nine children born to the Rev. Samuel Booth and his wife, Emma, is believed[1] to have been born Deaf. He grew up in Sydney and in Parramatta, a suburb of Sydney, in New South Wales, Australia. His close-knit family was very supportive and had strong ties to the Wesleyan Church and later the Church of England. It seems that the whole family could communicate with Booth through signs and fingerspelling, as his sisters were well-known sign language interpreters in both Sydney and South Australia.

From the age of seven, Booth was educated at the New South Wales (NSW) Institution for the Deaf, Dumb, and Blind in Sydney. He attended this school for about eight years. When he left at the age of fifteen, he trained as a draftsman and an architect and worked for several architectural companies in both Parramatta and Sydney. His main interests were reading (the Bible, newspapers, and books); doing crossword puzzles; boating (he owned a boat then); and socializing with Deaf people in Sydney and with his extended family.[2]

He married Laura A. Begent, one of the very few Deaf teachers in Sydney at this time, when they were both in their thirties. Booth had two sons with her, one of whom was Deaf. Laura died in 1946 after a short illness, and Booth died ten years later at the age of eighty-six in a nursing home for Deaf people in Strathfield, in the Sydney area. It appears that this family may have carried a deafness gene, as the subsequent generations include at least one or two family members with hearing loss.

Dorothy Evelyn P. Shaw, née Johnston (1921–1990)

Dorothy Shaw was born into a family of four that included a Deaf younger brother and Deaf parents, named James (Jim) and Evelyn Johnston (née Hair) in Melbourne, Victoria, Australia. Dorothy grew up in a household that used Deaf Sign Language, an old name for Australian Sign Language (Auslan). During her childhood and young adulthood, the family participated in many activities within the Victorian Deaf community.

She attended the Victorian Deaf and Dumb Institution (now known as the Victorian College for the Deaf) at St. Kilda, in the Melbourne area. She started her schooling when she was six and graduated with a certificate of merit when she left at the age of fifteen, as she was the dux, or top student. Shaw's dream was to be a teacher of Deaf children; however, her financial situation and the distance prevented her from attending Gallaudet College (now Gallaudet University) in the United States. Her interests were reading books, *Reader's Digest* magazines, and

newspapers; playing sports; hiking in the bush; writing stories and letters; and spending time with family and friends.[3]

From the age of nine, her family lived on the grounds of the
Victorian Deaf Adult Society in Jolimont Square in East Melbourne.
Thus, Shaw was influenced by a variety of individuals and organizations
as well as by her experience and training. Her father, Jim, was employed
as an assistant missioner and was responsible for assisting the missioner
(an early-day welfare worker) in looking after the welfare of deaf people,
residential officer, and caretaker of the Victorian Deaf Adult Society,
which had a church for Deaf people and a club building for Deaf adults'
social meetings. Her family also participated in Deaf sports clubs and
attended the Australian Deaf Games for many years.

Shaw married John (Jack) Shaw in 1943. The family moved to
Sydney from Melbourne and had three Deaf children. The Shaws are a
five-generation Deaf family (so far), as each generation has at least one
or two family members with hearing loss.

How Did They Contribute to the
Australian Deaf Community?

Organizations

From the age of twenty-one, Fletcher Booth was a leader of the Sydney
Deaf community and over the next few decades became its spokesman,
diplomat, and advocate. Booth was the first native Sydneysider who was
paid to take charge of "the uplift of the Adult Deaf." He noted the lack of
support for Deaf adults after leaving school and that many Deaf adults
were still being guided by the people at the NSW Institution for the Deaf,
Dumb, and Blind. From the 1890s on, he was paid the nominal sum of
£1 per month[4] for a couple of years to provide club meetings on Friday
evenings and assist with the religious services at various local nondeaf
churches in the Sydney area on Sunday mornings. In the beginning Booth
assisted the nondeaf ministers and interpreters at the church services;
eventually he assumed responsibility for church services for the adult
Deaf community, which took place after the church services for hearing people. He received mentoring support mainly from Samuel Watson,

superintendent of the NSW Institution for the Deaf, Dumb, and Blind, who also acted as an interpreter during the Sunday services.[5]

Recognizing the lack of services and specialized support for Deaf adults in Sydney, Booth offered to find solutions. With assistance from Watson, he provided space for Deaf adults on the grounds of the NSW Institution for the Deaf, Dumb, and Blind by erecting the first building for this purpose. The building, named Adult Deaf, had space for a printing machine, which was used to publish several Deaf journals (discussed later), a reading room, and a room for club and social meetings and church services.[6]

After Watson's death in 1911, the location of the Adult Deaf building on the grounds of the NSW Institution proved to be problematic for the Deaf community, so Booth sought to have an independent support service organization for Deaf adults established apart from the control of the NSW Institution and its board.

After the first public meeting with many deaf and nondeaf people in 1913 in Sydney's town hall, the proposal to form the Adult Deaf and Dumb Society of New South Wales was successful.[7] However, as was common practice with other charitable Deaf organizations in Australia, nondeaf people rather than Deaf adults themselves were appointed to the board, which created friction and power struggles for many years. Booth encountered this issue several times during his tenure with the board of management of the Adult Deaf and Dumb Society of NSW, so he and other Deaf and nondeaf adults who were dissatisfied with how the group was catering to the Deaf adults in NSW decided to form an independent, Deaf-controlled organization, called the New South Wales Association of Deaf and Dumb Citizens (also known as the Association). This new organization, established in 1929, had a Deaf majority on its board, with only one or two hearing men (as representatives of the public as well as interpreters). Predictably, this new organization was met with resistance from the board of management of the Adult Deaf and Dumb Society of NSW since it meant serious competition for the provision of services, especially with regard to government funding and charitable donations to the Deaf adults in New South Wales.

Later, Booth, with the support of Australian Deaf adults, formed and presided over a national organization named the Australian Association for the Advancement of the Deaf (AAAD), which was designed to be run by and for Deaf people and was intended to counterbalance the hearing-dominated, state-based Deaf societies. However, this association turned out be short lived, as the newly revised Charitable Collections Act of 1934 (NSW) stipulated that only one service organization could provide for the needs of the group it represented. Thus, after several years of negotiations, a forced amalgamation of the NSW Association of Deaf and Dumb Citizens and the Adult Deaf and Dumb Society of NSW took place without any Deaf board members in the leading Adult Deaf and Dumb Society of NSW.

After the 1940s Booth reduced his political involvement in the Deaf community and, until his death in 1956, attended only the Deaf club at 5 Elizabeth Street in Sydney (the same building that he originally helped to select, renovate, and work in as part of the offices for the Adult Deaf and Dumb Society of NSW).

❀

Dorothy Shaw became active in several Deaf organizations when her three Deaf children attended the NSW Institution for the Deaf and Blind. However, her potential as an influential leader, mentor, and activist for the Sydney and Australian Deaf communities was not apparent until the 1970s, when she attended an educational conference and presented what would be the first of many papers.

Shaw believed strongly that language fluency is the key to independence for Deaf people and that Deaf people needed to take responsibility for the progress of their community. From 1947 on, she was a board member of several organizations such as the Deaf Tennis Club, the Deaf Women's Guild, the Deaf General Committee of the Deaf Society of NSW, and the NSW Committee of the Australian Sign Language Development Project (ASLDP). However, she was proudest of her integral involvement with four important organizations. The first of these was called Concerned Deaf for Total Communication in Education, which Shaw initiated and presided over from 1981 to 1984.[8] This group declared that it would focus on the development of Total Communication for Deaf children in educational institutions throughout Australia and promote the use of both sign language and English. This group's work resulted in the creation of the Signed English dictionary (still in use today in most areas of Australia) and the use of Signed English in classrooms for Deaf children everywhere in Australia, displacing pure oralism as the core of the national education policy.

Next, Shaw lobbied for and assisted with the formation of the Australian Caption Centre, the launch of telephone typewriters (TTYs) in Australia, the research and development of an Auslan dictionary, and the recognition of Auslan as the official language of the Australian Deaf Community in the 1990s.[9]

The last and the two most significant organizations Shaw helped to establish were the Australian Association of the Deaf (AAD) in 1986 and Deaf Action Books in 1983 (the latter was later renamed Deafness Resources Australia, or DRA). Shaw believed that Deaf people needed to educate society and lobby for better living standards for Deaf people across Australia. Thus, the AAD covered the political aspect of lobbying for services for Deaf people, while DRA focused on increasing access to information about and for the Deaf community by providing products and equipment. Since that time, the AAD has become Deaf Australia (DA) and taken over the DRA as part of its services, naming it the Auslan Shop.

Publications for the Deaf Community

Fletcher Booth, with his fluency in both Auslan and written English, was the driving force behind two publications: the *Silent Messenger* and the *Deaf Advocate*. The former, which, as far as can be ascertained, is the first publication in NSW for Deaf people by Deaf people, was first printed in 1906 in Sydney and is still in circulation today. Although many stops and starts have occurred over this Deaf journal's life span, its main aim has been to inform and educate Deaf adults about current affairs, personal news of the members of the NSW Deaf community, and issues that affect them. Booth was officially its editor for many years, perhaps until the late 1920s, and contributed photos, informative articles, and religious passages.

The *Deaf Advocate* was another publication by and for the NSW Deaf community. It was started in 1929 after Booth and company formed the NSW Association of Deaf and Dumb Citizens, with Booth as its coeditor. The aim of this publication was similar to that of the *Silent Messenger*, and for about ten years before the forced amalgamation of the two NSW Deaf organizations, these two publications competed with one another. The *Deaf Advocate* stated that it aspired to be the voice of "deaf aims and ambitions and the deaf spirit of independence."[10] Its circulation had expanded from three hundred readers at the start to four thousand at its peak, and the paper was initially sent to readers in NSW but later expanded to an Australia-wide readership. It is believed that some issues may even have reached other countries.

Booth also wrote about the history of the Adult Deaf and Dumb Society of NSW from 1938 to 1943, describing his involvement with and the development of the Deaf community in NSW. One detects a certain shift in the tone of these historical papers from pride in the details of the organization to a stifled impartiality in several versions of those papers.[11]

Booth wrote several letters to the newspapers of his time, mainly the *Sydney Morning Herald*, clarifying or reporting on the progress of Deaf adults and their organizations and on church services.

Dorothy Shaw was a prolific writer of letters and stories. However, she also wrote speeches; papers for local, national, and international conferences; articles; and a short autobiography for an edited book of autobiographical stories called *I Always Wanted to Be a Tap Dancer*.[12] The letters varied widely from personal and supportive (such as those to soldiers during World War II) to political (regarding the need for Auslan recognition, services for Deaf persons, and education for Deaf children). She started writing in her early twenties and continued until her death in 1990.

After her one-year attendance at a technical college, where she took a creative writing course, in 1985 Shaw set up the Deaf Writers Group, which continued for a few years. This group published several issues of the Deaf literary journal *Sound Off*, in which Shaw shared her stories with other Deaf writers.[13] In the conference papers she wrote, she raised various issues, such as Deaf children's access to education, Deaf people's access to sign language, and access to services such as captions and other resources. She was very vocal about the concerns that she was passionate about and attended many mainstream and Deaf conferences. Shaw submitted articles and letters to the *Silent Messenger,* encouraging Deaf adults to be more proactive about the issues that affected them and to take responsibility for the needs of the Deaf community.

What Have They Left Behind?

Booth's and Shaw's activism resulted in an interesting array of both organizations and resources that are still in existence today and of benefit to the present members of the Australian Deaf community regardless of whether they are aware of this. The known organizations are Deaf Australia (the successor of the AAAD, which was cofounded by Booth, and the AAD, which was cofounded by Shaw); the Australian Captions Centre (cofounded by Shaw); the Auslan Shop (the successor of DRA, cofounded by Shaw); and the Deaf Society of NSW (cofounded by Booth).

The known resources are the publications the *Silent Messenger* (Booth); stories and papers by Shaw and Booth; the *Australian Signed English Dictionary* and the *Auslan Dictionary* (Shaw); and *Heritage in Our Hands,* a video documentary of recollections by Deaf adult members of the NSW Deaf Community (Shaw).

Recently Booth was posthumously recognized for his services to the Deaf Society of NSW, which named its boardroom after him, while Shaw was also honored for her services in numerous ways. She was awarded two prestigious medals, the Queen Elizabeth Silver Jubilee medal in 1977 and the Order of Australia in 1987 (she was the first Deaf Australian to be awarded this medal) for her services to Deaf people in Australia. Deaf Australia has a perpetual Dorothy Shaw Deaf Australian of the Year Award in memory of Shaw as "a tireless worker for Deaf rights in Australia."[14]

Notes

1. Nancy Booth [Fletcher Booth's granddaughter], interview by author, 2012.
2. Ibid.
3. Informal interviews with Shaw family members.
4. Notes on Origins and Growth of Adult Deaf.

5. Ibid.

6. Fletcher Samuel Booth, History of the N.S.W. Adult Deaf Society Organisation Work.

7. "Adult Deaf and Dumb Society: Meeting at the Town Hall," *Sydney Morning Herald* (October 21, 1913), 10, col. 4, http://trove.nla.gov.au.

8. Shaw, Correspondence and Papers.

9. Ibid.

10. Carty, "Managing Their Own Affairs," 151.

11. Fletcher Samuel Booth, History of the N.S.W. Adult Deaf Society Organisation Work.

12. Lawrence and Edwards, *I Always Wanted to Be a Tap Dancer.*

13. Shaw, Correspondence and Papers.

14. Deaf Australia Inc., *Deaf Australian Awards.*

References

Booth, Fletcher Samuel. History of the N.S.W. Adult Deaf Society Organisation Work. Unpublished. Archives of Deaf Society of NSW, 1943.

Carty, Bridget Mary. Managing Their Own Affairs: The Australian Deaf Community during the 1920s and 1930s. PhD diss., Griffith University, Brisbane, 2004.

The Deaf Advocate. 1929 to 1935? Edited by Fletcher Booth and Ernest Quinnell. Archives of Deaf Society of NSW.

Deaf Australia Inc. Deaf Australian Awards. Accessed May 2012, http://www.deafau.org.au/community/awards.php.

Heritage in Our Hands. Stories of the Deaf Community of NSW. Transcripts of *Heritage in Our Hands,* a series of seven videotapes of interviews with senior Deaf people in Auslan. Sydney: Adult Education Centre for Deaf and Hearing Impaired Persons Inc. with support of the N.S.W. Assoc. of the Deaf, 1990.

Lawrence, A., and S. Edwards, eds. *I Always Wanted to Be a Tap Dancer.* Parramatta, NSW: Women's Advisory Council, 1989.

Notes on Origins and Growth of Adult Deaf Society. Unpublished. Archives of Deaf Society of NSW, n.d.Shaw, Dorothy E. P. Correspondence and Papers. Dorothy Shaw Collection. NSW State Library.

The Silent Messenger. 1906–present. Edited. Archives of Deaf Society of NSW.

Laurent Clerc: A Complex and Conflicted Deaf Man in America

Christopher A. N. Kurz and Albert J. Hlibok

The unexamined life is ignorance. In the 1970s Robert F. Panara, a renowned deaf professor of literature at the Rochester Institute of Technology, acknowledged the depressing lack in both American and world literature of the genuine life stories of deaf people: "[I]t is time that the deaf are studied as the human beings that they are—as a living representation of the experience of Everyman in his journey through life."[1] Since then, postrevisionist writers have brought hundreds of deaf persons to light in the literature.[2] In this chapter we draw on primary sources to examine Laurent Clerc's inner self, his successes and struggles as a deaf man in the New World, and how he dealt with issues relating to family, religion, deafness, and the growing Deaf community.

Family: Deaf Wife, Hearing Children, and Hearing Grandchildren

As a young, single, Catholic man in a growing country, Laurent Clerc desperately needed someone with whom he could share life and rear a family. When Clerc first taught at the Hartford school, he was thirty-one years old. His deaf female pupils ranged in age from nine to forty. Naturally, the pupils, female and male alike, looked up to Clerc as their role model, for he was deaf, communicated in sign language, and knew about the world. After school they would visit him in his apartment for conversation in sign language. In September 1817 school board member Nathaniel Terry, whose deaf daughter attended the school, wrote a letter to Thomas H. Gallaudet accusing Laurent Clerc of fraternization with students. The issue was later resolved when Gallaudet responded, in writing, and defended Clerc's character:

> to have an opportunity out of school hours, of enjoying the pleasure of social conversation with the young ladies. They esteem this, too, a peculiar privilege, & I may add, also, that it is a singular advantage to them, in as much as their chief business here is to acquire language, & his language of signs is the foundation of all their improvement. . . . the origin of the charge, which has been made, that he is too attentive to them. I know his disposition well. He is as far aloof from any petty jealousy or retaliation as any man I was ever acquainted with.[3]

Well into retirement, Clerc continued his habit of welcoming groups of students to his home after class for a chat. It is certain that one of the ladies who frequented Clerc's social affairs was Eliza Crocker Boardman from Whitesborough, New York, who enrolled at the Hartford school in 1817 at the age of twenty-four. Of Laurent Clerc, Eliza wrote the following in a letter to Thomas Hopkins Gallaudet: "Mr. Clerc made signs and teaches the deaf and dumb about God and Jesus Christ . . . I believe Mr. Clerc will go to France in one year. We are sorry it."[4] Clerc, love struck by Eliza's beauty, intelligence, and character, needed to wait until Eliza's graduation in 1819 to share his love. Clerc was relieved when Eliza told him that she felt the same way. They were married at her uncle's house at Cohoes Falls near Watertown, New York, on May 3, 1819, one month after graduation.

Clerc was shocked when Gallaudet advised him not to marry a deaf woman for fear that they would produce deaf children or encounter more inconveniences in society as a deaf couple.[5] When Gallaudet, upset that Clerc was ignoring his advice, declined to be part of the wedding, Clerc asked Lewis Weld, one of the teachers at the Hartford Asylum, to help celebrate the wedding with him. Weld was his best man, not Thomas Hopkins Gallaudet, for whom Clerc held a high respect. This was a heartbreaking moment for Clerc, but he knew he needed Eliza Crocker Boardman to love for the rest of his life. After all, they possessed a shared deaf experience and conversed in sign language.

From his perspective, Laurent Clerc was vindicated when all of his children and grandchildren were hearing. In his April 28, 1858, retirement address Clerc related that "the first thing he did, on the birth of his child, was to satisfy himself by experiment that the child could hear, and how pleased he was to find that the discouraging predictions of his friends had failed to come to pass."[6] During his time, many deaf-mutes were happily married. In fact, several of his hearing friends had married deaf-mutes and had only now and then a deaf child among their offspring. In a letter to a friend, Clerc wrote: "I have now four grandchildren, all blessed with the sense of hearing, as well as their parents."[7]

On the day of Laurent Clerc's death, he had outlived four of his six children and his parents and sisters. The passing of his children, Helen (1822), John (1831), Charles (1852), and John's twin sister, Sarah (1869), must have been heartbreaking for Clerc and his wife, although the mortality of children was high at the time. The passing of his two sisters in France and the faltering health of another sibling, also in France, prevented Clerc from visiting that country for a fourth time. In his 1857 letter to a friend, Clerc wrote of the death of his sisters and the cancellation of his anticipated trip to France. As his childhood family and relatives in France passed away, the sense of nostalgia for France and family faded as there would be no communication support from extended family.[8] At the time of letter writing, Clerc knew he would never visit France again or see his old friends and family relatives.

Religious Conversion

At a time when religion defined a person's identity, one's religious association was usually passed along by family and/or political ties. Laurent
Clerc was born to a Roman Catholic family and educated as a Catholic
at the Institut National de Jeunes Sourds de Paris under the supervision
of the Abbé Roch Sicard. For Clerc, the world could be comprehended
by an understanding of God and Jesus Christ. As Clerc's writings demonstrate, difficult life conditions were alleviated by one's faith in God.[9]
Fearing that Clerc would convert to Protestantism should he accom-
pany Thomas H. Gallaudet, a Congregationalist, to a country where
Catholicism was not highly regarded, Abbé Sicard had Clerc promise
to be faithful to Catholicism: "[Y]ou would lose faith, you would have
embraced a false religion for sure . . . which would be fatal if you go to
a country of heretics or you would lose yourself for an eternity. I never
will cry over your fate. And I never will regret the pain and care that I
had given you as a good Catholic and a good Christian."[10] In a conversation with Gallaudet, Sicard was adamant that Clerc "not . . . be called
upon to teach anything contrary to the Roman Catholic religion which
he professes, and in which faith he desires to live and die."[11]

Arriving in New York City from Le Havre, France, Laurent Clerc
noticed numerous church steeples throughout the town, indicating the
American belief that people should have freedom of religion. During
his first years of teaching at the Hartford school, Clerc taught Catholicism to his deaf pupils.[12] One of his first religious struggles came when
he fell in love with Eliza Crocker Boardman, an Episcopalian. Although
his May 3, 1819, wedding was conducted as an Episcopalian ceremony
at the home of his fiancé's uncle, Benjamin Prescott, Clerc remained a
Catholic. Although he wrestled with his promise to Sicard, Clerc knew
he would have to answer to him when he visited France after the expira-
tion of his first contract with the Hartford school. In 1820, one month
after his first daughter's birth, he visited France for a year. In Paris he
reaffirmed to Sicard his Catholic religion. After the death of his parents in the late 1810s and then Sicard in 1822, Laurent Clerc was at last
free from any binding promise. He became an Episcopalian several
years later: "In middle life he became a communicant of the Episcopal

church, and ever after retained his connection with it."[13] In addition, Clerc attained US citizenship on December 11, 1838, thereby forfeiting his loyalty to the sovereign of France, King Louis Philippe, but gaining religious freedom.[14]

Language Use: The Unfortunates

From August 1816 to March 1817, the first seven months of Laurent Clerc's time in the United States, he accompanied Thomas Hopkins Gallaudet and Mason F. Cogswell (a wealthy physician and a father in search of a better education for his deaf daughter, Alice) up and down the Eastern Seaboard on a fund-raising and marketing drive to establish and recruit pupils for a new school for deaf children.[15] While in the eastern cities for legislature sessions and public audiences, Clerc gave addresses in sign language with Thomas Gallaudet's voicing and, with chalk and slate, exhibited his knowledge of and perspectives on the world. In his addresses Clerc would categorize deaf people as "unfortunates." In an address in New York City on August 19, 1816, Clerc concluded: "I thank you for it, and the interest you express for us poor unfortunates."[16] In Hartford he urged the audience to be benevolent to the deaf and dumb: "Be then so good as to hasten their happiness; your countrymen have been too negligent of that unfortunate class of deaf and dumb."[17] In Boston on September 10, 1816, he opened his address to a male audience in similar fashion: "[I wish to] speak to you more conveniently of the deaf and dumb, of those unfortunate beings who . . . would be condemned all their *life,* to the most sad vegetation if nobody came to their succor, but who entrusted to our regenerative hands, will pass from the class of brutes to the class of men."[18] To a female audience in Boston the following day he reiterated his address: "[Yesterday we spoke] of the poor deaf and dumb who abound in your own country" and of the "more than two thousand unfortunate deaf and dumb in the United States . . . While it lies in your power to contribute to render them happy here below, will you leave them to die in this sad state?"[19] Clerc's constant portrayal of deaf people as "poor unfortunates" stemmed from his experiences in France and England as part of a traveling exhibition with his mentor, the Abbé Roch Sicard, director of the Paris school for Deaf children. In the exhibitions Roch Sicard routinely portrayed deaf people as "the unfortunate," "the abandoned," and "strangers to society." Witnessing the success of Sicard's emotional appeal, perhaps Clerc adopted the same approach.

Laurent Clerc was an educated person with a brilliant mind; however, he did not cease to make negative generalizations about deaf people as a group. At the age of eighty-three Laurent Clerc wrote in a letter to a friend, "Thanks to God, I still enjoy good health and wish I had not retired so early as I could have continued to do more good to my unfortunate fellow Beings and to teach new teachers how to teach well."[20] His conviction was that uneducated deaf people may have more limitations in different aspects of life and that deaf people without knowledge or understanding of God are doomed in the afterlife. He strongly believed that deaf children need a good education so that they will be able to open their eyes to God and live independently in society through the use of reading and writing. In fact, Laurent Clerc, educated at the Paris school and an esteemed teacher, referred to himself as an "unfortunate." While in New York City during his first days in the United States, he met with Nathaniel F. Moore, a professor at Columbia College, and communicated with him by writing with chalk and slate. The day after, Nathaniel wrote a letter to the Reverend John McVickar about his meeting with Clerc: "We all are very much interested in this poor unfortunate, as he calls himself; though he has, as I told him, almost lost all claim to that name."[21] Moore himself did not see Clerc as a poor unfortunate, but Clerc thought otherwise. It is possible that Clerc continued to make emotional appeals to hearing people because he believed that, if he did so, society would help people in need.

Deafness, Deaf Community, Audism

Deafness can be perceived as a cultural identity, a biological condition, a disability, or a trait. Living in a society that highly values audiological input and spoken language can be a struggle for many deaf people. Some find it gratifying to be different from the norm and have unique experiences; others find it frustrating in terms of not being able to overcome societal obstacles or stigma. Laurent Clerc became deaf at a very early age, possibly at birth, from a fever or, as his family maintained, a fall into a fireplace. In spite of his many successes as a deaf person, Clerc would often wonder whether the grass was greener on the other side. During his second visit to France in 1843, he saw an opportunity to cure his deafness:

> One day, in walking through Lyons, seeing a crowd of persons reading a notice stuck on the wall at the corner of a street, I had the curiosity to examine it. It announced that a Mr. LaFontaine would give in the evening, at the hotel Du Nord, an exhibition of experimental magnetism, at which he would operate on a young girl and present the physical phenomena [sic] of magnetism, and produce ecstasy under the influence of music; that he would also introduce a deaf and dumb young man of Lyons, whom he said he had succeeded in making hear by magnetism, and submit to the magnetical operation many other deaf and dumb, whom he would try to enable to hear also. I immediately concluded to attend the exhibition, and to request Mr. LaFontaine to experiment upon me, should he succeed, that the operation might be decisive.[22]

However, Clerc was prevented from attending the exhibition when his son, Charles, became ill. He later learned from deaf students at a nearby school that the experiment was a total failure. Clerc felt that God had a better plan for him, which was to continue educating deaf people.

Sign language is the lifeblood of the Deaf community. Laurent Clerc was proud that he brought his sign language from France to the United States. In his teaching, he employed the methodical signs, that is, English-order signing, as he believed it was the only way for students to learn reading and writing. His educational experience dictated this belief, as he had learned French through the methodical French signs. Occasionally, he would criticize his students for sign production errors and for not adhering to his sign repertoire. A former student wrote the following:

> It seemed to distress him [Clerc] to see me make any sign wrong, or in a clumsy manner. I remember well how I once met him in a street in a great hurry, and told him my mother was visiting me. I was going to

run right by, but he stopped me, and made me repeat what I had said, and then corrected one or two faults, nor would he let me go until I had made every sign to his satisfaction.

During that incident, Clerc became upset when the student signed MOTHER with an open-palmed hand (5) with a thumb resting on the cheek rather than the old sign with two productions, MOTHER-BABY (the baby symbolizes motherhood). Though he was the originator of the modified French American Sign Language, Clerc struggled with the natural evolution of this language. He did not realize that languages must evolve if they are to survive; all he wanted was for everyone to use the same language.

A few years after Clerc arrived in the United States, he conceived the idea of establishing an exclusive community of, for, and by deaf people, where they would find jobs and communicate in sign language. In 1819, after he found that a land parcel in Alabama had been put aside for funding the Hartford School, Clerc suggested "the plan of selling such part of the land . . . for the Asylum, and then having the rest as *head quarters* for the deaf and dumb, to which they could emigrate after being educated." The idea was tabled until John Jacobus Flournoy, a deaf Georgian and former student of the Hartford school, picked it up in 1855 and petitioned for the formation of a deaf colony in the West; Oregon was the destination. In the Deaf community, the deaf colony debate intensified, and Clerc felt obliged to respond to it. He realized it would take a miracle to make this colony happen, especially when deaf parents have hearing children. What would become of these youngsters? Clerc pointed out this problem: "It was very convenient to have some hearing persons within call in many cases, as for instance, *sickness* and *fire*."[23]

Clerc acknowledged the potential of deaf people, as when, in his 1816 Philadelphia address, he described French deaf people in early 1800s: "Many are married and have children . . . Many others are employed in the offices of the government, and other public administrations. Many others are good painters, engravers, workers in mosaic, and printers. Some others . . . are merchants, and rule their affairs perfectly well."[24] However, he believed deafness imposed job-related limitations in terms of deaf people's ability to work as doctors and firefighters. During his 1843 visit to France, he stopped by a school for deaf children in the suburb of Lyons. The school was run by a deaf couple, a Mr. Forestier and his wife.[25] Before Clerc left the school to visit his family in Le Balmes, he advised Mr. Forestier to "associate with him a clergyman, or a gentleman of respectability and talents, who could hear and speak, for the greater prosperity of the school and the better improvement of the children in written language and religious knowledge; my opinion being that, however instructed a deaf and dumb person might be, he was still less so than those who hear and speak."[26] Convinced he could run the school independently, Mr. Forestier naturally dismissed Clerc's advice. Another example of Clerc's belief that deaf people have limitations comes up in his 1864 address to the First Presbyterian Church in Washington, DC, for the inauguration of the National College for Deaf-Mutes. Near the close of his address, in which he pointed out the importance of higher education for deaf people in their pursuit of happiness and independence, he signed, "The degree of Master of Arts can be conferred on the deaf and dumb when they merit it; but, on account of their misfortune, they cannot become masters of music, and perhaps can never be entitled to receive the degree of Doctor in Divinity, in Physic, or in Law."[27] His belief that deafness imposes such limitations is a classic example of *audism*.[28] "when deaf and hearing people have no trust in deaf people's ability to control their own lives."[29] Although he had directed and transformed the Philadelphia School for the Deaf in almost eight months, he had worked under the supervision of hearing people for most of his life. What he experienced and believed was not uncommon among deaf people of the nineteenth century.

Elitism in Two Communities

Throughout his life Laurent Clerc learned the importance of being affiliated with people in upper-class society, for it brings advantages in terms of opportunity and recognition. During his traveling exhibitions, he was no stranger to royalty and people of affluence in Europe. In the United States, through Thomas Hopkins Gallaudet, Clerc met, conversed with (through writing), and gave exhibitions to wealthy people, religious leaders, professors, politicians, and presidents.[30] His comfortable salary, in addition to what he earned as a private sign language tutor at the Hartford school, afforded him a life of prosperity. He traveled to Europe three times, owned a house and a pony, and attended social events in Hartford and elsewhere. Through his contacts in Philadelphia, Clerc met Charles Wilson Peale, who painted a portrait of Laurent and another of Eliza with baby Elizabeth Victoria Clerc.

Laurent Clerc maintained his elite status in the hearing community until the resignation in 1830 of Thomas Hopkins Gallaudet, his gatekeeper to upper-class society for almost fourteen years. Clerc was upset when Gallaudet decided to resign from his principal position: "We had been so intimate, so harmonious, so much attached to each other; we had labored together so many years; that I parted with him with unspeakable grief."[31] After his resignation, Gallaudet chose to take up writing, support women's education, and become a minister at a mental asylum. Laurent Clerc could no longer rely on Gallaudet for communication and networking. His status in the hearing community gradually diminished, and he continued to maintain his networks only through his children and their extended families.[32]

As the number of educated deaf people was growing exponentially, Laurent Clerc was christened by younger deaf leaders as the "Apostle to the Deaf People in the New World."[33] Clerc was invited to give presentations at events held by deaf organizations and teachers' groups. At conferences he was often given an honorary chair while the meetings were in session. Although his status in the hearing community began to decline, his standing in the Deaf community increased. In one situation during the 1850s he repeatedly petitioned the Hartford school's board of directors to help pay the maintenance costs for his house. Although he was drawing a pension from the school, he could not afford the house repairs, but, to Clerc's utter frustration, the board denied his requests. In response, the Deaf community initiated a fund-raising drive to cover the cost of the repairs, posting announcements in deaf newsletters and Hartford newspapers. Clerc was upset with the notice in the Hartford newspapers, preferring that hearing people not know of his financial problems. He was embarrassed by this fund-raising drive because it put him in the spotlight in the Hartford community. In the Deaf community, Laurent Clerc was highly respected, as he remains today.

✦

Every human being has successes and struggles. Even the apostles of Jesus Christ had internal struggles as they wrestled with faith, family, and money. The Apostle to the Deaf People in the New World was first and foremost a human being who happened to be deaf and who was the right man in the right time and place to bring bilingual teaching methods to the United States. As mentioned earlier, some of Clerc's experiences and perspectives on the world are not uncommon among deaf people, especially the belief, rooted in audism, that deafness is inferior to hearing. On his deathbed on July 18, 1869, at the age of eighty-four, Clerc had fulfilled his dreams: finding love, home, and a growing community that continues to venerate him as the Apostle to the Deaf People in the New World.

Notes

1. Panara, "Deaf Studies in the English Curriculum," 15. Panara has published articles and books on deaf Americans and deaf characters in literature. See Robert F. Panara. *Great Deaf Americans* [Rochester, NY: Deaf Life, 1996]; "The Deaf Writer in America from Colonial Times to 1970: Part 1," *American Annals of the Deaf* 115, no. 5 (1970): 509–13; and "The Deaf Writer in America from Colonial Times to 1970: Part II," *American Annals of the Deaf* 115, no. 7 (1970): 673–79, for examples.

2. Postrevisionism was a movement in the 1970s and 1980s that held that history should stick to actual facts [who, what, and where] to explain the effects of incidents or political contexts. See Harry G. Lang, *Silence of the Spheres: The Deaf Experience in the History of Science* [Westport, CT: Bergin and Garvey, 1994], and Jack Gannon, *Deaf Heritage: A Narrative History of Deaf America* [Silver Spring, MD: National Association of the Deaf, 1981]. In *When the Mind Hears: A History of the Deaf,* author Harlan Lane (1984), from the vantage point of Laurent Clerc, reconstructed historical events from primary sources and from Lane's own political agenda on how deaf children should be taught.

3. Thomas H. Gallaudet, letter from Thomas Hopkins Gallaudet to Nathaniel Terry, Thursday, September 1817. American School for the Deaf Library Archives.

4. Eliza Crocker Boardman, letter to Thomas H. Gallaudet, April 3, 1818.

5. Clerc, "Autobiography," 111.

6. Porter, "Retirement of Mr. Clerc," 181.

7. Clerc, "Autobiography," 111.

8. Clerc, letter to B. Hudson.

9. Baynton, "Abraham Lincoln, Laurent Clerc, and the Design of the Word."

10. Sicard, conversations with Laurent Clerc.

11. Gallaudet, "Conversation with the Abbé Sicard."

12. Clerc, contract between Thomas Gallaudet and Laurent Clerc, June 13, 1816.

13. Turner, "Laurent Clerc."

14. U.S. Citizenship Certificate, Laurent Clerc, December 11, 1838.

15. The group visited Boston, Salem, Hartford, New Haven, New York City, Albany, Philadelphia, and Burlington, NJ.

16. Clerc, "Address concerning the Deaf and Dumb in America."

17. Clerc, "Address."

18. Clerc, "Autobiography," 107–108.

19. Ibid., 109.

20. Clerc, letter to Parson.

21. Moore, letter to Reverend John McVickar.

22. Clerc, "Visits to Some of the Schools for the Deaf and Dumb," 66.

23. William M. Chamerlain, "Proceedings of the Third Convention of the New England Gallaudet Association of Deaf-Mutes," 212.

24. Laurent Clerc, "Publick Meeting," *Poulson's American Daily Advertiser*, December 12, 1816.

25. Mr. Forestier was a former teacher at the Paris school and moved to Lyons after the sign language debate at the institution.

26. Clerc, "Visits to Some of the Schools for the Deaf and Dumb," 66.

27. Laurent Clerc, "Address," 43.

28. Tom Humphries, "Communicating across Cultures [Deaf/Hearing] and Language Learning" [PhD diss., Union Graduate School, Cincinnati, OH, 1997].

29. Ibid., 13.

30. Some of these people were Yale president Timothy Dwight, Noah Webster, Speaker of the House Henry Clay, and President James Monroe.

31. Clerc, "Autobiography," 112.

32. Elizabeth Victoria Clerc, his first child, married George Webster Beers, a prominent merchant from Litchfield, CT. Sarah Clerc married Henry Champion Deming, mayor of Hartford and a Civil War general. Francis Joseph Clerc was an Episcopalian priest, and Charles Michael Clerc worked as a silk merchant in New York City.

33. Abbé Roch Sicard coined the honorific in his 1816 letter to the bishop in Boston.

References

Baynton, Douglas C. "Abraham Lincoln, Laurent Clerc, and the Design of the Word: Lincoln Day Address at Gallaudet University, February 11, 2009." *Sign Language Studies* 10, no. 4 (2010): 396–408.

Boardman, Eliza Crocker. Letter to Thomas H. Gallaudet, April 3, 1818. American School for the Deaf Archives, Hartford, CT.

Chamerlain, William M. "Proceedings of the Third Convention of the New England Gallaudet Association of Deaf-Mutes," *American Annals of the Deaf and Dumb* 10, no. 4 (1858): 205–219.

Clerc, Laurent. "Address." *Connecticut Mirror,* October 28, 1816, 1.

———. "Address." In *Inauguration of the College for the Deaf & Dumb, at Washington, District of Columbia, June 28th, 1864,* 41–43. Washington, DC: Gideon and Pearson, 1864.

————. "An Address concerning the Deaf and Dumb in America." August 19, 1816. American School for the Deaf Archives.

————. "Autobiography." In *Tribute to Gallaudet: A Discourse in Commemoration of the life, character and services of the Rev. Thomas H. Gallaudet, LL.D., delivered before the citizens of Hartford, Jan. 7th, 1852. With an appendix, containing the history of deaf-mute instruction and institutions, and other documents*, edited by Henry Barnard, 102–22. Hartford, CT: Brockett and Hutchinson, 1854.

————. Contract between Thomas Gallaudet and Laurent Clerc, June 13, 1816. Yale University Library Archives.

————. Letter from Laurent Clerc to John C. Parson, June 3, 1868. New York Public Library Archives.

————. Letter to B. Hudson, May 8, 1857. New York Public Library Archives.

————. "Visits to Some of the Schools for the Deaf and Dumb in France and England—I." *American Annals of the Deaf and Dumb* 1, no. 1 (1847): 62–66.

Gallaudet, Thomas. "Conversation with the Abbé Sicard." In *Journal and Letterbook, 1815–1816*. In *Tribute to Gallaudet* ed. Henry Barnard.

————. Letter from Thomas Hopkins Gallaudet to Nathaniel Terry, Thursday, September 1817. American School for the Deaf Library Archives.

Lane, Harlan. *When the Mind Hears: A History of the Deaf*. New York: Random House, 1984.

Moore, Nathaniel. Letter from Nathaniel Moore to Reverend John McVickar, August 21, 1816. American School for the Deaf Library Archives.

Panara, Robert. "Deaf Studies in the English Curriculum." *Deaf American* 26, no. 5 (1974): 15–17.

Porter, Samuel. "Retirement of Mr. Clerc." *American Annals of the Deaf and Dumb* 10, no. 3 (1858), 181–83.

Sicard, Roch. "Conversations with Laurent Clerc." Sicard Papers, F-0035. Institut National de Jeunes Sourdes Archives.

————. Letter to the Bishop of Boston, 16 June 1816. Clerc Papers, Yale University Archives.

Turner, William. "Laurent Clerc." *American Annals of the Deaf and Dumb* 15, no. 1 (1870), 16–28.

U.S. Citizenship Certificate, Laurent Clerc, December 11, 1838. Yale University Library Archives.

PART 3

Deaf Community Collective Histories: Stories from the Continents

The Siege of Leningrad and Its Impact on the Life of a Deaf Family

Tatiana Davidenko

I am Deaf from a Deaf family. In this essay I depict the lives of Deaf people in Leningrad (now Saint Petersburg) immediately before and during World War II. In doing so I relate the biographies of my mother and our relatives and friends. My mother, Ekaterina or Katya, was born in Leningrad in 1923. She came from a family of eleven children, two of whom died in infancy. Three of the surviving children were deaf: Aunt Marina, Uncle Vova, and, of course, my mother, Katya. Their oldest hearing sister, Valya, who left home in the early 1930s, had a deaf son, Boris. My hearing grandmother, Maria Ottovna Evert, who had Estonian and German roots, came from Narva, a town in Estonia. She married Alexandre Lepeshkin from Tver. Both of them had several deaf family members. The couple opened a bakery in Vasilievsky Ostrov (the name sign is fingerspelled v-o), a nice area of Saint Petersburg (the wrong sign for "Saint Petersburg" is EPAULETTE; the older and correct sign is the right hand configuration 2 upside down on the open palm of the left hand). My grandparents were said to make the best bread and

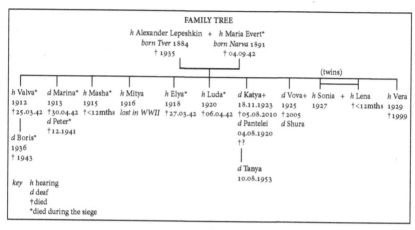

FIGURE 1. *Katya's family tree*

cakes in the area. They were comfortably well off with a big apartment over the bakery, and even after the Communist Revolution of 1917 they managed to keep the business afloat for some time.

However, the peace of the family was disturbed during the Stalin era of oppression and execution. My grandfather was arrested, put into prison, and then sent to a concentration camp. Perhaps his only fault was that he had an apartment and sold bread and other food that he and his family prepared. At the time it was common for innocent people to be arrested, exiled, and executed. Although my grandfather was able to come back to Leningrad, he died of tuberculosis soon afterward, in 1935. The family's life changed dramatically after Alexandre's arrest. My grandmother Maria and all eight of her children had to move from their nice apartment into one room in a different block of the same street. Because the family members were considered to be *lishentsy* (the "people's enemy") and therefore deprived of all rights, no one could get a job or attend the university. This is why Valya, the oldest hearing daughter, remained out of touch with her family; she joined the Komsomol (a young Communists' organization) and wanted to go to the university.

The Bolsheviks confiscated everything. Even the sewing machine, which could have supported the family, was taken away. Starvation was horrible. Somehow Maria, my grandmother, got a job in a biological lab, where she was able to steal mice, newts, and frogs and cook them at home for the children. One night, when everyone was asleep, my grandmother

FIGURE 2. *Family gathering, May 1, 1941. Front row, on the right, Maria; behind her Vova and Katya, and Marina, a young woman in the middle of the front row.*

was so overcome with desperation that she turned on the gas stove, hoping that everyone would be asphyxiated and that no one, including my grandmother, would wake up in the morning. However, that very night my grandmother's sister Anya unexpectedly came to see the family, pulled them out of the room, and saved everyone. This happened in beautiful Leningrad between 1935 and 1937.

Marina, the elder Deaf daughter, went to the first Russian school for deaf students, which had opened in 1810, on Gorokhovaya Street. Katya and her brother Vova went to the school for hard of hearing children, although both were Deaf and had used sign language from birth. Perhaps being exposed to sign language communication between family members and having an older Deaf sister boosted their literacy and other skills. At that time the midday meal was not provided at school, so both Katya and Vova had to go without. They both remember a kind hearing teacher who shared her own poor lunch with them.

When World War II began, most of the family was in Leningrad. The Deaf uncle, Vova, had luckily been sent to a Young Pioneers summer camp, and these children were then moved to the Urals near Cheliabinsk, where they survived the war.

From August 1941 until January 1944 the Germans blockaded Leningrad, which remained cut off from the rest of the country. The siege began when Nazi troops completed their encirclement of the city on September 8, 1941, severing all outside connections to Leningrad, and ended 872 days later. The only supply line lay to the northeast of the city across the thirty miles of Lake Ladoga. Food shortages were acute, the electricity was cut off, and temperatures often dropped to minus thirty degrees Celsius (minus twenty-two degrees Fahrenheit). During the nearly nine hundred days of the siege of Leningrad, one-third of the population died, mostly of starvation. More than a million civilians perished, killed by hunger or artillery fire, which was unceasing for the duration of the blockade. No city in modern times has seen famine and loss of life on this scale, and yet many survivors believed the authorities intentionally underestimated the number of casualties. From 1941 to 1942 the daily food ration was 125 grams of bread. The people of Leningrad could not have imagined that while they were starving and freezing to death, the Communist party heads were enjoying black caviar, fruit, and wine in well-lit halls. The worst months were from November 1941 to April 1942, when practically all of the family died.

My grandmother was the last to die. Because she had dropsy, or edema, she was hospitalized, but the hospital was destroyed by a German bomb. Before that, she had witnessed the deaths of her children and grandchildren from hunger. Valya, who had a complicated relationship with the family, visited her mother on March 25, 1942, the night before Valya died. Her deaf son, Boris, died later. My Deaf aunt, Marina, had married the Deaf son of a famous art collector named Dudin. Several items from his collection are now in the Hermitage, the famous art museum in Saint Petersburg. Both Marina and her husband died, but luckily their hearing son had been sent to a summer camp before the siege and survived. There were three survivors of the siege: the hearing daughters, Vera and Sonia, and the Deaf daughter, Katya.

As the eldest of the three, Katya had to wrap her relatives' bodies in cloth and place them outside the entrance of the apartment building. A special truck collected corpses in the mornings, and sometimes someone checked the apartments for dying or dead people. Katya said that the worst thing was that one was so weak that one felt no emotion at all—no pity, no joy, nothing. Even having to bring water from the Neva River, which flows through Saint Petersburg, was a horrible ordeal; if one fell down, one would die because passersby would not have enough strength to help one get up, and one would die there of hunger and cold. Katya recalled various incidents: At the beginning of the siege they thought of eating their cat, but the cat died; at another time a little girl stole a small ration of bread from Katya and ate it. Eventually the coupons for bread rations were eliminated, which meant more starvation. When Katya was strong enough, she would go to the hospital to help the patients and for her effort would receive extra grams of bread for the day. Soon she became very weak and stayed in bed, which meant the end was near.

She had many Deaf friends but was not strong enough to visit them. Nonetheless, she was actually saved by them and by the Leningrad branch of the VOG, the All-Russian Society of the Deaf. Katya was discovered by some of the members of the organization, among them her friend Maria Rezvan. They persuaded her to leave Leningrad on a boat that would be crossing Lake Ladoga. Since she did not want to leave her mother, Katya at first resisted, but at the end of July 1942 she received a place in a "Deaf boat." A general rescue campaign was under way, and the Deaf organization managed to get one boat for its members. This route, known as the Road of Life, was the only one that was not entirely controlled by the Germans. Along this route hundreds of thousands of civilians were killed by bombs and famine. Each boat carried about thirty people. Many such vessels tried to cross the Ladoga, and the Deaf boat was one of them. The line was bombed by the Germans. Lying in the bottom of the boat, Katya witnessed other boats with children and sick people sinking, but she felt no emotion. The Deaf boat luckily reached the other side of the lake.

Katya was then sent to the town of Barnaul in southern Siberia, nearly a two-month train ride away. Although more food was available in Barnaul, her body was unable to accept much food for more than a year after she escaped from the siege. Katya was placed with an ordinary village family, and because she was good at counting and could read and write, she got a job in a factory store. The family did not want her, however—because she was deaf and because they thought she was a shabby old woman of sixty. In 1942 my mother was only nineteen years old and weighed thirty-eight kilograms (about eighty-four pounds). She recovered and worked in Barnaul until the end of the war and was very popular in the Deaf community. Local Deaf people wanted to elect Katya as the head of the Deaf club, but she was preoccupied with thoughts of Leningrad and declined.

Katya, who was not a Communist party member then, described the cruelty of the times. She recalled a young Deaf man who was sentenced

FIGURE 3. *Katya in 1949*

to ten years in a concentration camp for stealing a plain quilted overcoat from the factory. Katya wanted to close her eyes to the theft, but her Deaf colleague, a Communist and a very important figure in the Deaf organization (leaders of the Deaf organization had to be Communist party members), accused the poor Deaf man and betrayed him to hearing people. The sentence was ruthless. The war among the country's people continued—even in peaceful Siberia.

Time passed, and Katya managed to return to Leningrad. This was not an easy task as no adult relatives were left, and no one could provide her with the special pass needed to reach her native city. Her friend Maria Rezvan once again assisted her. Finally Katya was reunited with the only survivors of her family: her Deaf brother, Vova, and her younger hearing sisters, Sonia and Vera. She also met some of her school friends who had survived the siege and those who had luckily been living elsewhere during the blockade. She heard about other Deaf people who had been executed just before the war. She became reacquainted with her older friend David Ginzburgsky, later one of the first Deaf historians in Russia, who had managed to move to Moscow during the siege. She found out that both leaders of the Leningrad Deaf association, M. Vishnevsky and N. Nekrasov, had starved to death in December 1941. She also learned the fates of many young deaf people from the Leningrad vocational college.

It is impossible to describe the horrors of life in Leningrad during the siege. My mother always told me about the cold and hunger, but more details of life at this time were revealed later, when she was rather

FIGURE 4. *Mother and daughter in 1969*

old. I understand now that I might be the only person whom she trusted and could talk openly with about her shocking experiences, sharing with me all of the particulars. When she got together with her Leningrad friends, they seemed to want to avoid discussing the war. For a long time I could not understand why they refrained from talking about the siege or if they did, used the clichés that one reads in Soviet books about the war. This was especially true when they were participating in official interviews or appearing in front of a camera. An exception was my mother's 1997 talk on May Victory Day to Deaf children from the bilingual school, but I used to work there, and the other teachers were our friends. These survivors of the siege were all very careful about food, and my mother kept saying, "I wish there were no war ever again."

Now it is clear to me that it was a combination of many factors: fear of the Stalin era, when one had to keep silent and never tell the truth; absolutely horrible experiences that were too hard to mention even after many years; and, alas, the betrayals by and wrong attitudes of many of the people around them at that hard time. The Deaf monthly magazines from 1968 to 1974, which were official publications from Soviet times of Deaf witnesses' memories of the siege, showed a different picture. The magazines depicted hungry but dignified Deaf fighters supporting the nation in its struggle with world evil: Deaf vocational school students working overtime at war factories, dancing for wounded soldiers in hospitals, supporting each other, and so on. Even the diary of my mother's friend David Ginzburgsky, which was published in 2004, when all the secrets of the siege had been revealed, depicted life during that period in polished clichés. Was this due to fear? Desire for oblivion? An unwillingness to trust any writing, which was also used in the 1930s for anonymous reports of other people's activities? However, it was Ginzburgsky who first spoke openly about the deaf-mute case in 1937 (see V. Palenny, this volume). Official and personal history sometimes contradicted each other.

Katya met my father, Pantelei, and I was born in Leningrad in 1953. Pantelei, who came from a Cossack family, hated the wet Leningrad climate, and the family moved to Moscow in 1958. Katya worked in a factory with Deaf colleagues and was very popular among her friends for her kindness and generosity. A wonderful storyteller, she retired at the age of seventy-nine. Practically every day until her death in 2010, she would feed stray dogs and cats by cooking food for them. She also collected stale bread and fed birds, who always recognized her when she was out in the courtyard and took the pieces from her hands—much more than the Leningrad siege ration of 125 grams.

References

Ginzburgsky, D. "I Would Like to Name All of Them." In *Proceedings of the 1st Moscow Symposium on Deaf History*, 109–22. Moscow: Zagrey, 1997.

Istorija Vserossijskogo obshchestva glukhikh. Edited by V. Palenny. Vol. 1, 399–471. Moscow: Author, 2007.

Komarova, A. "Sud'ba blokadnitsy." *V edinom stroju* 10 (2010): 23 (Deaf monthly magazine *VES*, in Russian).

Lepeshkina, Katya Davidenko. "Katya's Story." In *Deaf Identities*, edited by G. Taylor and A. Darby, 167–72. Coleford, UK: McLean, 2003.

The Oral History and Experience of the Deaf Community in Russia

Victor Palenny

In 1999, while working at a school for Deaf students, I videotaped short stories in Russian Sign Language (RSL) by Leonid Kamyshev, a physics teacher. Kamyshev is a Deaf man from a Deaf family and a gifted storyteller. This was the first time that sign language storytelling by a Deaf person had been filmed in Russia.

The feedback from this filming was very positive. Deaf people have since come to realize that besides so-called official history, their own history—that which they themselves experience and is told by Deaf people in their own language—exists as well. This history, which sometimes does not coincide with common values and assessments, incorporates unusual experiences that researchers previously ignored.

For example, the oral short stories told by Kamyshev revealed the scale of the shadow business conducted by the Deaf community (i.e., selling cards and postcards) and helped to reveal different ways of escaping the reach of

Leonid Kamyshev

various criminal statutes. The experience of the older generations of the Deaf community is reflected in the following stories:

My father finished his studies at the Lublino School for the Deaf before the war and started working. Actually, he had two jobs; one was an "official" job, and the other one was "unofficial," and he used to sell cards as well. That job was connected with spring and autumn recruiting by the army. My father used to work at his usual job before spring came; in the spring time he would quit this job and start selling postcards at the railway stations near the trains on which recruits were sent to their army locations. The postcards depicted various activities but were mainly about love, trains, meetings, dating, and so on. He used to sell them through the windows of the trains. He earned his living this way. During Stalin's time, life was very difficult; my father had to feed his family, and we were very poor. Do you think selling postcards was an easy job? It was very hard! And why? My father briefly told me about it. For example, future frontier guards were recruited (they were called "green caps"); these people were easy to work with; they were honest and paid with real rubles. My father was rather confident working with them. But the sailors were a different story. They were like a criminal gang; they would readily deceive you: First they would buy and then steal from you. My father was well aware of this. So he used the following approach: He would choose the leader of the group of sailors and offer him many good postcards. Then he would give him the postcards for free and ask him to persuade other sailors to buy cards—excellent goods—from my father. The sailors would start buying the cards while their leader would listen to what they were saying. When he heard that the sailors were planning to rob my father, he would make a secret sign to my father to disappear. When my father had made enough money, he would acknowledge the secret sign, and he would tell everyone that he would be back with more postcards, but instead he would disappear. So he never got robbed. At that time that sort of business was okay. . . . Even Saveliev, a true leader in the Deaf world and one of the founders of the Deaf association, used to sell cards when he was young. But his cards were not about love but depicted the fingerspelling alphabet. Hearing people were surprised that the Deaf had an alphabet of their own, and by using it they could communicate with Deaf people. So Saveliev did a very useful thing when he advertised fingerspelling.

Storytellers give their own assessments of different facts and events, and it is obvious that Deaf people find their identity through both flexibility and resistance. The Deaf persons described in these stories lived in Soviet times, when issues of disability, difference, and deafness were taboo. Despite the dominance of the hearing world, these people demonstrated a positive attitude toward the cultural traditions and experiences of the Deaf community as well the value of sign language. One very important example is the story by David Ginzburgsky about a "deaf-mute case" in Leningrad:

In 1937 fifty-four Deaf people were arrested, and thirty-five were shot. There could have been many more people executed, as the NKVD (the KGB of the time) was ruthless. But it was sign language that actually helped the Deaf people involved. The NKVD arrested people one by one, as if in a chain, and interrogated them, demanding the names of the "participants." A person under investigation would give some names, and these people would be arrested, and the process would go on and on. An experienced prisoner advised one Deaf person to give the names only of those who had already been arrested. In this prison the doors of cells used to be opened for a short time to air them out. Deaf people stood by the doors and in sign language passed along this message about names. Other Deaf people could see them from the peephole opposite the cells. This is how the arrests stopped.

Since then I, with the help of my friends and colleagues Roman Parfenov and Dmitry Rebrov, have been videotaping oral stories told by older Deaf people. The aim of this project was to record people's experiences of events during World War II and the period of industrialization. It allows us to unite and compare macro- and microhistories and to generalize from microsubjects. This biographical method allows for the drawing out of general themes from people's experience and reveals how and why these people have succeeded in realizing certain social possibilities. This approach makes it possible to understand people's stories through communication, revealing how important life events shape their identity.

Nearly all newspapers of the time published a photograph taken by a war correspondent, Evgenij Khaldej, that was titled "22 June 1941. Muscovites are listening to the radio bulletin." The photograph was taken at midday, when the chairman of the government, V. M. Molotov, addressed the nation. In the picture one can see Muscovites, busy with their daily chores, who are suddenly frozen in a tragic silence as they hear of the fascists' attack on their country. A young woman on the left touches her face and is bending over sadly. This is Nina Zvorykina, a member of the All-Russian Society of the Deaf (VOG), the national Deaf association. Here is her story.

> My child was nine months old. I took some dairy products for him and wanted to leave. But Zina [Nina's hearing friend] stopped me: "Molotov will be talking soon . . . Big trouble in Kiev." Then she said, "War!" Oh, no! Horrible! It will be dangerous in Moscow . . . I was very much worried and thought, what is ahead of us?

Here are two more stories told by Leonid Kamyshev about World War II:

> A Deaf woman from Belarus was telling her story. During the war she was very young and lived in a village similar to the famous village of Khatyn. As you know, the latter village was burned down, and the people of the village were killed [shot]. It was very similar for this girl in her village. The Germans had surrounded the village

"22 June 1941. Muscovites are listening to the radio bulletin." Photo by E. Khaldej.

and told the townspeople to go and pick potatoes in the field. When everything was collected, all the villagers were locked in a shed. They were likely to be shot and incinerated soon. The little Deaf girl was with her mother in the same shed. The villagers in the shed (who were ignorant people) teased and insulted the girl; they called her dumb and made rude signs. The girl cried loudly. Her mother could not bear it and started hammering at the door, "Help! Open the door!" The Germans heard the noise, but at that very moment the chief SS officer came by the shed in his car. He knew the Russian language well and decided to find out what was wrong. The mother complained that her Deaf daughter was being teased and hurt. The SS officer listened to them, then called a soldier and asked him to take them as far as possible out of the village. The mother and the little Deaf girl could not understand why they were being followed by the soldier. It turned out that there were German guards at checkpoints near the village, and they shot everyone who tried to leave the village on their own. But the mother and daughter were guarded by the German soldier and were able to pass all the checkpoints until they were finally free. Everyone in the shed was killed and burned. If the girl had not been insulted, she would have died with all of them, but she survived.

This sort of story where Russian village people are shown as cruel and stupid and a German SS officer as an understanding and merciful person would have never appeared in official publications in Soviet times.

> It was before World War II in the town of Rostov-on the Don. A very beautiful young Deaf woman lived there; she went out with many different men and was considered to be a prostitute. Everyone knew of her. But it so happened that one Deaf Jewish man liked her; he observed her and decided that she was good enough to marry. Everyone tried to talk him out of this and told him that the girl was "dirty," but he did not listen to anyone: "I like her, that's it! I will marry her!" And they got married. The girl turned out to be a wonderful housewife who washed the dirty clothes and cooked tasty food; she was a really great housewife. Time passed, and the Germans got closer to Rostov-on the Don and occupied it. First, the Germans started to arrest Jews. They put them into prison, planning to shoot them later on. This Deaf woman went to the Germans and pleaded: "He is Deaf, he cannot be blamed!" The Nazis replied: "If he is a Jew, he has to be shot." The girl said: "If so, okay, I want to die with my husband!" The Germans did not object; they told her, you are welcome to do so. The next day there was a column of Jews; Deaf people were trying to find the Deaf Jew, and when they saw the couple they could not understand. "Isn't she stupid? So foolish!" But she ignored everyone and followed her husband to be killed with him. This was true love!

The same thing holds for this story. During Soviet times, neither Deaf nor hearing people would have be able to read anywhere about a Deaf prostitute as a true, devoted character.

A number of interviewees had good jobs with the VOG. Because of this, their stories are largely similar and are linked to their views of the main events of the twentieth century. Their stories are united by pride in their role in strengthening the VOG and the socialist system. The idea of being part of the group of "constructors of socialism" was crucial for many people of the time, and Deaf people were no exception.

One typical example is the life story of one of the Deaf leaders who used to occupy a top position in the VOG.

Pavel Isaev

Pavel Isaev was born on January 26, 1912, in the town of Saratov, to the family of a worker. He lost his hearing at the age of twelve and became apprenticed to a Deaf shoemaker. In 1927, at the age of fifteen, he organized some craftsmen and unemployed Deaf people in a cooperative workshop called "Energy," where he worked as both a shoemaker and the group's secretary. In 1929, following a decision by the Central Board of the VOG, he set up a regional branch of the association in the autonomous republic of the Volga Germans. Then, for a year, he studied at the technical-vocational school in Leningrad. When Isaev worked for the Volga German Republic, he organized a network of local VOG branches, Deaf clubs, evening classes for Deaf adults, and workshops. In the local town of Engels he was elected as a deputy to the municipal council along with various hearing officials.

In 1931, at the third VOG congress, Isaev was elected a board member. The Central Board's decision was to move Isaev to the huge, industrial Ivanovo region. From 1936 to 1943 Isaev was the head of the Ivanovo branch of the VOG. In 1937 he became a Communist Party member. In 1940 he was elected a deputy to the Ivanovo city council. He initiated the opening of the regional orphanage and the construction of the boarding school for Deaf children in Ivanovo. As he had done for the Volga Germans, he developed local and regional branches, clubs, and evening schools and classes for Deaf adults. In Ivanovo and Kineshma, he was in charge of building two factories with hostels, blocks of apartments, clubs, and canteens for Deaf workers. In 1941 Isaev initiated an appeal to all VOG members by the Ivanovo Deaf community to collect money to build a tank called "Vogovets-2" (described later). At the end of 1943 Isaev was nominated as the first deputy chairman or vice president of the All-Russian Society of the Deaf. In 1959 he was elected chairman of the Moscow regional branch of the VOG. During Isaev's time, the network of regional and local branches of the VOG grew, new classes and vocational schools were opened, and more attention was paid to Deaf sports. The result of his energetic activity in the Moscow region was, among other accomplishments, two boarding schools and an orphanage, the construction of a Deaf factory in Podolsk with two blocks of apartments (one containing eighty and the other one hundred apartments), a club, canteen, nursery school, vocational school, and a hostel for young workers. Deaf workers were provided with private plots of land for dachas, or country houses. In 1976 Isaev retired. He remained a very active member of the VOG, working with Deaf senior citizens practically until his death in 2010 at the age of ninety-eight.

Here is a story from an interview with Pavel Isaev, who is proudly telling about the Deaf community's aid to the front lines during the war:

> Because of the Germans' attack near Moscow, Stalin and Molotov requested help from the Soviet people, who started collecting money to manufacture planes. At the Deaf community's meeting in Ivanovo, we decided to collect money to build the tank Vogovets-2. We sent letters to VOG branches in different parts of Russia, asking for support for our initiative. The tank was built very quickly. In response, Stalin sent a thank-you telegram to the Deaf people of Ivanovo. In July 1942 Saveliev asked me to donate the tank to the front lines. I went to Moscow bearing goodies: some pork and five boxes, or one hundred bottles, of vodka We were taken to Mozhajsk. The delegation consisted of Saveliev, an interpreter named Zelinskaya, and me. In his speech Saveliev related how the VOG members had raised the money for the tank, and I read an address to the tank officer: "Beat the enemy cruelly!" Then we organized a banquet with a barbeque. The officer of our tank was in Berlin.

This long interview with Isaev makes it quite clear that his identity was typically Soviet. Although he was devoted to Deaf people and his work for the Deaf community, he used the standard rhetorical clichés of the time. For example, his term for the Deaf people who were not skilled, active, or literate enough to manage the VOG branch during his absence was the "people's enemies." In Isaev's view these "people's enemies" caused much harm. But Isaev, as a true Soviet patriot, worked hard to restore the country's economy.

One of the interviews with David Ginzburgsky, where he talked at length about his hard work at an industrial plant making airplanes, also shows him to be a Soviet thinker:

> I tried hard and worked rather well. I worked for myself and for a guy who was at the front. I filled three times more orders than was the plan at the factory, and sometimes five times more. We made engines for bombers, which were much needed at the front.

In this excerpt Ginzburgsky mentions nothing about his personal feelings but simply makes a statement about one of the ideals of the Soviet nation: collective happiness and welfare.

The shadow economy of Deaf people follows a completely different model. These quasi-legal ways of raising income ran counter to the disciplinary model of the totalitarian state. At any rate, both groups of Deaf people strongly expressed a feeling of Deaf identity and of belonging to the Deaf world in all its unique features.

In Moscow in the spring of 2012 we organized the first festival of sign language storytellers, which became tremendously popular. Interviews with Deaf people, which constitute the oral folklore of the Deaf community, are becoming a legitimate topic of linguistic and sociological research.

These videos are a good basis for developing an RSL corpus because they enable linguists to trace old signs and to observe the evolution of signs and concepts in RSL. For example, in the interview with Pavel Isaev, I discovered that the original sign for COMMUNIST was the same sign as HERO. Later on, COMMUNIST changed to BUREAUCRAT and then LECTURER (as in "chatterbox"). And what about the attitude of the hearing majority toward Deaf people in Soviet times? One will not find any information about this in books. Sociologists can learn a lot about this history from storytellers. Through sign language stories we can see that hearing people were not sympathetic toward Deaf people and treated them as strangers in their midst. Perhaps the hearing majority subconsciously understood that Deaf people are different from blind people or people who have a physical handicap; they may have felt that deaf people inhabit a separate world with its own language and culture. Stereotypes about Deaf people used to be very strong.

The events depicted by Leonid Kamyshev in his stories are both revealing and typical, as these excerpts show:

> I started working at a factory called "Rubin" (or "Ruby"). I worked there as an engineer. There were a lot of funny cases. For example, I had problems with my bosses because I read newspapers at my workplace. I like reading and can read very quickly. I can read the whole newspaper in five or ten minutes. After that I would start working. My boss did not like a Deaf person reading newspapers all the time. Once, he could not stand it and took the paper out of my hands, meaning "I forbid you to read newspapers in the workplace!" I was really surprised. Okay, I thought. We'll see what happens. I then got up and switched off the radio: listening to the radio is forbidden here! The boss shut up . . .
>
> There were only two Deaf people in our big factory. I was an engineer, and the other one was an assembly-line worker. The worker used to drink a lot and everyday used to lie down drunk. The boss liked to talk to me in this way: "Your Deaf-mute friend drinks a lot, and you do not help him. What a shame!" And he went on and on like this. I told him many times, "He is not my friend!" but the boss stubbornly repeated the same words. One day the boss and I were walking out of the factory together through the turnstile. Suddenly I saw a hearing person lying on the ground completely drunk. I was very happy to have the opportunity to tease the boss. I asked him, "Why aren't you helping him? Why aren't you taking care of him?" The boss replied, "I do not know him. He is a stranger!" I said, "No, no, he is your friend!" But the boss did not agree. I said, "But he is also HEARING like you. You must help him!" The boss got mad but then understood and stopped nagging me after that.

Then there are stories about boarding schools. In the manuals about Deaf education, one cannot find any information about what was going on inside these fortresses and their dormitories. For many Deaf people these school memories are very special. In the Baku school the children had lice. Doctors came and put plaster casts on the children's heads and then took the casts off along with all the hair from their heads. The bleeding heads were then covered with iodine. There are so many stories like these, and often the teachers were not on the deaf children's side.

Russian Deaf historians are just now beginning to conduct research on oral Deaf history, but I am deeply convinced that personal biographies and Deaf folklore are an invaluable source of information, without which our knowledge of Deaf history and culture will not be complete. Other academic disciplines like linguistics, sociology, anthropology, and psychology will also benefit from this research.

References

Ginzburgsky, D. "Pomnju tragicheskii 1937-j." In *Leningradskii martirolog, 1937–1938,* vol. 4. Saint Petersburg: Rossiiskaia natsionalnaia biblioteka, 1999, 675–78.

Palenny, V., ed. *Istorija Vserossijskogo obshchestva glukhikh,* vol. 1. Moscow, 2007, 340–43.

———. "100 let Pavlu Isaevu." *V edinom stroju* 1 (2012): 16–19 (Deaf monthly magazine VES, in Russian).

Signs of Freedom: Deaf Connections in the Amistad Story

Kim A. Silva

In 1839 the capture of the Spanish schooner *La Amistad* by the US Navy in Long Island Sound revealed the United States' first successful mutiny by rebel Africans under the leadership of Sengbe Pieh, or Cinque. Were these captives Cuban slaves who defied their masters? Or were these free Africans who had been unlawfully kidnapped from their country in violation of international law? The Amistad affair became an international case tried by the US Supreme Court and defended by former president John Quincy Adams. The crux of the case rested on the identification of the language used by the Amistad captives. Where the Amistad Committee's African-language translators failed, the signs used by the Deaf succeeded. Deaf educators Thomas H. Gallaudet and George E. Day relayed riveting stories of the captives to the newspapers and helped to identify the elusive Mende language. The charismatic and controversial leader Cinque ultimately became known as the "Black Prince" in the popular press.[1]

Oral history from the American School for the Deaf (ASD) affirms that the founders of the school, Laurent Clerc and Thomas H. Gallaudet,

Clerc and Gallaudet meeting Cinque. Painting by author.

were the first interpreters for Cinque, the leader of the Amistad revolt. In 1839 Clerc and Gallaudet went to New Haven, Connecticut, to meet with the Amistad Africans and help with communication since the captives' spoken language was unknown by their captors. Clerc and his students met Cinque and the Amistad Africans again in 1841, when they harvested crops together at Austin F. Williams's farm in Farmington, Connecticut. It was easy for the Africans and the Deaf students to communicate because both used sign language and gesture. During this visit, the men's gymnastic-like dancing astonished these students.[2]

Although this oral history did not include the name of the African people aboard the *Amistad,* the history of the Amistad case identifies most of the captives as being Mende. Mende people are historically renowned for their artistry in mime, storytelling, and dance.[3] Once these details were confirmed, my research led to the writing of a manuscript that I titled "A Sign of Freedom," which turned out to be an amazing detective story with tantalizing clues.

How should oral history via the unwritten sign language of Deaf people be evaluated? What criteria and validation tools determine the accuracy of this information? Answering these questions not only serves to illuminate and enhance the history of the Amistad affair but also guides others to recognize and validate Deaf oral history in their own communities.

The author of *A Guide to Historical Method,* Gilbert J. Garraghan, a Jesuit priest, succinctly describes the criteria for evaluating the veracity of oral history. Oral history may be accepted if it satisfies two broad conditions. The first is "an unbroken series of witnesses beginning with the first reporter to the living mediate witness," or Deaf oral historian. The second condition for evaluating oral history is "several parallel and independent series of witnesses testifying to the fact." Garraghan suggests that other means of verifying oral history may exist, and I maintain that family ties, shared professions (e.g., teachers of deaf people), and genealogy are all effective tools.

The Witnesses

Using the oral history method, I identified Samuel Porter (1810–1901) as the "first reporter" of Amistad history. Porter was a Deaf teacher at both ASD and the New York School for the Deaf and a professor at Gallaudet College. In March 1841, after the Supreme Court verdict of freedom for thirty-six Amistad Africans, the men, one boy, and three girls from the ship were sent to Farmington, Connecticut, until funds could be raised for their return to Sierra Leone. During the same year, Porter was living in his family home when his parents, the Reverend Noah Porter and his wife, Mehitable, who were abolitionists, agreed to care for the youngest Amistad captive,[4] a nine-year-old girl named Margu.[5] At this time Porter had resigned from teaching Deaf students to pursue a career in the ministry. His increasing hearing loss, however, caused him to leave his theological studies at Yale, and he became editor of the *Congregational Observer*. After the Amistad Africans left for Sierra Leone in November 1841, Porter accepted a position as teacher at the New York School for the Deaf. When a teaching position became available at ASD, Porter returned there and later became an esteemed professor at Gallaudet College. The Yale Obituary Record of 1902 describes Samuel Porter as carrying "within his recollection almost the entire history of the movement for the education of the Deaf. . . . He retained to a remarkable degree, to the close of his life, his powers of body and mind."

David Halberg, curator emeritus of the ASD museum, is recognized as the "living mediate witness" or Deaf oral historian of Amistad history at ASD. At the age of seven, Halberg became fascinated with ASD Deaf history when his Deaf teacher, Mary Emma Atkinson (class of 1883), and his woodshop teacher, Charles Dermody (class of 1892), told him stories. He graduated from ASD in 1948 and was a classroom teacher for thirty-nine years. In 1955 Halberg joined Loy E. Golladay as ASD museum curator. Golladay himself worked as curator from 1944 to 1969. From 1963 to 1998 Halberg also worked with a hearing teacher, Frank Asklar,

Samuel Porter. Gallaudet University Archives.

in the museum. These men were interviewed for Harlan Lane's famous book about the history of Deaf people, *When the Mind Hears*.

The "unbroken series of witnesses" who related the Amistad story to Halberg were his Deaf teachers, house parents, and volunteers, most of whom graduated from ASD and/or did research in the ASD museum. Other Deaf historians and witnesses include Walter G. Durian (curator 1917–1958), Walter C. Rockwell (class of 1909), James Sullivan (class of 1911), Joseph Bouchard (class of 1915), Algot Anderson (class of 1917), and Marie Szopa (class of 1919).

In April 1998 the National Association of the Deaf held Laurent Clerc Headstone Restoration unveiling celebrations at Spring Grove cemetery, the Connecticut Historical Society, and ASD. During this week Halberg related Amistad history and cited Reuben Morris, who graduated in 1926 with an ASD certificate, as his authoritative source of information. Morris, who was from a multigenerational Deaf family, stated that his great-grandmother was a student under Laurent Clerc. Genealogical research proved that Morris's great aunt, Emeline Elmina Robbins, and cousin, Charles Augustus Jack, were both students at ASD in 1846.

Deaf Oral History and the Abolitionist Movement

Garraghan's "particular conditions" for evaluating the veracity of oral history also corroborate the oral history shared here. Three of the particular conditions require the oral history to report an important public event, be generally believed, and be one of a limited duration, a maximum of 150 years from cultures that excel in oral remembrance. The Amistad affair satisfies the first requirement. The mutiny and the trial of the Amistad captives were widely reported in the news as the case moved from Circuit and District to Supreme Court trials. In 1839 the American public did not discuss slavery, as speaking out for abolition was dangerous and often risked violent destruction from anti-black and anti-abolitionist mobs. Connecticut had sixteen episodes of anti-racial violence from 1833 to 1837. Abolition was also feared to cause a schism in the nation's unity. Prior to 1839 illustrations of American slavery show a benign system or depict Africans as animals or buffoons. During the Amistad affair, African American Abolitionist, Robert Purvis, commissioned the artist, Nathaniel Jocelyn to paint the first heroic portrait of an African, *Portrait of Cinque*. After the rebellion, sympathetic illustrations of the horrors of enslavement began appearing in publications in the United States, and people began to move from having a private opinion to taking action. The Amistad affair may have been a catalyst for the Civil War.[6]

Garraghan's fifth particular condition is that the necessary critical spirit and means of investigation be at hand to evaluate the evidence preserved through storytelling. Gary E. Wait, archivist of the ASD museum and the Hartford History Center, embodied this critical role during my fourteen years of research for my unpublished manuscript, "A Sign of Freedom." Wait, who is renowned for his research, has served as editor for many authors of prominent books on Deaf history, including *A Deaf Artist in Early America* and *People of the Eye,* both by Harlan Lane; *Edmund Booth, Deaf Pioneer* by Harry G. Lang; *Samuel Thomas Greene* by Clifton F. Carbin; *My Heart Glow* by Emily McCully; and *Words Made Flesh* by R. A. R. Edwards.

Returning to Garraghan's "broad conditions," what independent and parallel witnesses support the oral history of Clerc's and Gallaudet's roles as the first interpreters for Cinque, the Amistad leader? In 1825 ASD enrollment records show that African American students were accepted and fully integrated. In 1828 Gallaudet was active in the American Colonization Society and worked together with Lewis Tappan to ransom Abduhl Rahhaman, the Moorish prince. Rahhaman, who was from Teembo, Foota Jalloh, was rescued from forty years of slavery in Natchez, Mississippi, and returned to Liberia. This points to Clerc's and Gallaudet's sympathy for the abolitionist cause.[7]

There is also evidence for Clerc's and Gallaudet's facility in and promotion of signed communication between individuals who do not speak the same language. In 1834 the *Literary and Theological Review* published Gallaudet's "Language of Signs Auxiliary to the Christian Missionary," in which the use of sign language by missionaries was promoted. Gallaudet described various examples of successful signed communication between Clerc and a Chinese man, as well as his own success with more than twenty youths sponsored by the American Board of Commissioners for Foreign Missions. In September 30, 1839, the *New York Commercial Observer* published an article about Gallaudet's visit with the Amistad Africans during the Circuit Court trial held in Hartford. The article stated that "he [Gallaudet] finds little difficulty communicating with them [Amistad Africans] using the signs . . . employed with deaf."

In 1839 Gallaudet's colleague Tappan headed the Amistad Committee, a group of abolitionists dedicated to publicizing and defending the Amistad Africans. Tappan worked closely with Theodore Dwight Weld, chief editor for the American Anti-Slavery Association. Theodore Weld's brother was Lewis Weld, principal of ASD. Lewis Weld married Mary Cogswell, the oldest sister of Alice Cogswell, the first pupil enrolled at ASD. In a letter dated April 29, 1841, Austin F. Williams wrote to Lewis Tappan and stated that "Bro. (Theodore) Weld" accompanied the Amistad Africans, Cinque, and Kinna to an antislavery meeting in Bloomfield, Connecticut.

During the three trials the Amistad Africans were imprisoned in New Haven from August 1839 to March 1841. Two professors from Yale, Josiah Willard Gibbs and George E. Day, worked together to decipher and identify the captives' unknown spoken language. An October 9, 1839, article titled "Plans to Educate the Amistad Africans in English" in the *New York Journal of Commerce* stated that Professor Gibbs, who was working day and night, was assisted by Professor Day. After learning the numbers "*Eta, fele, sauwa . . .* one, two, three?" Gibbs went to the New York harbor and approached every black person with this question.[8]

After locating James Covey, a Mende African working on a British ship, and soliciting his aid as a translator for the Amistad trials, Gibbs testified in court and then pursued publication of his Mende/English vocabulary lists. Meanwhile, Day and his student assistants from Yale held classes in the New Haven jail six days a week for the Amistad men. Day's letter to Tappan on October 19, 1839, states that "in accordance with the advice of Mr. Gallaudet, we have procured (20 to 30) pictures of single objects . . . at the close of the day many of them [Amistad Africans] had learned committed all the words." More cards were needed but could not be found in New Haven; however, "if Mr. Bartlett or Mr. Cary, Instructors of the Deaf & Dumb Institution . . . were to undertake to search for them [word cards]. Either . . . would willingly engage in the business." Day, who was a former teacher at the New York School for the Deaf, used Gallaudet's *Elementary Book for the Use of the Deaf and Dumb at the Connecticut Asylum* as a textbook. Many of the exercises in this book include references to the use of sign language (e.g., "your signs are clear"; "your signs are obscure"; "do you know our manual alphabet?"). Day's earliest connection to ASD was through his father's rental of the Day House as a second building for the growing institution.

After a verdict of freedom, thirty-six Amistad Africans were sent to the town of Farmington until funds could be raised for their journey home to Sierra Leone. The three girls lived with abolitionist families while the men, including the adolescent, Ka-le, had their own quarters above Samuel Deming's store. Later, Austin F. Williams built a dormitory on his farm for the men's use. This was the farm that annually donated food to ASD.

The youngest Amistad captive, nine-year-old Margu lived with Samuel Porter at his father's home. Samuel's sister, Rebecca Porter, was engaged to John Keep, the minister of the Unionville Congregational Church. From 1834 to 1835 Keep and Day were both teachers at the New York School for the Deaf. From 1852 to 1880 Keep returned to teaching deaf students in Ohio, New York, and Connecticut. Porter and Keep taught together at ASD from 1854 to 1860.

John T. Norton's family soon became favorites of the leader, Cinque, and his second-in-command, Grabo. One reason for these friendly relations was that the Norton family had a son the same age as Cinque's own son in Sierra Leone. Charles Ledyard Norton wrote about his reminiscences of his close relationship with the two Mende leaders. During the

Civil War, Col. Norton helped organize and commanded the Twenty-ninth Regiment, Conn. Volunteer Infantry (Colored.).

The other reason for the friendly relations between the Norton family and Cinque was ease of communication. The Amistad leaders were not fluent in spoken English, but the Norton family could sign. Elizabeth Cogswell Norton, John's wife, was the older sister of Alice Cogswell. John T. Norton was a friend of Dr. Cogswell, and a family letter mentions Mr. Norton's inclusion at a tea at the family's home. Alice's journals describe her as a young Deaf woman who was always willing to teach sign language to her hearing friends. This indicates that the Norton family had access to learning sign language.

The *Phrenological Journal and Magazine of Moral Science* for the year 1845 describes a visit by the Amistad Africans to the Hartford Retreat for the Insane, now known as the Institute of Living. Of this visit Dr. Amariah Brigham wrote, "They [Amistad Africans] saw many patients and stated that insanity was rare in Africa. Cinquez [*sic*] stated that he had seen one case." In 1830 Gallaudet retired from his position as principal and teacher at ASD. He later accepted the position of chaplain at the Hartford Retreat and recommended many humane practices and activities for patients suffering from mental illness. Brigham and Gallaudet worked closely together, and Gallaudet's ability to communicate would have been an asset when the Amistad Africans visited this hospital. Coincidentally, Dr. Mason F. Cogswell, the father of Mary, Elizabeth, and Alice Cogswell, was one of the founders of both ASD and the Hartford Retreat for the Insane.

Minorities are underrepresented in history, and the Deaf community has faced discrimination against both their sign language and their culture. Even as Deaf storytelling is revered, its accuracy and its contribution to authentic history have often been doubted, disparaged, and overlooked. Historians have only recently come to value the importance of oral history as a complement to the written form. Although sign language is for the most part an unwritten language, Deaf culture excels in oral remembrance. Deaf oral history deserves respect and critical analysis so that a more complete history, including Deaf community connections, will be restored and retold.

Resources

The American School for the Deaf Museum contains a wealth of artifacts and archives related to the first school for Deaf students and to Deaf history in general. It has documents from the school's antecedents in Europe as well as other state schools for Deaf students whose founders came from ASD. This repository of information is highly recommended as a resource for both the serious historian and visitors. For more information, contact the following:

American School for the Deaf
139 North Main Street
West, Hartford, CT 06107
museum@asd-1817.org
(860) 570-2300 Voice

For those who are interested in the Farmington Historical Society's Amistad tours in Farmington, Connecticut, or in an Amistad PowerPoint presentation, please email the author at ksilva@farmingtonhistoricalsociety-ct.org or contact the following:

Farmington Historical Society
P.O. Box 1645
138 Main Street
Farmington, CT 06034
(860) 678-1645 Voice

For more information about the ASD/Amistad connections please visit the following website: www.deafis.org/.

David Halberg, curator emeritus of the American School for the Deaf museum, is willing to share his oral history with other interested historians. Museum archivist Gary E. Wait is now retired. Researchers interested in requesting an interview should contact ASD or Kim A. Silva.

Reuben Morris Family Genealogy

Reuben Morris's maternal genealogy links him to his great aunt, Emeline Elmina Robbins, who entered ASD in 1846. Morris had Deaf parents who were both ASD alumni and Deaf relatives of the Jack family in Maine.

Reuben Blake Morris*(Deaf ASD alumnus)

Born 1909

Mary Isabella Davenport (Deaf ASD alumna)

Born 1884

Nellie A. Purrington Gale Davenport (partially Deaf) (Deaf sister's name unknown)

Born 1859

Sarah Isabella Robbins Purrington - **Emeline Elmina Robbins** (Deaf younger sister; ASD alumna)

Born 1834

Augustus Jack (Deaf cousin; ASD alumnus)

Born 1835

* Boldfaced font indicates that the person was deaf.

Notes

1. "An Incident," *New York Commercial Observer* (September 30, 1839).

2. David Halberg, curator emeritus of the ASD museum, interview by Luisa Gasco Soboleski and Kim A. Silva, Amistad oral history interview video, filmed and edited by Krystina S. Carver, presentation at the Deaf History International conference in July 2012.

3. Sankofa Kuumba Mende Artists' workshop, August 5, 2000.

4. John Treadwell Norton to Lewis Tappan, March 22, 1841, Amistad Research Center, Tulane University.

5. John Swaray, Mende preceptor, interview by Kim A. Silva, March 20, 2013, stated that the American spelling of "Margru" is incorrect.

6. Arthur Abraham, *The Amistad Revolt: An Historical Legacy of Sierra Leone and the United States*, accessed July 20, 2013, www.sierra-leone.org/Books/Amistad.pdf.

7. "The Unfortunate Moor," *African Repository and Colonial Journal* 4, no. 8 (October 1828).

8. Leslie M. Alexander and Walter C. Rucker, eds., *Encyclopedia of African American History*, vol. 3 (ABC CLIO LLC) 314, accessed July 22, 2013, books.google .com/books?isbn=1851097740.

Bibliography

Abzug, Robert H. *Passionate Liberator: Theodore Dwight Weld and the Dilemma of Reform*. New York: Oxford University Press, 1980.

"American Era, The." Magazine of the American School for the Deaf (1921–1969).

Amistad Research Center, Tulane University New Orleans, LA. Letter from George E. Day to Lewis Tappan, October 19, 1839. Letter from Austin F. Williams, to Lewis Tappan April 29, 1841.

Barber, J. W. *A History of the Amistad Captives: Being a Circumstantial Account of the Capture of the Spanish Schooner Amistad by the Africans on Board, Their Voyage, and Capture near Long Island, New York, with Biographical Sketches of Each of the Surviving Africans, also, an Account of the Trials had on Their case Before the District and Circuit Courts of the United States for the District of Connecticut.* New Haven, CT, 1840. Electronic ed., accessed July 21, 2013, docsouth.unc.edu/neh/barber/barber.html.

Boone, Sylvia Arden. *Radiance from the Waters: Ideals of Feminine Beauty in Mende Art.* New Haven, CT: Yale University Press, 1986.

Clark, A. S. "John Robinson Keep." *American Annals of the Deaf and Dumb* 30, no. 1 (January 1885): 34–44.

Father and Daughter: A Collection of the Cogswell Family Letters and Diaries, 1772–1830, edited by Grace Cogswell Root. West Hartford, CT: American School for the Deaf, 1924.

Exploring Amistad: Race and the Boundaries of Freedom in Antebellum Maritime America (Mystic Seaport). http://www.mysticseaport.org/amistad .online/overview.html.

Gallaudet, Edward Miner. *The Life of Thomas Hopkins Gallaudet.* Henry Holt, 1888.

Gallaudet, Thomas Hopkins. "Abduhl Rahhaman, the Moorish Prince." *African Repository and Colonial Journal* 51 (May 1829).

———. *An Elementary Book for the Use of the Deaf and Dumb in the Connecticut Asylum.* Hartford Hudson, 1817. This is an authorized facsimile of the original book from the Clark Collection, Wallace Memorial Library, Rochester Institute of the Deaf Archives, Rochester, New York.

———. "The Language of Signs Auxiliary to the Christian Missionary." *Literary and Theological Review* 1, art. II (June 1834).

Garraghan, Gilbert J. *A Guide to Historical Method,* edited by Jean Delangez, 260–61. New York: Fordham University Press, 1946.

Gibbs, Josiah Willard. "A Gissy or Kissy Vocabulary," "A Vai or Vei Vocabulary," "A Mendi Vocabulary." *American Journal of Science and Arts* (April 1840). Accessed 1998, http://amistad.mysticseaport.org.

Goodheart, Lawrence B. *Mad Yankees: The Hartford Retreat for the Insane and Nineteenth-Century Psychiatry.* Amherst: University of Massachusetts Press, 2003.

Lane, Harlan. *When the Mind Hears.* New York: Random House, 1984.

Lepore, Jill. *A Is for American: Letters and Other Characters in the Newly United States.* New York: Knopf, 2002.

Mende Artists Workshop. Sponsored by Sankofa Kuumba and held at the Connecticut Historical Society (August 5, 2000).

Normen, Elizabeth J., with Katherine J. Harris, Stacey K. Close, and Wm. Frank Mitchell. *African American Connecticut Explored.* Middletown, CT: Wesleyan University Press.

Norton, Charles Ledyard. "Cinquez, the Black Prince." *Farmington Magazine* (February 1901) 4: 2–5. *Farmington, Connecticut,* reprinted by the Farmington Historical Society, 1997.

Obituary Records of Graduates of Yale University Deceased during the Academic Year Ending in 1902. No. 2 of the Fifth Printed Series, and no. 61 of the whole record, 115–16.

Phrenological Journal and Magazine of Moral Science for the Year 1845 18 or 8 of the New Series. Edinburgh: Maclachlan, Stewart.

Rediker, Marcus. *The Amistad Rebellion: An Atlantic Odyssey of Slavery and Freedom.* New York: Viking Penguin, 2012.

Wait, Gary E. "A Sound Mind: Beginnings of Humane Treatment of the Insane in America, 1800–1860." Speech presented to the Farmington Valley Unitarian-Universalist, 2000.

Wyatt-Brown, Bertram. *Lewis Tappan and the Evangelical War against Slavery.* Cleveland: Press of Case Western Reserve University, 1969.

Yung, Marguerite, and Jean B. Johnson. *Farmington's Freedom Trail: The Amistad Story and the Underground Railroad.* Farmington, CT: Farmington Board of Education and the Farmington Historical Society, 2005.

The Cosmopolitan
Correspondence Club

Melissa Anderson and Breda Carty

Deaf people have a long tradition of seeking contact with others like themselves, creating signed languages, and sharing their experiences. Much of this has necessarily taken place at a local level, but deaf people have also pursued wider spheres of contact. This is obvious today in the way deaf people exploit social media and the Internet to connect with each other and exchange information, stories, art, and resources related to their history and current status. Murray (2007) has documented some of the early transnational gatherings of deaf people in the nineteenth and twentieth centuries, and the ways in which deaf people of the time shared national periodicals, traveled, and organized international meetings and conferences: "[Deaf people have] consistently maintained connections with their counterparts in other nations, participating in the development of a transnational Deaf public sphere" (4).

Another way in which deaf people of this period developed transnational contacts and shared experiences has received relatively little attention: Many deaf people were also enthusiastic letter writers. This is most visible in the letters they sent to periodicals, but exchanges of personal letters were also important. Most of their personal letter writing was probably carried out within the confined circles of friends or family members, but it also extended into transnational spheres and was at times planned with the explicit aim of furthering contacts and extending their knowledge of deaf people in other countries.

Letters are an important primary source in much historical research and writing, but they feature less in Deaf history. In part, this may be because of deaf people's fraught relationship with literacy. But because letters also tend to be easily lost or destroyed, it is possible to underestimate the role they may have played in deaf people's lives. An example of "telling Deaf lives" and building transnational networks by writing letters is found in the Cosmopolitan Correspondence Club of the early twentieth century.

Beginnings

The Cosmopolitan Correspondence Club was initiated in 1912 by Daisy Muir (née Damman) of Melbourne, Australia. Muir was a leader in her Deaf community, an active deaf woman articulate in both Australian Sign Language and English. She wrote to deaf people in several countries to invite them to join her in establishing a correspondence group. It seems that she identified possible members of the group by reading newspapers such as the *Silent Worker* (from the United States) and the *British Deaf Times*. These newspapers were widely disseminated and read by deaf people outside their countries of origin. If Muir did not herself subscribe to these newspapers, she would have had access to them at her local Deaf mission, the social and welfare center of the Deaf community. As one of the earliest formalized ways of "telling deaf lives," these newspapers helped to stimulate other transnational activities.[1] This role was a conscious one; for example, the deaf editors of the *Silent Worker* "underlined the shared interests of deaf men and women around the globe and actively strengthened a tradition of international activity among deaf people."[2]

Ella Florence Long was an American deaf woman who wrote a regular column for the *Silent Worker* called "Stray Straws." In June 1912 Muir wrote to Long inviting her to join the new club, and soon afterward found herself mentioned in "Stray Straws." Long described receiving a letter from a "deaf stranger," which brought "a whiff of ocean breezes from far-off Australia." She quoted Muir's letter in her column:

> I am starting a Deaf International Correspondence Club and should like you to join it if you can. The object of the club is to obtain new ideas and interests and establish friendships between the deaf of far lands. Each member is asked to make his or her letter as interesting as possible and send it on to another who adds his or her contribution to this and passes them to the next and so on.[3]

The name of the Cosmopolitan Correspondence Club may have been influenced by the Cosmopolitan Clubs or international associations that emerged at universities in the United States in the early twentieth century. Their intent was to "promote international understanding and good will."[4] Since 1907 a loose international organization of university Cosmopolitan Clubs had published a journal called the *Cosmopolitan Student,* which carried news from around the world. These clubs had no particular aims apart from promoting international goodwill, and they have been described as reflecting the "optimistic, vaguely progressive, world view which prevailed in the middle classes during the early twentieth century."[5] We have no confirmation that these clubs influenced the choice of the name of the fledgling deaf letter-writers' group, but Daisy Muir's aspiration to "obtain new ideas and interests and establish friendships between the deaf of far lands" was similar to that of the Cosmopolitan Clubs.

How the Cosmopolitan Correspondence Club Operated

In the time of steamship transport, the Cosmopolitan Correspondence Club established firm guidelines about how the rounds of correspondence should proceed. Daisy Muir began each sequence by writing a lengthy letter, attaching clippings and illustrations of interest, and sending it to the next person in the group of eight to ten people. Each person would write a letter and add it to all the others and then send the "budget" on to the next person until the package returned to Muir. As the rounds progressed, each person would remove his or her previous letter from the budget, write a new one, and send the whole package on again. This meant that each club member would periodically receive a bulky package with the contributions of all the other members since that person's last participation.[6]

In order to keep the package circulating at a reasonable pace, each member was asked to send it on, with their own addition, within two weeks of receiving it. A package was said to take between six and ten months to circulate from Muir in Australia to France, Scotland, Wales, England, Canada, the United States, and back to Muir.

The club began with eight members and expanded to ten the following year. According to John Bodvan Anwyl of Wales, who was one of the members, it was mutually agreed at this time "not to add any more correspondents for the present, as that would only delay the receipt of the budget, which is looked forward to with eagerness."[7] During the first few years, new members seem to have been recruited only when another member withdrew from the club.

The Membership of the Cosmopolitan Correspondence Club

This was a small, select club, and evidently some care was given to the choice of members. In order to achieve the club's aims as set out by the founders, each member needed to be literate in English, willing to write at length, knowledgeable about the lives of deaf people and the issues that concerned them in his or her own country, and interested in and open minded about the lives of deaf people in other places. Each member was also likely to have achieved some prominence in his or her own community—enough to have been featured in national deaf newspapers—as this seems to be how the member came to the attention of Muir and other club members, as happened with Ella Florence Long. The following are some brief descriptions of the club members between the years 1914 and 1916.

Daisy Muir

Daisy Muir (1874–1970), the club founder, was born deaf to German immigrant parents in Melbourne, in the Australian state of Victoria,

FIGURE 1. *Daisy Muir*

and lived there all her life. She was educated at the Victorian Deaf and Dumb Institute, which was established in 1860 by Frederick J. Rose, a deaf teacher. This school would have been relatively new and small when Muir was a pupil, but it provided the genesis of a sizeable and thriving Deaf community in Melbourne. Many deaf leaders emerged in Melbourne in the late nineteenth century, among them three brothers: Adam, William, and John Muir. Daisy married John Muir in 1902, and she would have been closely involved while he worked with others to establish Melbourne's Adult Deaf and Dumb Mission, which was the first such organization in Australia.[8] Still new and evolving, Melbourne's Deaf community lacked the large schools and national Deaf organizations of other Western Deaf communities. Isolated by distance and slow communication, Australian deaf leaders learned all they could about other Deaf communities by reading newspapers such as the *British Deaf Times* and the *Silent Worker* and by importing the occasional British missioner (the contemporary term for superintendents of Deaf clubs and societies, who filled religious, educational, and social support roles). Daisy Muir established many clubs and organizations under the auspices of the Adult Deaf and Dumb Mission, including the Deaf Workers' Club, the Deaf Ramblers' Club, and the Deaf Women's Guild. She encouraged young deaf women in particular and mentored and organized adult education classes for many of them. She is regarded as a pioneer of the Victorian Deaf community[9] (see figure 1).

FIGURE 2. *Yvonne Pitrois*

Yvonne Pitrois

Yvonne Pitrois (1880–1937) was a well-known deaf writer and activist in France in the early decades of the twentieth century. Often compared to Helen Keller, she had a similarly high profile in France at this time. Pitrois became deaf and blind at the age of seven. She recovered her sight at the age of twelve but remained deaf throughout her life. After her recovery, she maintained her interest in the lives of deaf-blind people and was a lifelong advocate for them. Pitrois was a regular contributor to deaf periodicals in other countries, including the *Silent Worker* in the United States and the *British Deaf Times*. She published biographies of Helen Keller, the Abbé de l'Epée, the deaf-blind French poet Bertha Galeron de Calonne, and other individuals such as Abraham Lincoln. She published two series of periodicals in France: one for young deaf girls, which had more than nine hundred subscribers, and the other for deaf-blind people. She actively helped deaf refugees from Belgium during World War I by raising funds for them through her international contacts, assisting them with schooling and employment, and writing about their plight in deaf newspapers. Pitrois received several awards and honors for her humanitarian work and her writing and was made an officer of the French Academy.[10] (See figure 2.)

FIGURE 3. *John Brodie*

John Brodie

John Brodie (1865–1926), a Scotsman, had a long and active involvement in the Edinburgh Deaf and Dumb Benevolent Society, which included establishing and editing its quarterly newsletter, the *Albany*. He had become progressively deaf since the age of ten and also had one eye removed by surgery when he was seven. Like Yvonne Pitrois, he was an advocate for deaf-blind people, and he managed the Braille printing department of the Royal Blind Asylum in Edinburgh. He lost his sight completely during the last few years of his life. After his death, a memorial fund was established in his honor for the benefit of deaf-blind members of his church.[11] (See figure 3.)

Douglas Tilden

Douglas Tilden (1860–1935) was a well-known deaf sculptor in the United States. His larger-than-life statues are still on display in several locations around San Francisco. Tilden, who became deaf at the age of five, worked as a teacher at the California School for the Deaf, his alma mater, for a number of years before leaving to pursue his interest in sculpture. He later moved to Paris for seven years to study and develop his craft. He exhibited his sculptures widely in the United States and Paris and was active in Deaf organizations such as the US National Association of the Deaf.[12] (See figure 4.)

FIGURE 4. *Douglas Tilden*

We have varying amounts of information about the remaining members of the Cosmopolitan Correspondence Club. As mentioned earlier, Ella Florence Long (United States) wrote a regular column in the *Silent Worker* and was active in the Gallaudet College Alumni Association. She wrote about the club a number of times in her "Stray Straws" column. She lived in Iowa with her deaf husband, Joseph Schuyler Long, who was principal of the Iowa School for the Deaf and author of an early dictionary of American Sign Language.

The Reverend John Bodvan Anwyl (Wales), who lost his hearing as an adult, was a missioner at the Glamorgan Mission to the Deaf and Dumb at Pontypridd. Recommended to the club by John Brodie, he joined the second round of letters. As a noted lexicographer, Bodvan Anwyl also edited an English-Welsh dictionary and several other Welsh publications.

Two members of the club taught deaf students. Sylvia Chapin Balis, who became deaf at the age of eight, was employed as a teacher along with her husband at the Ontario School for the Deaf in Belleville, Canada. Bessie Edgar, from the United States, became deaf as an adult and taught deaf children in Columbus, Ohio.

Two other club members were regularly referred to as "globetrotters." Ethel Egan Desmond, an Irishwoman, frequently traveled around Europe and was variously reported as living in Paris or London. Based in New Jersey in the United States, Annabelle Kent was another world traveler. In 1911 she published a book about her journeys called *Round the World in Silence.*

In 1914 Howard L. Terry (1877–1964), an American writer, published a novel titled *A Voice from the Silence*. He also published numerous volumes of poetry. Terry, who was deaf and partially blind, was an alumnus of Gallaudet College. He joined the club in 1916 when Douglas Tilden retired from the group.

Some writers have reported that Helen Keller was a member of the Cosmopolitan Correspondence Club.[13] Keller did correspond extensively with Yvonne Pitrois and was known to have addressed a "Cosmopolitan Club" in Maine in 1913,[14] but she has not appeared as a member of the Cosmopolitan Correspondence Club in the surviving records.

All of the club members were deaf, although more than half of them had been deafened in middle childhood or early adulthood. Although this high proportion of deafened members would be unusual for modern deaf social networks, it was much more common in the early twentieth century, when a higher percentage of the deaf population was deafened after early childhood by illness or accident. As well as being fluent in English, most of the club members seem to have used sign language (for some, this was perhaps predominantly fingerspelling). Most of them had clear connections with Deaf communities, organizations, or schools. Several had professional roles such as teachers or mission- ers, and others, such as Daisy Muir, who had more limited educational opportunities, were very active in a volunteer capacity.

In a 1913 article about the club, John Bodvan Anwyl wrote, "Correspondence seems the very thing for deaf people, especially deaf peo- ple of culture."[15] He identified a shared interest in arts and culture—especially writing—among the club members as a key factor in the group's success. As their voluminous letters reveal, several members were published authors, newspaper editors, or columnists. Although most of them did not travel, they were interested in the world beyond their immediate environment. In many ways they could be called an elite group of deaf people, but most of them would have had limited opportunities to enjoy such company in their home environments. It is likely that they relied on deaf periodicals to find other deaf people like themselves. Atherton (2006) remarks that "deaf newspapers helped foster feelings of community cohesion and member- ship amongst deaf people who might not otherwise have any direct contact with people from similar backgrounds who lived outside their immediate location" (3). Deaf community newspapers played a vital role in bringing these people together.

When we compare this small group with Murray's (2007) account of other deaf people who were active in building early transnational networks, it is a striking difference that most members of the Cosmopolitan Correspondence Club were women. At the time, women rarely attended international gatherings or had prominent roles in national deaf organizations. They were more likely to be regular letter writers, a role that served as an alternative channel for building networks that extended around the world.

What Did They Write About?

Ella Florence Long reported that the Cosmopolitan Correspondence Club's first round of letters focused on members' "life stories . . . with descriptions of their school lives, social lives, travel and conditions in their countries."[16] These topics continued to interest the group throughout its life span. The globetrotters recounted their travels, and many wrote about their work; for example, Tilden described his progress with some of his sculptures and included photographs of clay models for some of these works.[17]

The club discussed significant deaf people within the members' home communities. Bodvan Anwyl reported that the new institute for his mission was opened by a deaf peer, Sir Arthur Fairbairn: "It was something for the hearing people here to see what respectability attached to the deaf and dumb. They might have seen that from our ordinary members, but then they are not titled."[18] A subtext of such comments is the insistence that deaf people can perform in almost any role and that it is important to demonstrate this competence to the wider public—a preoccupation that is still common in Deaf communities today.[19]

Helen Keller was another significant person of the time whom the members, especially North American members of the club, commented on in some of their letters. Sayers (2008) notes that deaf Americans in the early twentieth century were extremely interested in Helen Keller and wrote about her extensively in periodicals like the *Silent Worker*. They were concerned about Keller's use of oral communication and about the possible misconceptions of deaf people in general that she might give the public. Regarding Keller's vaudeville-style performances, Sylvia Chapin Balis commented as follows in one of her letters: "I do not at all approve of the way they are exploiting [Helen Keller] now. Because she has been such a remarkable success is no proof that all deaf persons can accomplish as much."[20] Balis's remarks seem to reflect the social pressure felt by many deaf people who believed they had to live up to the expectations Keller created. Other members wrote about meeting Keller or seeing her at public appearances. Bessie Edgar, a late-deafened teacher from Ohio, reported, "Helen Keller was in my city last month— on exhibition one might say. One dollar was charged to hear, or rather to SEE her . . . Those who could hear her said her voice was very strong and filled the large hall. But her words were very indistinct and few could catch what she said. Whatever her voice her mind is a wonder."[21] It is likely that the issue of deaf-blindness was raised in other ways in the club correspondence, as it was a strong personal interest of Yvonne Pitrois, John Brodie, and Howard Terry.

Contemporary issues such as women's suffrage were discussed by some of the correspondents. In the third round of letters Daisy Muir wrote, "Talking of suffragettism! Australia is regarded as a most advanced and desirable country by the English suffragettes, because Australian women have enjoyed the privilege of voting for many years."[22] Sylvia Chapin Balis of Canada responded as follows: "I hope to live to cast my vote in this country or the United States of which I am a native and property owner. My sister and mother all vote in the United States. I am glad to know that the Australian women have the power."[23] Douglas Tilden, however, was unconvinced: "For all that [the wisdom of women], I hardly approve of Suffragists."[24]

Ella Florence Long described a round of letters in 1916, in which the club members shared their experiences of the war then raging in Europe and their concerns about its progress. John Brodie wrote of his son, who was serving at Gallipoli, and Sylvia Chapin Balis reported that two of her former pupils from the Ontario School for the Deaf were serving in the army, one with the ambulance corps and the other with the military paymaster.[25]

These exchanges build a picture of observant, aware, socially progressive people who were for the most part allied with established institutions such as schools, churches, and welfare organizations for deaf people.

They aspired to better conditions and wider participation in society for deaf people, but they rarely wrote of frustrations or disappointments. A determinedly cheerful approach prevailed. At the simplest level, the members were entertained and heartened by the letters, and they committed to following Daisy Muir's original exhortation to make the letters "as interesting as possible." Club members were intrigued by the descriptions and pictures of each other's home countries, and their imaginations were sometimes fired, as this comment from John Bodvan Anwyl reveals: "Sometimes I try to imagine myself in your place, say roughing it in a log cabin in the backwoods, or strolling leisurely beneath the southern cross with a kangaroo leaning upon my arm!"[26]

The Impact of the Cosmopolitan Correspondence Club

The emerging "transnational Deaf public sphere" (Murray 2007) served not only to expand Deaf people's interests and connections but also to provide political and moral support for Deaf communities in times of crisis. The Cosmopolitan Correspondence Club seems to have fulfilled this role in at least one case. During World War I Yvonne Pitrois sought support for her work with Belgian deaf refugees by requesting financial contributions from her international contacts, including the Cosmopolitan Correspondence Club. Daisy Muir evidently wrote to several Deaf communities in Australian states, asking them to raise funds to support Pitrois's work. In a 1915 letter to the *South Australian Deaf Notes*, she thanked the South Australian Deaf community for raising forty pounds and mentioned that deaf people in two other states had done the same. She explained, "I may mention that I have known, though I have never met, Mlle Pitrois, and corresponded with her for many years. I have grown to love this sweet lady through her beautiful descriptive letters."[27]

The members of the Cosmopolitan Correspondence Club did not keep their activities or even their letters to themselves. They were obviously proud of the club and encouraged other deaf people to establish similar letter-writing networks. As John Bodvan Anwyl urged readers of the *British Deaf Times,* "Any friends can start a similar circle. It need not encircle the globe. It may be a mere interchange of letters among friends. Where the territory

covered is not so great, the number of members can easily be increased."[28]
Bodvan Anwyl's exhortations may have had an effect. In 1914 Martha Overend Wilson, an Australian deaf woman, wrote to the *Silent Worker* seeking
interested people to help her start a second correspondence club:

> My good friend Mrs. J. E. Muir, of the Cosmopolitan Correspondence
> Club, has got the flower of American correspondents: let me see if there
> are still some left. I hear rumours of a very desirable correspondent in
> the Winnipeg School, Canada, and there are clever folk in California
> whom I could name. I know a lot about my clever cousins and I want
> them to help in forming a magic ring of Deaf literature round the globe.[29]

We do not know whether Wilson was able to establish a new correspondence club. However, her phrase "a magic ring of Deaf literature round
the globe" (note the capitalized "Deaf") suggests the value that deaf people of the time placed on transnational connections and conveys their
belief in the potential of letter writing to create these connections.

Conclusion

When the Cosmopolitan Correspondence Club began in 1912, Ella
Florence Long wrote perspicaciously in the *Silent Worker:*

> It would be a good idea for Mrs. Muir, when the budget reaches her,
> to make copies of the letters and later print the more interesting parts
> and publish in book form. This first round of letters contain[s] life
> stories of the writers with descriptions of their school lives, social
> lives, travel and conditions in their countries which are too varied and
> full of interest to be thrown away or lost.[30]

As is the fate of most letters, those of the Cosmopolitan Correspondence
Club do indeed seem to have been lost, although we are fortunate to have
extensive extracts from one round reprinted in the *Silent Worker* in 1914
and references to the club's activities in various periodicals. These extracts
hint at a rich layer of autobiographical writing by deaf people and their
interest in the lives of other deaf people around the world, and demonstrate
a lively debate about important issues of the time. They show that women

as well as men were interested participants in these debates and that letter writing made a vital, if underappreciated, contribution to the emerging "transnational Deaf public sphere" in the early twentieth century.

Notes

1. Atherton, "Deaf Newspapers"; Buchanan, "*Silent Worker* Newspaper."

2. Buchanan, "*Silent Worker* Newspaper," 178.

3. Long, "Stray Straws" (1912), 2, 28.

4. Altbach, *Student Politics in America*, 28.

5. Ibid.

6. Bodvan Anwyl, "Cosmopolitan Correspondence Club."

7. Ibid.

8. Flynn, *No Longer by Gaslight.*

9. Anderson, "Daisy Muir."

10. Hartig, *Crossing the Divide.*

11. *Albany*; Hay, *175 Years of Deaf Action*, 14.

12. Lang and Meath-Lang, *Deaf Persons in the Arts and Sciences.*

13. See, for example, Hartig, *Crossing the Divide*, and Lang and Meath-Lang, *Deaf Persons in the Arts and Sciences.*

14. *Helen Keller Newspaper Notices*, 82ff.

15. Bodvan Anwyl, "Cosmopolitan Correspondence Club."

16. Long, "Stray Straws" (1912), 2, 32.

17. Ibid. (1914), 5, 96.

18. John Bodvan Anwyl, reprinted in ibid., 5, 95.

19. Witness the popularity of I. King Jordan's 1988 comment, "Deaf people can do anything except hear."

20. Sylvia Chapin Balis, reprinted in Long, "Stray Straws" (1914), 5, 95.

21. Bessie Edgar, reprinted in ibid., 5, 96.

22. Daisy Muir, reprinted in ibid., 5, 94.

23. Sylvia Chapin Balis, reprinted in ibid., 5, 95.

24. Douglas Tilden, reprinted in ibid., 5, 96.

25. Long, "Stray Straws" (1916), 8, 142.

26. John Bodvan Anwyl, reprinted in Long, "Stray Straws" (1914), 95.

27. Muir, "Correspondence."

28. Bodvan Anwyl, "Cosmopolitan Correspondence Club."

29. Wilson, "Another International Correspondence Club."

30. Long, "Stray Straws" (1912), 2, 32.

References

Albany 37 (July 1926): 3–7.

Altbach, Philip G. *Student Politics in America: A Historical Analysis.* New Brunswick, NJ: Transaction, 1997.

Anderson, Melissa. "Daisy Muir: A Remarkable Influence in the Deaf Community." Master's thesis, La Trobe University, 2001.

Atherton, Martin. "Deaf Newspapers: A Cornerstone of the Deaf Community." Paper presented at the Disability Studies Association Conference, Lancaster University, September 2006.

Bodvan Anwyl, John. "The Cosmopolitan Correspondence Club." *British Deaf Times* 10 (December 1913): 120, 268.

Buchanan, Robert M. "The *Silent Worker* Newspaper and the Building of a Deaf Community: 1890–1929." In *Deaf History Unveiled: Interpretations from the New Scholarship*, edited by John V. Van Cleve, 172–97. Washington, DC: Gallaudet University Press, 1993.

"Deaf Correspondence Club." *Our Monthly Letter* 9 (February 1913): 5–6.

Flynn, John W. *No Longer by Gaslight: The First 100 Years of the Adult Deaf Society of Victoria*. East Melbourne: Adult Deaf Society of Victoria, 1984.

Hartig, Rachel. *Crossing the Divide: Representations of Deafness in Biography*. Washington, DC: Gallaudet University Press, 2006.

Hay, John A. *175 Years of Deaf Action: From Benevolence to Empowerment 1835–2010*. Edinburgh: Deaf Action, 2010.

Helen Keller Newspaper Notices. Vol. 11, Samuel P. Hayes Research Library, Perkins School for the Blind, 1913. http://archive.org/details/helenkellernewsp11unkn.

Kent, Annabelle. *Round the World in Silence*. New York: Greaves, 1911.

Lang, Harry G., and Bonnie Meath-Lang. *Deaf Persons in the Arts and Sciences: A Biographical Dictionary*. Westport, CT: Greenwood, 1995.

Long, E. Florence. "Stray Straws." *Silent Worker* 25 (November 1912): 2, 28–32.

———. "Stray Straws." *Silent Worker* 26 (February 1914): 5, 94–96.

———. "Stray Straws." *Silent Worker* 28 (May 1916): 8, 141–42.

Muir, Daisy. "Correspondence." *South Australian Deaf Notes* (July 1915).

Murray, Joseph J. " 'One Touch of Nature Makes the Whole World Kin': The Transnational Lives of Deaf Americans, 1870–1924." PhD diss., University of Iowa, 2007.

Sayers, Edna Edith. "What's Up with Helen Keller?" In *Proceedings of Deaf Studies Today! Conference*. Orem: Utah Valley University, 2008.

Terry, Howard L. *A Voice from the Silence: A Story of the Ozarks*. Santa Monica, CA: Palisades, 1914.

Wilson, Martha Overend. "Another International Correspondence Club." *Silent Worker* 26 (April 1914): 7, 140.

PART 4

Deaf Arts Evolution

The History of Poetic Style: De'VIA Poetry

Theara Yim and Julie Chateauvert

This chapter provides an overview of the techniques developed by certain sign language poets in order to see how their poetry reflects the De'VIA manifesto, which was issued in 1989 during the first Deaf Way gathering at Gallaudet University. Because it is not possible to exhaustively describe the evolution of techniques and styles in signed poetry, we have narrowed our topic to a partial analysis of a specific temporal and stylistic context. As a result, we do not touch on the period of creation preceding the 1880 International Congress on Education of the Deaf in Milan, Italy. Although we mention a number of characteristics of sign language poetry from 1880 to 1960, we mainly focus on original poetry composed in American Sign Language (ASL) after the 1960 publication of Stokoe's first study.[1] Through this overview we show how this evolution enabled poets not only to express Deaf lives but also to achieve emancipation.

The De'VIA Manifesto

The Deaf View/Image Art, or De'VIA, manifesto was authored by nine artists who came together for a four-day workshop during the first Deaf

Way conference at Gallaudet in 1989.[2] The conference took place the year after the Deaf President Now movement, which was a high point in the worldwide Deaf community's political struggle for recognition. The De'VIA manifesto was an emblematic moment. It took what came before and put it into overt written form. Prior to the De'VIA manifesto, Deaf artists had already been working in its direction, and the actual authoring of the manifesto was a moment of synthesis for a movement whose momentum continues even now. This manifesto is at once political and aesthetic. At the political level, De'VIA represents and affirms perceptions specific to Deaf people's experiences and affirms them. At the aesthetic level, the signatories of the manifesto identified several formal elements as having a special importance in the work of Deaf artists: contrasting and intense colors and textures, as well as the accentuation of or disproportionate use of significant body parts (hands, eyes, mouth) in relation to the context. Themes of De'VIA artwork can include illustrative, metaphoric, or symbolic references to Deaf people's experiences anywhere on the continua between mundane and extraordinary, sensory and cultural, or individual and collective.[3]

In publishing the De'VIA manifesto, the signatories became heirs to a strong tradition in the visual arts of manifestos that were associated most notably with early twentieth-century avant-gardes and which marked the launching of artistic schools or movements.[4] In the same manner, the De'VIA manifesto concerns visual artistic disciplines and, although the signatories also worked in textile and video, De'VIA has for the most part been exemplified in painting, drawing, and sculpture. In 1984, the Bird Brain Society, a group including Peter Cook and Debbie Rennie, formed at the National Technical Institute for the Deaf and devoted to the exploration of sign language poetry, also drew up a poetic manifesto.[5] However, in order to explore the relationship between artistic disciplines, we use the De'VIA manifesto as our reference.

From the Perspective of Poetry

In poetic creation we find the very same political motivation. At an aesthetic level, questions of color and textures, in the sense understood in plastic arts, are obviously of no relevance. However, we can address the issue of form and ask, What are the formal tendencies of sign language poetry? We can approach this question from two critical standpoints. On one hand, we can observe affirmation and emancipation in poetry, juxtapose it with what we observe in the visual arts, and identify the aesthetic characteristics most used by sign language poets. This is a valuable and worthwhile approach. However, approaching the question from this standpoint continues to dissociate visual arts from poetry and to treat them as distinct categories. For us it seems that signed poetry is a unique art form in that it can simultaneously be considered as literary, visual, kinetic, and dramatic. By virtue of this, Deaf culture is the source and expression of an artistic discipline that emerges nowhere else and enriches artistic culture with a specific form of creation that critically examines the relation between the body and language.

After the Milan congress, Deaf literary creation began taking a path toward emancipation starting with poetic texts composed and published in written form, moving to translations of works from written to signed language, and arriving at the creation of works in sign languages. To take ASL creation as our example, the first stage follows the stylistic conventions of the English-language literary canon. We see here at once an approach to research and a strategy of legitimization. With that recognition the constraints lose importance, and we develop our own forms, giving them pride of place. The more we advance, the stronger the basis becomes for developing our own techniques and styles. It is important to note that this is obviously not a linear progression. Stylistic periods and developments overlap, and the motivations for taking advantage of one strategy or another vary.

We are currently witness to a profusion of poetic creativity in sign languages. With the increasing accessibility of video and the Internet, we are able to see the work of an ever-increasing number of artists. For the purposes of this chapter, we juxtapose the artistic approaches of two major figures of contemporary signed creation: Clayton Valli and the Flying Words Project.

Clayton Valli's "Snowflake" and the
Evolution of Critical Discourse

In Clayton Valli's work the processes of linguistic research and poetic creation evolve simultaneously. For example, Valli analyzed how verse functions in written poetry to examine the components of sign language poetry. These observations led him, for example, to identify what he called "parameter rhyme."[6] A *parameter rhyme* consists of periodically repeating a particular parameter that punctuates the rhythm and gives a formal regularity to a poem. At a theoretical level, Valli makes use of this repetition of form to propose hypotheses about verse segmentation markers, while from a creative standpoint he explores opportunities to play with formal constraints of this type. His approach is explicitly one of validation.

"Snowflake" is one of Valli's best-known poems. Alec Ormsby (1995) uses it as the basis of the first critical literary study of sign language poetry. Prior to this, all studies of sign language poetry were linguistic analyses of phonology or syntax.[7] None approached analysis at the level of discourse or narrative processes. Ormsby points out that "Snowflake" utilizes an ordinary romantic tripartite format (i.e., three stanzas of equal duration whose changes correspond to key points in the narration). Comparing "Snowflake" to "Frost at Midnight," a poem by Samuel Taylor Coleridge, he shows that, besides formal correspondences, the two poems also exhibit thematic similarities. In both cases, the author relates the experience of solitude during a stay at a residential school. Comparing the two poems also makes it possible to appreciate Deaf experiences, as when Valli describes seeing his own identity denied by his father. As Ormbsy argues, Valli's work aligns signed creation with a work from the English literary canon. In this way sign language poetry gains legitimization.

Additionally, a Deaf child's experience of alienation is a theme that corresponds to the call to artists in the De'VIA manifesto. Here we discuss whether the techniques used in this poem correspond to those emphasized in the De'Via manifesto. Clayton Valli did much to elaborate parameter rhyme, which had a clear influence on numerous poets after him. We suggest that formal work with the structural parameters of sign language poetry gives shape to Deaf experiences. However, our research also shows that Valli's poem displays forms found in written poetry. Valli is therefore both aligned with and dissociated from the De'VIA manifesto.

Bauman (2007) asks about "Snowflake": What if we reimagine a verse, taking its visual form, a line, as our point of departure? Would this not be a more relevant way to approach the analysis of signed works and allow us to escape from obligatory reference to written languages?

The opening and conclusion of the poem are marked by the drawing of diagonal lines that redirect the viewer's gaze from the periphery toward the center. In both cases the diagonal path is a classifier describing a falling snowflake. In the context of the poem, the snowflake represents a Deaf child. In the opening of the poem, the falling of the snowflake is a metaphor for solitude. In the conclusion the snowflake comes to rest on the snow already lying on the ground. Bauman interprets this gesture as a symbol of the dissolution of identity under the oppressive attitude of the father, as represented by the sun. It seems to us that we could also interpret this gesture as representing the integration of an individual into his or her community, as well as coming to rest in a tranquil landscape. The movement from the periphery to the center can also be interpreted as a consolidation of identity. These diagonal lines contrast with the straight, vertical lines that dominate the rest of the poem, which relates the child's painful experience of the father's oppressive attitude.

This approach shows us that the context for analysis of ASL poetry has evolved. And even if it is still necessary to demand recognition of one's existence, it is now more possible, when creating or critically deconstructing ASL poetry, to follow processes of affirmation that no longer refer only to written languages.

This analysis of the pictorial organization of the work opens up the possibility of enriching an endogenous critical discourse on signed works. By endogenous, we mean a critical discourse of sign language poetry that relies on a poem's own internal structures. A pictorial analysis is only one possible avenue; a movement-based study is another. We are already beginning to realize the potential afforded by these approaches, which, besides nourishing critical reflection and poetic creation in signed languages, also have the power to stimulate literary, cinematic, and pictorial critical studies of sign language poetry.

The Flying Words Project: The Realization of the De'VIA Manifesto

Like Clayton Valli, the Flying Words Project (FWP) has influenced not only the contemporary creation of ASL poetry but also teaching strategies used to promote awareness of poetic discourse. The approach taken by the FWP is more synthetic than analytic. The duo concerns itself with creating images. To do this, they draw on the iconicity inherent in sign languages. When Stokoe's first studies were published, the iconic character of sign languages was deemphasized. The linguistic community at the time considered iconicity to be a factor for exclusion when it came to deciding what could claim the status of a language. Stokoe, with the recognition of sign languages as full-fledged languages in mind, avoided referring to their iconic character.

Over the past decade, though, we have observed a growing recognition and increased study of iconicity's role in every language. The FWP turns this characteristic into a core stylistic element of its creative process. The duo develops cinematographic and transformative techniques and in this way, places itself in a dialogue with certain contemporary visual art forms. The transformative technique, which consists of creating a progressive transition from one sign to the next, is reminiscent of digital image morphing. The cinematographic technique recalls the editing techniques of contemporary cinema while remaining anchored in a tradition internal to Deaf communities and specific to poetic creation in sign languages. Here we are referring to the "visual vernacular," developed in the 1980s by Bernard Bragg.[8]

The FWP's approach is entirely endogenous and establishes a dialogue with the duo as an equal. The creative process no longer depends on spoken language as a reference but instead interacts and shares exchanges with it by choice. On a political level, the FWP's approach is one of radical affirmation. Its narrative, anchored in the body and the visual, always enacts Deaf cultural identity independently of the subject being dealt with. There is no more need to talk about it. The duo's work "Wise Old Corn" is a good illustration of this. This poem deals with a specifically political theme of emancipation and a history of struggle, although not directly with the history of Deaf people. It depicts the history of the aboriginal Delaware nation and the civil rights struggle of African American communities. As interpreted by Peter Cook, this narrative situates the history of Deaf people within a broader history of struggle. The duo succeed in this narrative of inclusion by inserting, through its technique and style, the Deaf community, uncompromisingly and with a sense of affirmation, in the history of humanity as a whole. In this sense it can be said that

FWP's approach operationalizes a revolution founded in creating and performing ASL poetry, one that is now achieved and contributes to its continued unfolding. The Flying Words Project is thus in a way the most masterful incarnation of the De'VIA manifesto.

Conclusion

We invite readers to imagine what will come next in ASL poetry. With the massive availability of and increased access to the Internet, we can foresee a new stage both in the development of poetic techniques and aesthetics and in the way Deaf culture affirms itself. We anticipate the appearance of new forms of creation that are not often seen in sign languages. We imagine, for example, the appearance of longer forms, hour-or-more-long narratives, novels, and so on. We also predict the development of new techniques placing sign language iconicity and image processing in a situation of dialogue. This is similar to hypertext on websites, and creative forms will likely exploit this possibility. And, as poetic techniques have evolved in dialogue with digital cinema and images, we envisage Deaf artists using existing forms of web art as a springboard to the creation of new, hybrid forms and syntheses. Since what is emerging in poetic creation in sign languages is unique, these are thrilling ideas. With its emergence, this creation continues to stimulate critical thought concerning artistic disciplines.

Acknowledgment

We would like to thank Christophe Miller for his help with this text.

Notes

1. Stokoe, *Sign Language Structure.*
2. The signatories were Dr. Betty G. Miller, painter; Dr. Paul Johnston, sculptor; Dr. Deborah M. Sonnenstrahl, art historian; Chuck Baird, painter; Guy Wonder, sculptor; Alex Wilhite, painter; Sandi Inches Vasnick, fiber artist; Nancy Creighton, fiber artist; and Lai-Yok Ho, video artist. The manifesto can be read here: http://www.deafart.org/ Deaf_Art_/deaf_art_.html.
3. In contemporary painting, the work of Nancy Rourke is one of the best representatives of this: http//:www.nancyrourke.com.

4. Among the best known are the surrealist manifesto, the futurist manifesto, and the seven Dada manifestos.

5. For further information see Bauman, Nelson, and Rose, "Introduction," in *Signing the Body Poetics*, 10.

6. Valli, "Poetics of American Sign Language Poetry."

7. Ormsby, "Poetic Cohesion in American Sign Language."

8. For a good explanation of the technique see Bauman, Nelson, and Rose, *Signing the Body Poetics*, clip 5.5.

References

Bauman, H-Dirksen L., Jennifer L. Nelson, and Heidi M. Rose, eds. *Signing the Body Poetics: Essays on American Sign Language Literature.* Berkeley: University of California Press, 2007.

Bauman, H-Dirksen L. "Getting out of Line: Toward a Visual and Cinematic Poetics of ASL." In *Signing the Body Poetics: Essays on American Sign Language Literature*, 95–117. Berkeley: University of California Press, 2007.

"The De'VIA Manifesto." *Www.deafart.org*, 1989. http://www.deafart.org/ Deaf_Art_/deaf_art_.html.

Ormsby, Alec. "Poetic Cohesion in American Sign Language: Valli's 'Snowflake' and Coleridge's 'Frost at Midnight.' " *Sign Language Studies* 88, no. 1 (Fall 1995): 227–44.

Stokoe, William C. *Sign Language Structure: An Outline of the Visual Communication Systems of the American Deaf.* Silver Spring, MD: Linstok, 1960.

Valli, Clayton. "Poetics of American Sign Language Poetry." PhD diss., Union Institute Graduate School, Cincinnati, OH, 1993.

Southwestern De'VIA: The Origin of Multicultural De'VIA

Tony Landon McGregor

The concept of southwestern De'VIA art originated at the 1999 Deaf Studies Conference in Oakland, California (Schertz and Lane 1999), where curator Brenda Schertz introduced the term. My southwestern De'VIA artworks were part of the national touring exhibition, a first of its kind, called "Elements of a Culture: Vision by Deaf Artists," sponsored by Harlan Lane and Northeastern University. It was shown throughout the United States from 1999 to 2001 (ibid.). Author Deborah Sonnenstrahl used the same term in *Deaf Artists in America,* which was published before the 2002 international Deaf Way II conference (Sonnenstrahl 2002). Afterward, Chuck Baird, artist, reintroduced the term in his "De'VIA: Art Talk" presentation at the 2004 Deaf Studies Today Conference at Utah Valley State University in Orem (Baird 2004). An imaginative juxtaposition of two cultures, Deaf and southwestern, created a new frontier in De'VIA art. This new style emerges in many of my gourd artworks as well as in my relief prints, drawings, and paintings. My acquaintances with American Indians, such as the Pueblo Indians in the southwestern part of the United States, inspired me to incorporate their culture into my artworks, which contain a unique blending of two cultures: the American Indian culture and my own Deaf culture. My wood-burned gourd artworks with ASL/southwestern motifs were the first to incorporate De'VIA symbolism into a specifically southwestern art form. Since 1999 my southwestern De'VIA art has matured, and I have received much support in promoting the general idea that De'VIA includes subcategories such as black or African American De'VIA, Mexican American De'VIA, and Asian American De'VIA. This idea promotes the understanding of multicultural De'VIA art, which combines experiences from the Deaf and other cultures.

Prior to the 1999 Deaf Studies Conference in Oakland, I had produced early artworks with southwestern themes during my teenage years, and my work won citywide recognition in the metropolitan Dallas area. Strong encouragement from family members and schoolteachers, and especially from my first Deaf teacher, Dr. Walter Kelley, helped me continue with my art. Dr. Kelley told me fascinating stories about the Deaf art movement, which was started by four Deaf student artists at Gallaudet University: Harry Williams, Ann Silver, John Darcy Smith, and John Canady (Van Manen 2012). This led me to become interested in Deaf art. In 1976 I enrolled at Gallaudet, where I took studio art and art history courses. At this time I met Dr. Sonnenstrahl, who was a professor of art history and museum studies. At the end of one class, she encouraged me to attend the University of Texas (UT) at Austin, for I was dissatisfied with the quality of Gallaudet's studio art program.

While attending UT from 1978 to 1980, I had the unique opportunity to meet Dr. Betty Miller and other Deaf artists, such as Chuck Baird, Sandi Inches, and Nancy Creighton. They were members of Spectrum: Focus on Deaf Artists, a nonprofit arts organization in Austin. One afternoon Dr. Kelley took me to Spectrum, for he knew Dr. Miller, a former professor of studio art at Gallaudet and in spring 1972 had seen her first art show, which was based on her Deaf experiences and perceptions. Also, I had an opportunity to meet Carol Addabbo, who was studying printmaking at UT and whose work consisted of images and fingerspelling. This exposure to Addabbo's art and Spectrum's Deaf artists, especially Dr. Miller, helped inspire me to create a body of drawings and paintings depicting Deaf experiences during my art classes at UT. These artworks were displayed in the office of Travis County Services for the Deaf in Austin. Also, under the guidance of visual arts coordinator Chuck Baird, Spectrum produced a statewide art exhibition featuring Deaf artists (Baird 2004). Baird had created a star-shaped exhibit panel that hung both his painting *The Mechanical Ear* and my southwestern-themed artwork.

Two years later, Paramount Theatre in Austin organized a national Deaf arts festival that featured the award-winning play *Children of a Lesser God,* a national Deaf artists' exhibition curated by Robert Roth, and a series of presentations by Sonnenstrahl and others. As part of the exhibition, Roth gave a docent tour and a public presentation called "Is There a Deaf Art Genre?" which featured artworks by Baird, Kelly Stevens, Ned Behnke, Theophilus Hope d'Estrella, and me (Roth 1999). Sonnenstrahl led a panel discussion on Deaf art history and possible art careers for Deaf people (Sonnenstrahl 1993).

One year later Sonnenstrahl and Gallaudet University's art department hosted a national Deaf art exhibition, "Spotlight on Deaf Artists II," which included Ned Behnke, Robert Peterson, and me. At the Execucom Gallery in Austin that same year I held my first one-man art show, which featured my computer-enhanced, predominantly southwestern works. Later I won international recognition through *Computer Graphics World* magazine's juried computer art competition for my computer-enhanced artwork "Octagonally Plottered." The following year I had my second one-man art show at the Eagles' Nest Gallery in Austin.

In 1987 gourds started to play an important role in my artistic life, and they still do today; at the same time, I began interacting with American Indians, especially the Pueblo Indians living in Arizona and New Mexico. I would purchase gourds from them and experiment by painting on the gourds in acrylic. I continued this technique until I was exposed to wood-burning tools, which are now my preferred art medium. I created my first wood-burned gourd in 1990. Today I handpick gourds at the annual Texas Gourd Society show, of which I am a founding member, and I sell these gourds after wood-burning them.

I first learned about the Deaf Way I conference from Dr. Patti Singleton, who had loaned my award-winning, computer-enhanced artwork

"Seascaplot" to Gallaudet University to be included in its international Deaf artists' exhibition (Miller 1989). Unfortunately, I was not able to participate in Deaf Way I, for I was working as a computer graphics designer for an airline manufacturing company in San Antonio. From Deaf Way I, I learned of the new term "De'VIA," and I fell in love with the wording of "Deaf View/Image Art," which described what I was doing with my own art (Sonnenstrahl 1996; Schertz and Lane 1999).

Ten years later Brenda Schertz was asked to curate a De'VIA art exhibit at the Pro Arts Gallery as a part of the Deaf Studies VI Conference in Oakland. The theme of this exhibition was "20 Deaf Artists: Common Motifs." In this exhibition, my southwestern De'VIA concept was unveiled to the public for the first time and created much discussion about the southwestern De'VIA concept and the inclusion of other cultures with Deaf culture (Schertz 1999). I had told Brenda Schertz before the show that De'VIA is not only about Deaf culture but also about other cultures that exist in the United States, like American Indian, Mexican American, and Asian American cultures. I had thought outside of the De'VIA box and come up with a new subcategory. This new De'VIA style created an original frontier, for it had a unique blending of American Indian and Deaf cultures (Schertz and Lane 1999; Sonnenstrahl 2002). This concept imaginatively juxtaposes different icons from both cultures; basically it is an aesthetic act of visually placing things, images, or ideas side by side or blending various icons into powerful and graceful images (Sylvester 2009). Also, it involves unexpected combinations of colors, lines, images, and/or ideas. The American Indian cultural icons derive from various sources, such as Mimbres art found in southwestern New Mexico and rock art symbols from Texas's Seminole Canyon State Park. Interactions with American Indians, especially the Pueblo Indians living along the Rio Grande in New Mexico, greatly influenced my artistic designs, while American Sign Language complements the other icons. The Pueblo Indians often invited me to participate in and observe their sacred dances.

Also in 1999 Harlan Lane and Brenda Schertz, with the support of Northeastern University, sponsored their national touring exhibition "Elements of a Culture." From 1999 to 2001 the tour traveled to seven cities throughout the United States (Schertz and Lane 1999). This historic Deaf art exhibition was the culmination of Spectrum's dream (Baird 2004).

In May 2002, after conducting my doctoral research on the life history of a Diné (Navajo) Deaf rug weaver on the Navajo reservation, I obtained a PhD from the University of Texas (McGregor 2002). During this time I learned much about the Navajo ways. A Diné Deaf rug weaver invited me to attend an annual Navajo fair, where I had an opportunity to see Navajo art and participate in their cultural activities. Also, I was able to witness the Diné Deaf rug weaver's code switching between two worlds, the Diné and the Deaf worlds. Afterward I added Navajo designs to some of my artworks.

In 2002 I was selected as one of the participating artists for Gallaudet's Deaf Way II international conference (Thornley 2002). Many attendees from all over the world came to witness my demonstration of wood-burning gourds at the Washburn Arts Center. In the meantime, DawnSignPress published the first-of-its-kind art history book focusing on Deaf artists from the colonial period to contemporary times: Sonnenstrahl's (2002) *Deaf Artists in America*. My works are included in this book, which also states that my southwestern De'VIA art has created a new frontier for De'VIA (ibid.). During the 2004 Deaf Studies Today Conference, Chuck Baird noted that I had brilliantly expanded the De'VIA concept by adding subcategories such as southwestern De'VIA, feminist De'VIA, American Indian De'VIA, African American De'VIA, and Mexican American De'VIA (Baird 2004). For example, Susan Dupor calls herself a feminist De'VIA artist since she often depicts women's issues in her paintings (personal communication, 2012). Zaurov (2012) states that another Deaf art category is Jewish De'VIA, which includes both Jewish and Deaf experiences. An example of Jewish De'VIA is seen in works by Deaf artist David Bloch that depict his experience during the Holocaust. Even though the De'VIA concept was created in the United States, it can be applied in other countries (e.g., French De'VIA, Russian De'VIA).

In the last ten years I have been exhibiting my southwestern De'VIA artworks at countless national and international group art shows, such as the 2012 National Association of the Deaf/DeaFestival Conference Kentucky in Louisville; the "Deaf Artists in the Community and Schools" exhibit at Lamar University's Dishman Art Museum in Beaumont, Texas; the Deaf Studies Today Conference art exhibit at Woodbury Art Museum in Orem, Utah; the "Images and Visions of a Culture" art exhibit at aND Gallery in Saint Paul, Minnesota; and many others. My southwestern De'VIA art has matured and become more refined over the years. My unique concept has inspired many other Deaf artists to look beyond their Deaf culture and include their different ethnicities in their artworks as a blend of icons. At the 2012 DeaFestival I unveiled two historical paintings featuring prominent Deaf artists from the Deaf art movement and De'VIA, spanning the period from the 1960s to today (Van Manen 2012). Some of these artists incorporated their diverse ethnicities and beliefs in their creations.

References

Baird, C. "De'VIA: Art Talk." In *Deaf Studies Today! A Kaleidoscope of Knowledge, Learning, and Understanding. Conference Proceedings,* edited by B. Eldredge, D. Stringham, and M. Wilding-Diaz. Orem: Utah Valley State College, 2004.

Durr, P. "Deconstructing the Forced Assimilation of Deaf People via De'VIA: Resistance and Affirmation Art." *Visual Anthropology Review* 15, no. 2 (1999): 47–68.

McGregor, T. "Should Home Culture Play a Role in Art Education for Diné Deaf and Hard-of-Hearing Children? A Life History of Coyote Eyes, a Diné Deaf Rug Weaver." PhD diss., University of Texas at Austin, 2002.

Miller, B. "De'VIA (Deaf View/Image Art)." In *Deaf Way: Perspectives from the International Conference on Deaf Culture,* edited by C. J. Erting, R. C. Johnson, D. L. Smith, and B. N. Snider, 770–72. Washington, DC: Gallaudet University Press, 1989.

Roth, R. "Deaf Art Criticism: Where Have We Been, Where Are We Going?" In *Deaf Studies Conference Proceedings,* edited by J. Mann. Washington, DC: Gallaudet University, College of Continuing Education, 1999.

Schertz, B., and H. Lane. "Elements of a Culture: Visions by Deaf Artists." *Visual Anthropology Review* 15, no. 2 (Fall 1999): 20–36.

Sonnenstrahl, D. *Deaf Artists in America: Colonial to Contemporary.* San Diego: DawnSignPress, 2002.

―――. "De'VIA: What an Odd Word! A Historical Perspective." Deaf American Monograph. Silver Spring, MD: National Association of the Deaf, 1996.

_____. "Visual Arts in Deaf Studies: Historical Perspectives on Deaf Artists." In *Deaf Studies III: Bridging Cultures in the 21st Century, Conference Proceedings, April 22–25, 1993*, edited by J. Cebe. Washington, DC: Gallaudet University, College of Continuing Education, 1993.

Sylvester, D. *Magritte*. Brussels: Mercatorfonds, 2009.

Thornley, M. "Deaf Artists at Deaf Way II." In *Deaf Way II: Featured Visual Artists*. Washington, DC: Gallaudet University Press, 2002.

Van Manen, J. *Ann Silver: One Way, Deaf Way*. Iowa City, IA: Empyreal Press, 2012.

Zaurov, M. "De'VIA and Jewish Deaf Art." In *Fifth Biennial Deaf Studies Today! Beyond Talk. Conference Proceedings*, edited by B. Eldredge and M. Wilding-Diaz.Orem: Utah Valley State College, 2012.

Photographing Deaf People: The Lives and Works of Three Pioneers in American Deaf Photography

Drew Robarge

The cliché "A picture is worth a thousand words" has been used but not taken to heart by researchers of deaf history. Precisely because they do not contain words, the visual record of photographs and the hidden details and messages that are embedded in them tend to be overlooked by historians. While deaf history books have extensively utilized photographs to bring their narratives to life, there has been insufficient documentation about the photographs and the deaf photographers who took some of them. These photographs are, in fact, primary sources and deserve to be examined closely in an attempt to understand the past and how deaf people used to live. This chapter brings to light the story of three deaf pioneers in photography, explains how their photographic experience fits in with deaf history as well as the larger history of photography, and reveals how we can "read" some of their photographs to gain an insight into deaf culture and the deaf experience.

Even though I discuss three male American photographers, there were also deaf international photographers during this same period, and the earliest prominent deaf female photographer, Maggie Lee Sayre, started photographing after this era. I begin this analysis with the first known deaf photographer in the United States, Ranald Douglas.

Ranald Douglas

Douglas was born hearing in Syracuse, New York, in 1853. Scarlet fever rendered him deaf at the age of five, and his mother enrolled him at the New York School for the Deaf in White Plains from 1862 to 1872.[1] It was during his time as a student at the school that he received his first photography outfit from the principal, Weston Jenkins, who would ten years later also advise Alexander Pach to work in photography.[2] After graduating, Douglas attended the National Deaf-Mute College (now known as Gallaudet University) from 1873 to 1875. There he continued to photograph and develop his skills. In 1896 he wrote to Edward Miner Gallaudet that the college put "facilities in my hand that made me a first class photographer."[3] It was likely that Douglas knew he wanted to be a photographer as soon as he entered the college and could not wait until his studies were finished to become a professional photographer. In the middle of the 1875 academic term, Douglas, with his career goal in mind, went to Wisconsin to pick up a photo wagon from his father. This left the college no choice but to expel him for nonattendance. However, the departure did not end his relationship with the college.[4]

Setting out on his own, Douglas became an itinerant photographer. Unable or choosing not to stay in one place, he went where there was minimal or no competition for his photographic services and moved on when he felt that the competition increased, which was common practice among professional photographers of the day.[5] Douglas established his first studio in 1875 in Livingston, New Jersey, which would be the place he called home and returned to many times throughout his life.[6] He had studios in Pennsylvania, Massachusetts, New Jersey, and Washington, DC. While the studios were in operation, he would also travel to take photographs at different deaf schools. One article claims that he photographed at almost all of the deaf schools.[7]

Douglas became the official photographer at the National Deaf-Mute College from 1878 until 1895, spending only a month or two in residence at a time. His photographs of the college's building and grounds, officers, students, and interior views were exhibited in 1893 at the Columbian Exposition in Chicago.[8] From 1894 to 1896, however, Douglas's relationship with the college soured. Douglas wrote several letters to Edward Miner Gallaudet, asking him to prevent the students from copying his photographs for the student publication, *The Buff and Blue*, as well as from taking photographs while he was on campus. He also asked Gallaudet to require the students to give Douglas credit for his works. We do not know how Edward Miner Gallaudet responded to his requests or whether any action was taken on this issue, but the situation was resolved in May 1896, when Douglas made a public apology for his written outbursts in a Brooklyn deaf newspaper, most likely in an effort to save face and continue photographing at the college.[9]

In 1900 Douglas moved to Ricketts, Pennsylvania, where he spent the rest of his life. In the ensuing years Douglas became a prominent photographer throughout the region, receiving recognition from two local historians for capturing the area's history. However, he continued to struggle financially until the end of his life. When he died of a kidney disease in 1910 at the age of fifty-seven, he lacked sufficient money for a proper burial.

Theophilus d'Estrella

While some individuals attempt to make a living from photography, others use it as an art medium or enjoy it as a hobby. As an instance of the latter, Theophilus d'Estrella was one of the first prolific deaf amateur photographers. His status as the first student to graduate from the California School for the Deaf, as well as the preservation of his photographs at the school, has inspired several scholarly works about his life and photography. Given the extent of the scholarly attention that has been devoted to him, I here provide only a summary of his biography and photographic works. However, I situate his experiences alongside those of the other two photographers featured in this chapter.

Born deaf in 1851 in California, d'Estrella was the first male deaf student to attend the California School for the Deaf in Berkeley in 1860, as well as the first student to graduate in 1873.[10] He attended the University of California in Berkeley, which made him the first deaf student to enroll, but he never finished his studies, citing the lack of support services.[11] While he was studying there, he taught art at the California School for the Deaf, which he would continue to do until his death in 1928.

In April 1874 the soon-to-be famous photographer Eadweard Muybridge[12] took photographs of the California School for the Deaf. This was d'Estrella's first encounter with photography. D'Estrella was fascinated by how Muybridge framed his shots, and Muybridge's influence can be seen many years later in one of d'Estrella's photographs in which he captures a dog leaping off the ground to grab a stick.[13] D'Estrella first learned how to take pictures in 1886 from Charles Wilkinson, who was the brother of Warring Wilkinson, the principal of the California School for the Deaf.[14] It was during this decade that taking and developing photographs became more accessible as photographers switched from the wet-plate to the dry-plate process. The latter process, along with the Brownie, made by Eastman Kodak, eased the would-be photographers' learning curve and made photography more enticing to more people.

In the years to come, d'Estrella would continue to learn techniques that would make him an "expert amateur." His photographs of nature often appeared as illustrations in the *The Overland Monthly*, a literary magazine, but the photographer's work frequently went unattributed, so it is difficult to verify which of his photographs he was able to publish.[15] Teaching at the California School for the Deaf allowed d'Estrella to have a steady source of income, and he did not depend on photography to make a living. This fact would grant him more artistic freedom as he did not need to take pictures in the hope that people would purchase them.

He also took photographs of students at the California School for the Deaf. Mildred Albronda and Terri Manning both argue that the photographs of school children have social meanings attached to them.[16] One that may be inherent in d'Estrella's photography is the desire to challenge the dominant culture's perception of deaf people. Virgil Williams was a mentor to d'Estrella when the latter attended the California School of Design in San Francisco, and Williams urged d'Estrella that if he could

"hit upon something that is pathetic, and yet unites beauty with affliction, you are sure to make a success of it."[17] Disagreeing with his mentor,
d'Estrella did the opposite and attempted to show deaf children as normal
individuals without any indication of their deafness or affliction.[18] It is
difficult to determine whether he had this in mind when he took the pictures absent any explicit statements by him or to know how he exhibited
the photographs, if at all. His photographic work was extensive, but it was
ended by a fire that destroyed the studio that housed his five cameras and
several thousand of his negatives. After that tragedy and until he passed
away in 1929, he never photographed again.

Alexander L. Pach

The legacy of Theophilus d'Estrella has continued in the institutional
memory of the California School for the Deaf, the grouping of several
prominent deaf artists in California, and the extensive research of
Mildred Albronda. Unfortunately, the same cannot be said for Alexander
Lester Pach, who was not only a reputable professional photographer but
also a prolific writer and commentator on many issues concerning deaf
people during his time. Alexander Pach was born hearing in Philadelphia
in 1864.[19] His father, Morris Pach, along with his brothers Gustavus
and Gotthelf, opened the prestigious Pach Brothers photographic
studio in New York City, which specialized in portrait photography.[20]
Many famous individuals came to have their likeness taken at this
studio.[21]

Alexander Pach became deaf at the age of seventeen after being
afflicted with cerebral meningitis, which lasted several months. At the
urging of his friends, he decided to enter the New York School for the
Deaf even though he had completed public school and begun taking
college courses.[22] In 1882, he graduated as valedictorian. In 1881, while
he was at school, he started working for his uncles in the printing
department at the Pach Brothers Studio.[23] After a year he was promoted
to manager of several branch studios in college towns such as Wellesley,
Amherst, Williamstown, Middletown, Hanover, and Schenectady.[24]
In 1888 he devoted his attention to his new acquisition, an unprofit-
able Pach Brothers branch studio in Easton, Pennsylvania, which Pach

immediately turned around and made profitable.[25] He became well known in Easton for providing quality portrait photographs, and his motto was "Not how cheap, but how good!" By 1893 he had six people working for him in the Easton studio taking, retouching, and printing photographs. Knowing the manual alphabet, his staff members would sometimes serve as interpreters for Pach, and his clients were often unaware that Pach was deaf as they rarely saw an assistant spell or sign what the clients said.[26] Pach said he was able to speak very well but proclaimed himself as being the worst lip-reader.[27]

For unknown reasons he sold his studio in 1895 to two photographers, one of whom was deaf. Pach then moved to New York City, where he opened and closed several studios before he returned in 1898 to work for his uncles at the Pach Brothers flagship studio, where he served as vice president of the printing department. This role was highly prestigious but did not allow him to take photographs as much as he had in the past. He must have missed doing so, as he left the studio in 1915 and established his own, which he would operate until his death in 1938. Just prior to his death he wrote that, in fifty years of photography, he had photographed twenty-five thousand people.[28]

Mainly because the Pach Brothers specialized in portraits, Alexander Pach acquired the same specialized set of skills. Through his work at the Pach Brothers studio and his own personal networks, he had the opportunity to photograph many famous individuals, such as Theodore Roosevelt, Alexander Graham Bell, and Helen Keller.[29] In addition to photographing individuals, Pach would often serve as the official photographer for many conferences that were hosted by deaf organizations, thereby traveling all over the nation. He accomplished all this despite having a family with four children, being the vice president of a prominent photography studio, serving as a ticket agent for different theaters and cruise lines in New York City and as an officer in different organizations, and writing an article every month for the *Silent Worker*, as well as contributing to other deaf newspapers. In fact, his participation was so extensive that his name appears in more than six hundred articles in the *Silent Worker*, a majority of which he penned himself. His articles often featured news of the deaf community in New York City and commentary on deaf issues. The pictures that we can positively identify as belonging to him, which were portraits, group shots, and convention photographs, were published in the *Silent Worker.*

Reading the Photographs

Now that we know the men behind the photographs, what do the photographs themselves say about the deaf community? It is imperative to look at a photographer's oeuvre as well individual photographs for clues and messages. Consideration of individual photographs must include the surrounding context, but a comparison of photographs with different contexts might reveal other information.

One example of the latter is two photographs of two baseball teams taken by Ranald Douglas. The first photograph, taken in the 1880s, is of the baseball team of the National Deaf-Mute College, and the other, taken in the 1900s, is of a hearing baseball team from Ricketts, Pennsylvania. Crucial to the interpretation of these photographs is the knowledge that Douglas composed his photographs in a certain style: the subjects look slightly away from the camera in a three-quarters pose, not making eye contact. This style was also used when he took his self-portrait in 1874 and can help identify photographs by Douglas at Gallaudet University. In the first picture, the college baseball team follows Douglas's trademark style of looking away from the camera; however, the Ricketts team does not: The players look directly at the camera. The change in styles for the two teams is quite jarring, allowing us to wonder whether the difference in the hearing status of the subjects influenced the way in which Douglas photographed them. While it may be premature to state that oppression appears in Douglas's photographs, it is worth comparing photographs of hearing and deaf people by the same photographer. Pach has photographed both deaf and hearing individuals, but there is no clear distinction between the ways in which they were photographed. Douglas's portraits raise interesting questions about his interactions with people and how his control over the quality of his work was affected.

As other scholars have noted, deafness is an invisible physical disability that the camera cannot capture.[30] This invisibility could be either useful or disadvantageous, depending on how the subjects felt about their deafness and whether they had a desire to show it. If one wanted one's deafness to be known in a photograph, one could show some sign of it in any of three different ways: contextual information in the photograph, the use of a hearing aid, and the use of sign language. Of these three, sign language, whether involving actual signs or fingerspelling, would be the best. A survey of our subjects' works shows that each photographer took only one photograph depicting sign language.

Ranald Douglas had an engraving in the *Silent Worker* showing a classroom of students fingerspelling at the New York School for the Deaf. Theophilus d'Estrella also took a picture of a classroom of students fingerspelling, but it was somewhat blurred, possibly due to motion. Alexander Pach took a group photograph of the American Association for the Promotion of Teaching Speech to the Deaf conference, where Alexander Graham Bell is looking at two individuals seated below him and signing to each other.[31] Of the many pictures that these individuals have taken, why do so few show sign language and fingerspelling?

The role of the photographer in composing the photographs and the photographer's professional or amateur status could perhaps explain this absence. Professional photographers such as Douglas and Pach were beholden to the customer's taste and style. Even though there is an underlying struggle between a photographer's artistic vision and a customer's artistic preference, in the end the customer has the final word. The lack of sign language in the three men's photographs could indicate that customers did not want to see it depicted, particularly if a portrait was involved. As a result, Pach and Douglas may not have had much input in this matter.

This does not appear to be true for amateurs such as d'Estrella, who did not have a customer to consider and thus could compose a photograph for his own amusement or to convey a message. Mildred Albronda has explained this omission of sign language from d'Estrella's photographs as adhering to Victorian morals and manners, which were prevalent in the United States at the time. These would have prohibited gesturing or any kind of movement that would make one appear inappropriate.[32] Terri Manning and Judith Tressburg have both made similar statements, although Tressburg has argued that the lack of signing was to impress parents, visitors, and legislators who supported the California School for the Deaf and to portray the students in a manner that was seen as appropriate.[33]

After the American Civil War, a shift in ideology occurred; as a result, immigrants and others considered outside the mainstream, such as deaf people, were expected to assimilate into American society. The oralist movement was one branch of that ideology, branding sign language as making deaf people isolated and different.[34] D'Estrella might have attempted to show that, in front of the camera, deaf people were normal, eschewing any imagery that would hint at a deaf identity or signs of being different.[35] Another, simpler explanation for this absence of sign language is the fact that photography during this era did not allow for the capture of slight movements, which may explain why these individuals chose not to take or publish many photographs of sign language.

Photography is not only an art form but also a business, making Ranald Douglas and Alexander Pach deaf entrepreneurs of the late nineteenth century. Studies of deaf people who owned their own businesses have yet to be undertaken, but the lives of Ranald Douglas and Alexander Pach provide contrasting case studies. These men were born hearing, but Douglas became deaf at five and most likely did not retain speech, whereas Pach became deaf at seventeen and had perfect command of his speech. The ability to speak would have some kind of impact on their relationship with their hearing customers, as Pach stated that some of them did not even realize he was deaf, thus reducing the bias that might be inherent in the customer's selection of business. Douglas did not have family with a background in photography, whereas Pach had an impressive photographic pedigree. Douglas was an itinerant photographer who struggled to make ends meet. He considered giving up photography more than once and considered learning engraving in order to supplement his income. Pach, on the other hand, stayed in one place for long periods of time, and all of his business ventures were successful. One fact that may be indicative of the demands of the profession is that both of the men's wives divorced them.

Conclusion

The lives and photographs of these three men serve as valuable sources in the exploration of deaf cultural sensibilities at the turn of the twentieth century. This chapter demonstrates how the field of photographic history is untapped and challenging, especially in the pursuit of answers to questions about the deaf community and its history. One hopes that more research will be done on deaf photographers, as additional photographers have been discovered during the research process, prompting more questions. Additional deaf photographers of a similar time period from around the world have come to light, inviting comparisons of their photographs to see whether they have something in common. Although deaf people might have embraced the invisibility of deafness in these photographers' works, that invisibility hampers researchers who are unable to distinguish between the deaf and the hearing in the creator and the subject. In addition, the frequent lack of attribution makes such research difficult. Nevertheless, this aspect of our history and our understanding of photography needs to be brought to light if we are to gain a better picture of our past.

Notes

1. Marriage Record for Ranald Douglas and Elizabeth Stevens, no. 972, 1892, Edward Fay Marriage Records, Gallaudet University Archives, Washington, DC; New York School for the Deaf Attendance Record of Ranald Douglas, October 10, 1862, Ranald Douglas Papers, Gallaudet University Archives, Washington, DC.

2. "Local News," *Silent Worker* [December 22, 1892].

3. Ranald Douglas to Edward Miner Gallaudet, June 6, 1896, Ranald Douglas Papers, Gallaudet University Archives, Washington, DC.

4. Peter Tomasak, *In Command of Time Elapsed: The Life & Times of Robert Bruce Ricketts* [Kyttle, PA: North Mountain, 2007], 197.

5. Robert Hirsch, *Seizing the Light: A Social History of Photography* [Boston: McGraw-Hill, 2000], 94.

6. Tomasak, *In Command*, 198.

7. This is presumably all of the deaf schools on the East Coast as it is very unlikely that he traveled to California. As of 1889, when the following article from *Silent Worker* was written, approximately forty-nine schools throughout the United States were in operation. See "About the Deaf," *Silent Worker* [September 26, 1889].

8. Columbia Institution for the Instruction of the Deaf and Dumb, *1893 Annual Report* [Washington, DC: Government Printing Office, 1894].

9. Ranald Douglas to Edward Miner Gallaudet, May 18, 1896, Ranald Douglas Papers, Gallaudet University Archives, Washington, DC.

10. Mildred Albronda, *The Magic Lantern Man: Theophilus D'Estrella* [Fremont, CA: California School for the Deaf in Fremont, 1985], 15, 21.

11. Ibid., 21.

12. Eadweard Muybridge is most notable for his work on animal locomotion using an instrument formally known as a zoopraxiscope, which he lectured about at the

California School for the Deaf in 1892. The most famous example is his series known as *Sallie Gardner at a Gallop* or *The Horse in Motion,* photographed in 1878.

13. Albronda, *Magic Lantern Man,* 21–23.

14. Ibid., 33.

15. Ibid., 48.

16. Ibid., 89. Terri Manning, "Theophilus Hope d'Estrella (1851–1929): Photography and Deaf School Life" [master's thesis, San Francisco State University, 1991], 7.

17. Albronda, *Magic Lantern Man,* 89.

18. Manning, "Photography and Deaf School Life," 7.

19. "Alexander L. Pach: An Interesting Sketch of a Prominent Deaf Man," *Silent Worker* (February 1893).

20. Often stamped "Pach Bros" on the back of their photographs.

21. "Guide to the Pach Brothers Portrait Photograph Collection 1867–1947," New York Historical Society Museum and Library, created January 3, 2012, http://dlib.nyu.edu/findingaids/html/nyhs/pach/.

22. "Alexander L. Pach: An Interesting Sketch of a Prominent Deaf Man."

23. Ibid.

24. Ibid.

25. Ibid.

26. Alexander L. Pach, "Outstanding Men and Women I Have Photographed," *Maryland Bulletin* (April 1938).

27. "Alexander L. Pach: An Interesting Sketch of a Prominent Deaf Man."

28. Alexander L. Pach, "Outstanding Men and Women I Have Photographed."

29. Ibid.; W. S. Runde, "Roosevelt and the Deaf," *Silent Worker* (February 1919).

30. Manning, *Photography and Deaf School Life,* 6.

31. This was most likely an unintentional shot of the group, but one that is ironic given that the organization advocates the use of the oral method rather than sign language in the classroom and the public sphere.

32. Albronda, *Magic Lantern Man,* 91.

33. Judith Tressburg, "Seeing in Deaf: Reading the Photographs of Theophilus Hope d'Estrella," unpublished paper, ca. 1992, 21; Terri Manning, *Photography and Deaf School Life,* 7.

34. Douglas C. Baynton, *Forbidden Signs: American Culture and the Campaign against Sign Language* [Chicago: University of Chicago Press, 1996], 150.

35. This applies only to the photographs taken by these three photographers from 1875 to 1910. Several photographs show the use of sign language, and, in fact, some of these photographs depict a sense of integration as well as difference. There are images of children signing the "Star-Spangled Banner" and students fingerspelling "victory," thereby showing, in their unique way, their pride in being an American.

The Vineyarders: A Fusion of History and Fiction

Veronica Bickle, Bob Paul, and Jennifer Paul

It [historical fiction] is a zone of freedom, a verbal realm apart from history, the limits of which are prescribed by the taleteller's imagination, where the ugly facts history throws in the way of the writer can be made into appealing, or at least consoling, stories about the past.

(Kerr, *Fiction against History*)

For us, the first and foremost challenge of writing *The Vineyarders* is that we are not professional historians. However, we enjoy history. We love good stories. As tale-tellers, we strive to recognize, on one hand, the history and "ugly facts" of oppression and, on the other, to show the human spirit, resilience, and creativity of Deaf people and nondeaf allies of the past in order to inspire and at the same time console us. To this end, we are making use of various genres—romance, comedy, mystery, and the picaresque (the latter usually involves traveling)—albeit within the context of the late nineteenth century in Massachusetts, specifically Boston and Martha's Vineyard.

This historical and geographical context[1] has a special meaning in the DEAF-WORLD.[2] *The Vineyarders,* as a work of historical fiction,[3] allows the reader to see what life was like for Deaf people and nondeaf allies during a specific time period. At the same time, in gaining insight into the history of the DEAF-WORLD, we make the past relevant to readers and create a comfortable environment for imagining the past.

The creation of such a setting is indeed what happens with Douglas Bullard's *Islay.* Unlike John F. Egbert's *Mindfield,* which is an apocalyptic story, *Islay* is a fictional story of a Deaf man who dreamed of a Deaf-run town and worked toward its establishment. Whereas *Mindfield* is very much science fiction, the story in *Islay* is not far-fetched, and it has a germinal seed in the canals of history. In the 1850s John Flournoy initiated intense discussions about a "state sovereignty" for Deaf people, with "our peculiar necessities and such arrangements." William Willard and Edward Fay also proposed, in 1858, less controversial structures to support a "neighborhood" of Deaf people (Padden and Humphries 1988, 112–14).

In the early 2000s Marvin T. Miller led a group of private investors to create a town in South Dakota for Deaf and hard of hearing people, as well as nondeaf ASL users. The name of the town was intended to be Laurent, after the first Deaf educator in the United States, Laurent Clerc. More than 150 people signed up to be residents of the proposed town. However, the plan did not pan out (Nomeland and Nomeland 2012, 86) because an investor who promised ten million dollars for the project did not follow through, and Miller then moved to Indiana. Although it is entirely fiction, *Islay* is an excellent journey into what could have been.

As tale-tellers in the process of journeying into the past, we are continually compiling historical information, working with various historical

1. In the eighteenth and nineteenth centuries, Martha's Vineyard had a larger-than-average population of deaf people due to genetics.

2. "DEAF-WORLD" derives from "the convention of identifying signs from signed language with English glosses (approximate translation equivalents) in small capital letters. The dash in 'DEAF-WORLD' indicates that this is a compound sign . . . This compound sign refers to 'a group possessing a unique language and culture. This language and culture have only become recognized and accepted of late' . . . In truth, however, this linguistic minority is not so new" (Lane, Hoffmeister, and Bahan 1996, ix).

3 *The Vineyarders* was originally a screenplay written by Sherry Lajiness, Barbara Munder, and Bob Paul in 2001. The screenplay was registered with Writers Guild of America, West, from 2003 to 2008.

societies and museums, poring over primary data, consulting historical publications, and taking trips to the locations relevant to the story. It is our hope that we will be successful in making entertainment out of this rich and inspirational historical information. We also believe that, as historical fiction, *The Vineyarders* has the potential to make a meaningful contribution not only to the literary field but also to the discipline of history.

The most significant historical contribution of *The Vineyarders*— and of historical fiction in general—is to offer hypotheses that fill in information gaps in history. For example, Gary Jennings, a famous author of historical fiction, lived in Mexico for twelve years to research the Aztecs. The result of his intensive research is his novel *Aztec,* which was published in 1980 and applauded for its historical detail. However, *Aztec* was also attacked by historians for including details that had not yet been proven. In particular, Jennings's plotline established a trading relationship between two formidable tribes, the Aztecs and the Tarascans, during a period when it is commonly held that no such connection existed. The Tarascan tribe was a powerful empire to the west of the Aztecs, and the two empires were at war with each other until the fifteenth century. The continuous animosity between these two polities has been emphasized in historical studies.

It was after the publication of *Aztec* that archaeologists found evidence of Tarascan trading objects at Aztec sites during the period in question (Smith 2001, 95–105). Michael Smith offers the following argument for the value of historical fiction in studying the past: "Authors of novels can flesh out the details of people's behavior and daily life by building upon a foundation of historical facts, and they can suggest plausible ideas (such as Aztec-Tarascan trade) that might not occur to scholars who are too bound to their sources" (ibid., 89).

The lack of information about Deaf history is one of the major challenges for us as writers. However, we know ourselves best. We know the norms of the DEAF-WORLD, Deaf people's capabilities, and Deaf people's inherently adventurous spirit. We are not fazed by accounts of Deaf people traveling to the far corners of the world or by the level of connectedness between members of the DEAF-WORLD regardless of geopolitical boundaries. We are also intimately familiar with nondeaf allies' learning process as they immerse themselves in the DEAF-WORLD.

For example, although there is no evidence for this, it is plausible that Laurent Clerc visited Martha's Vineyard. Clerc emigrated from Paris, France, to work with Thomas Hopkins Gallaudet to establish schools for Deaf children, demonstrating that he was an adept traveler. There is evidence of Clerc's visits to various parts of the Eastern Seaboard. The New England Gallaudet Association, led by grassroots Deaf leader Thomas Brown, honored Clerc for his leadership in the education of Deaf-mute children. Brown was married to Mary Smith, whose family was from Martha's Vineyard. After Clerc's death, his wife gave his watch to Brown, which signifies a close relationship between these two men of widely different backgrounds. With these and more factual pieces of information, as well as our familiarity with the norms of the DEAF-WORLD, it is not a big leap for us to imagine Clerc visiting Martha's Vineyard.

Furthermore, Smith (2001) recognizes the ability of historical fiction to reach a much wider audience:

> But perhaps the biggest contribution of good historical fiction to the study of the past is its role in communicating the facts and processes of history to a wide audience. The Aztec world constructed by Gary Jennings is remarkably accurate and true to what we know, and his biggest distortions are easily recognizable as novelistic devices. Jennings's book has reached millions of readers; the books that my scholarly colleagues and I have written have not. (103)

One can argue that it is not easy to make history popular. For instance, social critic Dwight Macdonald states that "popular culture is a debased, trivial culture that voids both the deep realities and also the simple spontaneous pleasures . . . The masses, debauched by several generations of this sort of thing, in turn come to demand trivial and comfortable cultural products" (quoted in van der Haag 1957, 529). In defense of popular culture, Wertz (2010) says it best:

> Despite its much-maligned image, popular culture, or "pop" culture as it is more commonly known, is a vital component in the story of humanity. For that reason, pop culture history warrants exploration . . . It doesn't cure diseases, topple nations . . . but pop culture reveals many facets of human behavior throughout history. It is hard to define the human experience without it.

The Vineyarders aims to bring to life a special time in the history of the DEAF-WORLD. The story takes place during the late nineteenth century, which was a turning point in Deaf history as a result of the emergence and effects of oralism and the changes that were taking place on Martha's Vineyard, where the farmlands were being supplanted by summer homes and attractions for visitors from the mainland.

The late nineteenth century also saw the advent of residential schools and the westward spread of Deaf-run organizations and newspapers. Among other significant historical events, we wish to dramatize these movements as the background to the main plot of *The Vineyarders*. The novel draws in a wider Deaf and nondeaf audience, both of whom, we hope, will view the history of the DEAF-WORLD as part of popular culture.

Envisioning the audience for *The Vineyarders* was also a challenge for us. Did we want to write for Deaf people or the majority (i.e., nondeaf people)? How much historical information did we want to include? How would we make these facts interesting to both Deaf and nondeaf readers? Ultimately, what does the telling of history entail, and for whom does it do so?

We decided to create a human story. To this end, we chose to make *The Vineyarders* relevant to readers of all backgrounds and experiences. On one side, nondeaf readers may learn along with the protagonist, who is a nondeaf oral educator, as she embarks on a journey with the original purpose of contributing to research that will help cure deafness; along the way, however, she becomes immersed in the DEAF-WORLD and undergoes a conversion. On the flip side, Deaf readers may follow the protagonist, hoping for validation by her, and watch her undergo this conversion as she learns about Deaf people's history, the level of connectedness between members of the DEAF-WORLD, and their ingenuity, humor, resilience, and, ultimately, humanity, all of which prevail in spite of oppression and threats.

The Vineyarders also offers readers an opportunity to learn about Deaf people and our contributions to mainstream society, as well as those of our nondeaf allies. Our wish to include this information is an exercise in *historical revisionism,* which is a response to the omissions in and misinformation presented by mainstream history, which severely underrepresents minorities such as women, people of color, the working class, and, of course, Deaf people. It is a challenge to work against the dominant culture's view of history, with its influence on our access to data, historical archives, and resources. But we are revisiting this information with our unique, fresh perspective, which is not shared by the majority, and this is to our advantage in terms of providing new historical interpretations of existing stories.

Another example of historical revisionism is the issue of name signs. It would be a challenge to incorporate name signs for different characters in *The Vineyarders*. Although we are limited only by our imagination and linguistic rules in coming up with name signs for fictional characters, there is no record of name signs for any real-life characters, including Deaf people residing on Martha's Vineyard, aside from Clerc and a few other prominent Deaf people of the late nineteenth century. Nora Groce's *Everyone Here Spoke Sign Language*, as comprehensive as it is, does not address the issue of the Deaf residents' name signs. Furthermore, we have no knowledge of the common patterns of assigning name signs to the Deaf residents of the island. By the time Groce was writing her book, the island people who had first- or even secondhand knowledge of name signs and the general patterns of assigning them had passed away. Therefore, we cannot rely on this type of source to suggest name signs that might realistically have been used on Martha's Vineyard and at the American School for the Deaf in the years before the development of arbitrary name signs.

We have our intimate knowledge of name sign conventions in the DEAF-WORLD, albeit they are not those of the island. We have also consulted Sam Supalla's (1992) *Book of Name Signs,* where we came across admission ledgers from the mid-nineteenth century from the Pennsylvania School for the Deaf; in addition to the usual information categories in the ledgers, such as students' names, causes of "deafness," and age at the time of enrollment, a column was devoted to the students' name signs. This column contained descriptions of the name signs and even illustrations of some.

Although the American School for the Deaf, which most of our Deaf characters attend or attended, does not have such information in either its admission ledgers or any other archived records, the enrollment documents of the Pennsylvania School for the Deaf helped us come up with name signs for the characters. In addition, we wanted to identify their distinguishing qualities (e.g., facial features). We also accessed various primary sources such as photos, journal entries, and historical publications related to the fictional figures featured in our story. In creating name signs based on the characteristics and personalities of our fictional characters and in giving name signs to the historical figures whose name signs are unknown, we based our choices on what we hope is a realistic pattern of name signs of the nineteenth century in this particular geographical region.

In a related manner, it is a challenge to confront the oppression evidenced and the misinformation contained in mainstream history in a way that is not defensive or negative. In fact, our attempt at confrontation is another example of historical revisionism. For instance, we are including Alexander Graham Bell's less-than-noble attitude toward Deaf people. He is renowned in mainstream society for his invention of the telephone and as a proponent of oralist education for Deaf people. However, there is more to Bell's stance regarding Deaf people that is familiar to historians of the DEAF-WORLD and most members of the DEAF-WORLD. Bringing forth Bell's insulting opinions of Deaf people's reproductive dignity, among other unpleasant truths, requires a strategy, which is an art in itself. As the story progresses, we hope to exercise this strategy in a reciprocal relation with readers' growing appreciation of Deaf people's humanity.

Essentially, the Bell challenge speaks to a bigger dilemma: We do not want to make *The Vineyarders* too preachy. We do not want the story to be marked in the same way Ayn Rand's (1957) *Atlas Shrugged* is marked. *Atlas Shrugged* was published in a post–World War II world during the "Great Society" initiative.[4] It protested against what Rand perceived as a threat to individual autonomy in innovation, business, and politics, especially in relation to income redistribution. We do not want *The Vineyarders* merely to be a protest against audism but rather have it as the backdrop against which the humanity of Deaf people prevails.

Fusing history and fiction for entertainment is no easy task. We cannot deny that we are in the minority vis-à-vis the mainstream. The consequences of our minority status have not always been pleasant, let alone entertaining, as they have led to omissions and misunderstandings in terms

---

4. Lyndon B. Johnson, the United States' thirty-sixth president, initiated major spending programs for freeways and public transit, compulsory education, old-age income, housing for poor people, and health care.

of historical information and to threats to and the constant oppression of Deaf culture. However, we hope to show, through *The Vineyarders,* that the human spirit, resilience, and creativity of Deaf people and our non-deaf allies of the past have prevailed and that this remains true to this day.

References

Bullard, Douglas. *Islay: The Novel.* Silver Spring, MD: TJ Publishers, 1986.

Carnes, Mark C. *Novel History: Historians and Novelists Confront America's Past (and Each Other).* New York: Simon and Schuster, 2001.

Cowart, David. *History and the Contemporary Novel.* Carbondale: Southern Illinois University Press, 1989.

Egbert, John F. *Mindfield.* Bloomington, IN: iUniverse.

Groce, Nora. *Everyone Here Spoke Sign Language: Hereditary Deafness on Martha's Vineyard.* Cambridge: Harvard University Press, 1988.

Jennings, Gary. *Aztec.* New York: Forge, 2007.

Kerr, James. *Fiction against History: Scott as Storyteller.* Cambridge, UK: Cambridge University Press, 2007.

Lajiness, Sheryl G., Barbara B. Munder, and Robert R. Paul. 2001. *The Vineyarders: A Screenplay.* Chicago: Writers Guild of America, West.

Lane, H., R. Hoffmeister, and B. Bahan. *A Journey into the DEAF-WORLD.* San Diego: DawnSignPress, 1996.

Lane, H., R. Pillard, and U. Hedberg. *The People of the Eye: Deaf Ethnicity and Ancestry.* New York: Oxford University Press, 2010.

Nomeland, M., and R. Nomeland. *The Deaf Community in America: History in the Making.* Jefferson, NC: McFarland, 2012.

Padden, C., and T. Humphries. *Deaf in America: Voices from a Culture.* Cambridge, MA: Harvard University Press, 1988.

Railton, A. *The History of Martha's Vineyard.* Beverly, MA: Commonwealth, 2006.

Rand, Ayn. *Atlas Shrugged.* New York: Dutton Plume, 1957.

Smith, Michael. "The Aztec World of Gary Jennings." In *Novel History: Historians and Novelists Confront America's Past (and Each Other),* edited by Mark C. Carnes, 95–108. New York: Simon and Schuster, 2001.

Supalla, Samuel J. *The Book of Name Signs.* Berkeley: DawnSignPress, 1992.

Van der Haag, Ernest. "Of Happiness and Despair We Have No Measure." In *Mass Culture: The Popular Arts in America,* edited by Bernard Rosenberg and David Manning White, 528–36. New York: Free Press, 1957.

Wertz, Jay. April 14, 2010. *Pop Culture History from Ancient Times to Today,* accessed August 12, 2012, HistoryNet.com.

PART 5

Preserving and Accessing Deaf History

Digital Personal Documents: Preservation Challenges

Marc-André Bernier

Individual and family documents and manuscripts related to Deaf leaders, Deaf individuals, and Deaf families are considered primary archival sources. Social science and humanities researchers use primary archival materials to conduct research to increase knowledge of the lives of individuals and families (Neuman 2006). Clifton F. Carbin (1996) illustrates the use of primary sources to extract information about historical Deaf individuals and families. After all, personal documents and manuscripts often help us to learn about people's activities (Cox 2008; Craven 2008). Traditionally, paper has served as a medium for putting factual and biographical information in writing (e.g., birth certificates, school notes, diplomas, handwritten letters, wills). But with the democratization of the Internet in the 1990s (Ferdinand 2000), Deaf individuals and families have been able to produce and receive numerous "born-digital" personal documents, which have been directly created with a computer or a smartphone. Unlike digitized materials, born-digital documents have no physical counterpart, which makes them more fragile than those in analog format (i.e., on paper). In addition, Web 2.0 technologies now provide new opportunities for Deaf individuals and families to share personal information through social networking websites. However, although these new computer and Internet technologies facilitate online communication and the dissemination of information, they also create challenges for the preservation of digital documents (Craven 2008; Millar 2010). How do we preserve them over time?

Types of Personal Documents

While conducting their everyday activities, Deaf individuals and families produce and receive different kinds of personal documents in both paper and digital formats. The following filing system, which is subdivided into twelve themes, has been proposed by the Bibliothèque et Archives nationales du Québec (2008):

Themes	Examples
history and genealogy	research files; personal journals and agendas
civil status, citizenship, and other official documents	birth, marriage, and death certificates; marriage contracts and common-law union agreements; passports, citizenship certificates; wills and mandates in case of incapacity; health records; driver's license
recreation and travel	subscription agreements and membership cards for sports, cultural, and social activities; entertainment and travel
family and social relations	correspondence; invitations and thank-you notes; obituaries and mourning cards; greeting cards; volunteer work and community involvement
education and training	schoolwork and class notes; educational diplomas and certificates; transcripts of credits; evaluations and reports cards; extracurricular activities; statements of loans and scholarships; alumni directories and school yearbooks
employment	résumés and related documents; work contracts; business cards; lectures and speeches; professional associations; awards and distinctions

Themes	Examples
housing and real estate	leases and lease-modification notices; purchases and sales contracts; tax receipts; invoices for repairs and maintenance; insurance contracts; claims; warranties; plans and architectural drawings
movable goods	purchase contracts; invoices for repairs and maintenance; warranties and certificates of authenticity; rental contracts; insurance contracts; claims; instructions for use; maintenance guides
professional services and service companies	contracts, bills (telephone, cable, Internet, electricity, heating oil, natural gas, etc.), and invoices (medical, dental, optical services; legal and landscaping services, etc.)
income, savings, and investments	income tax returns and related documents; paychecks; employment insurance (salary insurance); old-age security and pension statements; family allowances; deposits and investments; life insurance contracts
loans	mortgages, personal loans, and lines of credit
banking transactions	banking statements; statements of purchases and services paid by credit card; checkbooks and checks

Source: Bibliothèque et Archives nationales du Québec (2008).

Emergence of Personal Computer Technologies

For many centuries most kinds of information have been recorded on paper (Ritzenthaler 2010). Nevertheless, since the early 1980s computer technology has been employed to record digital personal documents. Although the computer was invented in the 1940s, it was not until the 1980s that the first personal computers were introduced in the home (Allan 2001). Moreover, even though the Advanced Research Projects Agency Network project led to the development of the Internet in the late 1960s, the World Wide Web did not become a popular means of communication until the 1990s (Ferdinand 2000). Equally important, with the emergence of Web 2.0 in the early 2000s, individuals and families have been able to interact with

Categories	Examples
social networking websites	MySpace, Facebook, Twitter, Instagram, Google+, LinkedIn, Viadeo, etc.
video-sharing websites	YouTube, Dailymotion, Vimeo, etc.
photo-sharing websites	Flickr, Picasa, Pinterest, etc.
blogs	Blogger (Google), TypePad, WordPress, Tumblr, etc.

others on the Internet and share information via networking websites such as Facebook and YouTube (Theimer 2010). The following table shows different categories of Web 2.0 technologies that are employed mainly for sharing personal information.

In addition to Internet technologies, other communication devices have entered the marketplace: smartphones (ca. 2007) (e.g., Apple iPhone) and tablets (ca. 2010) (e.g., Apple iPad). As a result of technological innovation in computers and the Internet, the growth of digital personal information has been exponential.

Digital Preservation Challenges

Gallaudet University Library Deaf Collections and Archives holds a body of valuable photographs, videotapes, documents, and manuscripts related to the worldwide Deaf community. In order to make these analog materials accessible to a wider audience on the Internet, it is necessary to digitize them. The digitized copies are used only for dissemination; the original materials are kept in the archives. As an example, the papers of Benjamin M. Schowe, Sr. have been digitized and posted on the website of the Washington Research Libraries Consortium.[1] Today, however, Deaf individuals and families directly create emails, word-processed documents, digital photographs and videotapes, and so on in digital format with a computer or a smartphone.

Born-digital documents are primary sources, as are documents in paper format. As such, in the decades to come researchers will need

---

1. http://www.aladin0.wrlc.org/gsdl/collect/schowe/schowe.shtml.

to have access to born-digital documents to conduct research on Deaf individuals and families. Unlike digital media, paper media can be kept in archives for hundreds of years by controlling both the external and internal environments (Ritzenthaler 2010). However, digital documents require different approaches to preservation. The volatility of digital information, the fragility of digital media, the various technological layers, and the obsolescence of computer technologies provide challenges for the safekeeping of such documents.

Volatility

Why are digital documents volatile or unstable? Computer technologies enable users to deliberately or accidentally alter digital information without leaving traces behind (Jones and Beagrie 2001). The concept of authenticity applies not only to paper documents but also to digital ones. *Authenticity* is defined as "the quality of archival documents to bear reliable testimony to the actions, procedures and processes which brought them into being" (Pearce-Moses 2005, 42). Indeed, researchers need to make sure that digital documents are authentic over time; evidence law also requires that digital documents employed as evidence in courts be authentic (Jones and Beagrie 2001). Hence, the authenticity of digital documents must be preserved. In addition, *metadata*—that is, data about data or information about information—provides information, such as provenance, access control, intellectual rights, technical requirements, to ensure the authenticity and the accessibility of digital documents. Metadata can be embedded in a digital document or stored externally, perhaps in a database (National Information Standards Organization 2004).

Fragility

Digital information is stored on magnetic and optical media. However, due to the fragility of both, loss and even destruction of digital information may occur (Jones and Beagrie 2001). For example, magnetic hard drives, on which digital information is stored, may break unexpectedly, leaving information irretrievable, and because CD-ROMs are sensitive to scratches, damaged CDs may become unreadable. "[E]ven under the best storage conditions . . . digital media can be fragile and have limited shelf life" (Commission on Preservation and Access and the Research Libraries Group 1996, 5).

Various Technological Layers

"[D]igital information today is produced in highly varying degrees of dependence on particular hardware and software" (Commission on Preservation and Access and the Research Libraries Group 1996, 5). Unlike documents in analog format, such as paper media, which are directly accessible to human eyes, a variety of technological layers is indispensible to enhance the readability and accessibility of digital files (Jones and Beagrie 2001; Millar 2010). Hardware, operating systems, and software are necessary to open and read digital files. Without these technological layers, it would be impossible to preserve these files. Moreover, in order for users to open digital files, compatible technological layers are essential. For instance, in order to open a Microsoft Office file (DOC), which is processed by a Macintosh computer, three technological layers are required: Microsoft Office software for Macintosh, the OS X operating system (software), and a Macintosh laptop or desk computer (hardware). Because of the different technological layers required to enhance the accessibility and readability of digital files, the preservation of technological layers is complicated. Both the digital files and the requisite hardware, operating system, and software must be preserved (Heslop, Davis, and Wilson 2002).

Technological Obsolescence

The preservation of various technological layers is further complicated by technological obsolescence (Commission on Preservation and Access and the Research Libraries Group 1996; Millar 2010; Heslop, Davis, and Wilson 2002). As mentioned earlier, the technological layers needed to enhance the accessibility and readability of digital files must be preserved. However, because corporations tend to rapidly develop new hardware and software technologies, technology cycles are often short. For example, digital data files stored on a 3.5-inch floppy disk are now difficult to access because few computers today have a disk reader to access this medium. In addition, "a file format may be superseded by newer versions, which may no longer be supported by the current vendor or relevant standards body" (Cornell University Library 2003).

Digital Preservation Approaches

Refreshing

Refreshing is a process consisting of "copying content from one storage medium to another" (Cornell University Library 2000). As digital media are not stable enough to ensure the accessibility of digital data files over time, refreshing is necessary to preserve these files (Millar 2010). For instance, as few current computers have a disk reader that accepts 3.5-inch floppy disks, data from a 3.5-inch floppy disk must be transferred to a current storage device, such as a USB flash drive, without any alteration in the *bitstream* (data structure). As another example, copying all of the pictures in JPG format from an old CD-ROM to a new DVD-ROM is also referred to as refreshing as there is no alteration in the bitstream.

Migration

Migration "is the process of transferring digital information from one hardware and software setting to another or from one computer generation to subsequent generations" (Cornell University Library 2000). When the software on which a data file depends is no longer available, migration is necessary to ensure its accessibility. A data conversion from an out-of-date database to a current Microsoft Access database is an example of migration. In addition, an out-of-date file format can be migrated to a current file format; this is known as *format-based migration* (e.g., a DOC extension-based file [Microsoft] can be converted to a DOCX extension-based file). Unlike refreshing, migration involves an alteration in the bitstream. With regard to technological obsolescence, migration is a way to ensure the accessibility of digital files.

Format Standard

Format standards ensure the preservation of digital files (Heslop, Davis, and Wilson 2002). Proprietary data formats such as PSD (Adobe Photoshop), WMV, and DOC (Microsoft), which are usually maintained by corporations and whose code is protected by intellectual property laws, cannot be shared with the public. In order to open and read files in proprietary formats, one must obtain a license to acquire the appropriate software applications. Corporations may decide for any reason not to support their proprietary software applications and withdraw them from the marketplace; as a result, proprietary data files may no longer be accessible. Therefore, proprietary data formats are not suitable for the long-term preservation and accessibility of digital files. In contrast to proprietary data formats, open data formats, such as JPG, PNG, HTML, and XML, are developed by international standards bodies and include code that is open to anyone. By using open data formats, digital files are more likely to continue to be accessible over time.

Backup

Backup consists of making physical copies of digital data files. The primary purpose of backup is to recover digital data files in the event that they are lost or in cases of corruption (errors in data structure). Because digital media are fragile, it is indispensible to have physical copies of data files. Otherwise, data may be lost forever; the loss of data without backup is irreversible. Refreshing data files can overlap with backup; however, refreshing and backup are different preservation approaches. Refreshing consists of transferring the content from a CD-ROM, for instance, to a DVD-ROM, whereas backup only makes many physical copies of the content stored on the DVD-ROM to make it recoverable in case of emergency.

Conclusion

Individual and family documents in both paper and digital formats are primary sources for researchers who wish to study the life stories of Deaf individuals and families. Due to advances in personal computer technologies over the last three decades, documents are changing to digital forms, thereby creating challenges in the preservation of born-digital personal documents. The volatility of digital information, the fragility of digital media, technological layers, and the obsolescence of computer technologies are among the challenges to preservation. To ensure the accessibility of born-digital personal documents, different approaches are being utilized. Admittedly, no perfect preservation approaches are currently available, but by using a combination of methods, born-digital personal documents can be preserved from generation to generation. In summary, how will you ensure the accessibility of your digital documents? Will you help the Deaf community of the future to understand who we are in the present day?

References

Allan, Roy A. *A History of the Personal Computer: The People and the Technology.* London, ON: Allan, 2001.

Bibliothèque et Archives nationales du Québec. *Safely Stored but Not Forgotten: A Guide to Conserving Your Personal and Family Documents.* Montreal, QC: Bibliothèque et Archives nationales du Québec, 2008.

Carbin, Clifton F. *Deaf Heritage in Canada: A Distinctive, Diverse, and Enduring Culture,* edited by Dorothy L. Smith. Toronto: McGraw-Hill Ryerson, 1996.

Commission on Preservation and Access and the Research Libraries Group. 1996. *Preserving Digital Information: Report of the Task Force on Archiving of Digital Information,* accessed August 17, 2012, www.clir.org/pubs/reports/pub63watersgarrett.pdf.

Cornell University Library. 2000. *Moving Theory into Practice: Digital Imaging Tutorial,* accessed August 10, 2012, http://www.library.cornell.edu/preservation/tutorial/preservation/preservation-03.html.

———. 2003. *Digital Preservation Management: Implementing Short-Term Strategies for Long-Term Problems,* accessed August 10, 2012, http://www.dpworkshop.org/dpm-eng/oldmedia/index.html.

Cox, Richard J. *Personal Archives and a New Archival Calling: Readings, Reflections and Ruminations.* Duluth, MN: Litwin Books, 2008.

Craven, Louise, ed. *What Are Archives? Cultural and Theoretical Perspectives: A Reader.* Aldershot, Hampshire, UK: Ashgate, 2008.

Ferdinand, Peter. "The Internet, Democracy and Democratization." *Democratization* 7, no. 1 (2000): 1–17.

Heslop, Helen, Simon Davis, and Andrew Wilson. (December 2002). *An Approach to the Preservation of Digital Records*. Canberra: National Archives of Australia. Accessed August 17, 2012, www.naa.gov.au/Images/An-approach-Green-Paper_tcm16-47161.pdf.

Jones, Maggie, and Neil Beagrie. *Preservation Management of Digital Materials: A Handbook*. London: British Library, 2001.

Millar, Laura A. *Archives: Principles and Practices*. London: Facet, 2010.

National Information Standards Organization. 2004. *Understanding Metadata*, accessed August 5, 2012, http://www.niso.org/publications/press/UnderstandingMetadata.pdf.

Neuman, W. Lawrence. *Social Research Methods: Qualitative and Quantitative Approaches*, 6th ed. Boston: Pearson, 2006.

Pearce-Moses, Richard. *A Glossary of Archival and Records Terminology*. Chicago: Society of American Archivists, 2005.

Ritzenthaler, Mary Lynn. *Preserving Archives and Manuscripts*. Chicago: Society of American Archivists, 2010.

Theimer, Kate. *Web 2.0 Tools and Strategies for Archives and Local History Collections*. New York: Neal-Schuman, 2010.

Finding Hidden Treasures: Research Help in the Library and Archives

Diana Moore and Joan Naturale

At the 2009 Deaf History International Conference, Ulf Hedberg spoke on the preservation of Deaf materials.[1] The objective was to promote the preservation of Deaf materials by individuals, institutions, and organizations and to encourage the donation of Deaf materials to libraries, archives, museums, or organizations. In this chapter our objective is to identify the numerous resources at the Gallaudet University Library Deaf Collections and Archives and the Rochester Institute of Technology's (RIT) Wallace Library, which are now on the Internet. The resources discussed here contain biographical materials that relate to this book's theme of telling Deaf lives. Since the year 2012, when the Eighth Deaf History International conference was hosted, was the three-hundredth anniversary of the Abbé de l'Épée's birth, several de l'Épée resources are identified. Many of the materials mentioned from the Gallaudet University Library Deaf Collections and Archives were made accessible online thanks to a generous grant from the Mellon Foundation.

Founded in 1967, the Gallaudet University Library Deaf Collections and Archives has the world's largest collection of materials related to the institute and the global Deaf community. It strives to collaborate with other repositories as well. Founded in 2006, the Rochester Institute of Technology and National Technical Institute for the Deaf's (RIT/NTID) Deaf Studies Archives focuses on collections and topics related to NTID at RIT and the Rochester community in New York State.

Deaf Rare Book Collection at Gallaudet

The Deaf Rare Book Collection contains publications dating from 1546; the materials cover various topics and languages from different countries. About 180 titles were selected to be scanned and digitized and are now available online in two databases. The first is the Gallaudet University Library Catalog, also known as ALADIN Catalog (http://www.gallaudet .edu/library.html), and the second is the Internet Archive (http://archive .org). An example of one title available online is *The Abbé de l'Épée, Charles-Michel de l'Épée, Founder of the Manual Instruction of the Deaf, and Other Early Teachers of the Deaf.*[2] Although the de l'Épée text is available at two online sources, the features of each are different. The ALADIN Catalog and the Internet Archive have a tagging feature and search box, which make searching easier. Another important resource available from Internet Archives is the *Deaf Mutes' Journal* (1874–1901). Issues from 1902 to 1938 will be added later to complete the series.

NTID Connection

Jeanne Behm, the coordinator of RIT's ASL and Deaf Studies Community Center (RADSCC) (http://www.rit.edu/ntid/radscc/), who was charged with hosting a celebration of de l'Épée's birth, asked us whether a play had been written about de l'Épée. After searching the Internet Archive, a play called *Deaf and Dumb or the Abbé de l'Épée; an Historical Drama, Founded upon Very Interesting Facts: From the French of M. Bouilly* was found and adapted for the celebration (http://ia701206.us.archive.org/10/items/gu_ deafdumbabbed00boui/gu_deafdumbabbed00boui.pdf). This play focuses

FIGURE 1. A Lesson with Abbé Charles Michel de l'Épée, *painted by Nachor Ginouvier, after a draft by Frédéric Peysson, 1891. Collection Institut National des Jeunes Sourds, Paris.*

on de l'Épée and the abandoned Count of Solar, Theodore (Joseph), a Deaf orphan who was brought to the school. The story tells how the Count finds his childhood home and dramatizes the court case to regain his lost title. The play also shows de l'Épée's incorporation of sign language in his teaching. This play was one of the first to include a signing Deaf character.[3]

The story is famously depicted in an innovative painting by Marie-Pierre Nicolas Ponce-Camus that shows the Count and de l'Épée at the Count's family home (figure 2). When Joseph recognizes his home, de l'Épée uses

FIGURE 2. *Marie-Pierre Nicolas Ponce-Camus, L'Abbé de l'Épée. Taken from the* Causes Célèbres, *1802 (Institut National des Jeunes Sourds, Paris).*

FIGURE 3. *De l'Épée sculpture by Eugene Hannan. Photgraph by Francis C. Higgins, Gallaudet University Historical Photograph Collection, Gallaudet University Library Deaf Collections and Archives, Washington, DC. http://dspace.wrlc.org/ view/ImgViewer?img=2&url=http://dspace.wrlc.org/doc/mainfest/2041/72566.*

a methodical sign for "heaven," pointing upward to the sky, and the Count, using a natural gesture, clasps de l'Épée's hand over his heart. This painting is an important work in the genre of historical art because of the depiction of sign language.[4] Because he was unable to travel himself, de l'Épée provided traveling companions for the Count when he went searching for his home.[5] The play was popular and was staged all over Europe and the United States to raise financial support for Deaf schools. Laurent Clerc, who wrote the preface to the play, had it performed in Hartford, Connecticut, to help raise funds for the American School for the Deaf.[6] After reviewing materials on this famous teacher, the de l'Épée committee decided to host a dinner-theater event.

Gallaudet Video Catalog

Many Gallaudet University film productions are online, as are other films such as those in the George W. Veditz Collection, produced by the National Association of the Deaf (NAD). Additional films in other formats have been preserved and digitized and can be viewed in the video catalog (http://videocatalog.gallaudet.edu). One may search among various categories, including alumni, biographies, Davila (president),

Deaf mosaic, and Deaf sports. Films of American and international guest lecturers and visitors are also included. All films are signed or have open captions. One such title is *A Plea for a Statue in Honor of Abbé Charles Michel de l'Épée* (http://videocatalog.gallaudet.edu/?id=2518).

NTID Connection

Saint Mary's School for the Deaf in Buffalo, New York, is the only site in the United States that has a statue of de l'Épée.[7] The film *A Plea for a Statue in Honor of Abbé Charles Michel de l'Épee* led to a request for proposals from sculptors, and Eugene Hannan (an alumnus of Saint Mary's School for the Deaf and Gallaudet University) was appointed to produce this sculpture. Since Saint Mary's is near NTID, trips to view the historic statue were planned during the International Week of the Deaf, which takes place in the last week of September. The RADSCC also planned to display a collection of papers compiled by Bernard Bragg when he was a Gallaudet student. The papers showed the development of the NAD statue project, proposals by sculptors, letters, and sketches. These documents are all from the Gallaudet University Library Deaf Collections and Archives.[8]

The de l'Épée committee asked whether there were any films about de l'Épée. Through international contacts, two important films were found based on the play *Abbé de l'Épée; an Historical Drama*. One is a British Broadcasting Corporation (BBC) film titled *The Count of Solar* (figure 5) (http://vimeo.com/39223648), and the other is *L'Enfant du Secret* (http://ph.bourdais.pagesperso-orange.fr/), a French film (figure 4). Both adaptations present different perspectives on the story, as there were several variations of the play in existence.[9] The BBC film shows the sister's denial of knowing her brother in court and incorporates the use of British Sign

FIGURE 4. *Photograph of characters (students and de l'Épée) in the film* L'Enfant du Secret. *Acbard and Privat (2007).*

FIGURE 5. Count of Solar. *Vimeo. Video file, 12:47. Posted by Tony Bloem, 2012. Accessed September 4, 2012. http://vimeo.com/39223648. Screen capture scene from the film clip.*

Language. All of the students in this film are boys. The French film shows the Deaf boy's mother denying knowledge of her son in court and illustrates the use of Langue des Signes Française (LSF). The students are a mixed group of boys and girls.

Other video sources are YouTube videos posted by Charles Katz and Bernard Truffaut on French Deaf history: http://infoguides.rit.edu/lepee. These videos introduce background information about de l'Épée and other influential historic figures from this era.

WRLC Libraries Digital and Special Collections

At the website http://aladin.wrlc.org/dl/ scroll down to "Gallaudet University Archives and Library," where you will find the following resources: Gallaudet University Historical Photograph Collection; *American Annals of the Deaf* (1847–1893); Gallaudet University alumni cards; and the *Silent Worker* (complete holdings, 1888–1929).

NTID Connection

To prepare background information for the de l'Épée committee, research was conducted using archived material from the *American Annals of the Deaf* and the *Silent Worker*. Articles about de l'Épée and French Deaf people were found and linked on the research guide. In 1834 the Deaf-Mute banquet began celebrating de l'Épée's birth anniversary.[10] The Parisian Deaf community organized these annual formal dinners to celebrate Deaf culture, sign language, and the achievements of Deaf leaders. This led to discussions about hosting a Deaf-Mute banquet at NTID. An interesting *American Annals of the Deaf* article about the Anniversary Festival of Deaf-Mutes in Paris can be accessed at http://dspace.wrlc.org/doc/bitstream/2041/56331/AADDvol09no3display.pdf#page=3. Readers can also learn about the first Deaf museum in a *Silent Worker* article titled "The World Museum of the Deaf in the National Institution at Paris" by Kelly H. Stevens: http://dspace.wrlc.org/view/ImgViewer?url=http://dspace.wrlc.org/doc/manifest/2041/40204.

Additional Resources

The Deaf Research Guide at Gallaudet (http://libguides.gallaudet.edu/deaf-research), the Gallaudet University Guide to Deaf Biographies (http://liblists.wrlc.org/deafbiog/), and the Gallaudet University Index to Deaf Periodicals (http://liblists.wrlc.org/gadpi/) assist researchers in finding biographical and other Deaf resources and information.

NTID Connection

Information about Deaf and influential hearing persons from France was found in the Gallaudet University Guide to Deaf Biographies database and assisted the de l'Épée committee in selecting live characters for their Deaf-Mute banquet. While dinner was served, these characters visited each table and explained their significance in Deaf history. Some examples of the characters involved were Ferdinand Berthier, founder of the Deaf-Mute banquets; Laurent Clerc, the first known Deaf teacher in the United States; Jean Massieu, the first Deaf teacher at the Institut National de Jeunes Sourds de Paris; Pierre Desloges, a Deaf writer who published the first book in defense of sign language; Émile Mercier, a Deaf winemaker from Champagne; Theodore, Count of Solar, the Deaf orphan; Frédéric Peysson, a Deaf artist who painted *Last Moments of the Abbé de l'Épée*; and Marie Pierre Pelissier, who was a Deaf teacher and writer at the

Institut National de Jeunes Sourds de Paris. At the end of the banquet, the English-translated French *Art Pi* (http://www.art-pi.fr/public/page/) special issue magazine on Abbe de l'Epee (https://www.dropbox.com/s/69rkc0v2nwwjtj6/artpi.pdf) was handed out to the participants.

LibGuides

Some examples of LibGuides are as follows:

- Gallaudet University Library: http://libguides.gallaudet.edu/searchtags.php?iid=642&gid=0&tag=research%20guide
- Rochester Institute of Technology's Wallace Library: http://infoguides.rit.edu/

LibGuides are resources that lead the researcher to information on various topics, such as de l'Épée and Deaf culture. These guides also sometimes identify specific materials in various formats. LibGuides are updated, and new topics are added regularly. One of RIT's LibGuides is about de l'Épée: http://infoguides.rit.edu/lepee. This LibGuide includes links to many of Gallaudet's online journals, books, and video resources and is freely accessible for curriculum planning. Several recommended books present biographical sketches. Others discuss French Deaf history, such as the prevalence of Deaf artists and sculptors in France. De l'Épée believed in training Deaf teachers who would establish Deaf schools around the world. These Deaf teachers brought LSF with them, which influenced the development of sign language in the countries they visited. In this LibGuide, the section on "Sign Languages in Different Countries" will assist those who are researching the historical roots of LSF. In addition, the LibGuide includes French Deaf poets, writers, educators, scientists, artists, and sculptors.

Genealogical Resources at Gallaudet University Deaf Library Collections and Archives

Alumni cards from 1866 to 1961, faculty/staff cards from 1910 to 1944, the Fay Marriage Index, Pennsylvania School for the Deaf applications from 1824 to 1938, and vital records are available in the collection at https://www.gallaudet.edu/library_deaf_collections_and_archives/ genealogy_resources.html. Vital records, an index found in many Deaf periodicals from 1847 to 2001, assists in locating dates of Deaf people's births, marriages, and deaths.

Art Print Resources at Rochester Institute of Technology/ NTID History and Deaf Studies Archives

The Deaf Studies Archives at RIT/NTID (http://library.rit.edu/depts/ archives/ritntid-deaf-studies-archive) collects original artwork and prints by Deaf artists. The de l'Épée committee looked for prints, which were shown during the dinner theater production of the Deaf-Mute banquets. Prints by Deaf artist Nachor Ginouvier, Frédéric Peysson's *A Lesson with Abbé Charles Michel de l'Épée* (figure 1), and *Abbé Roch-Ambroise Cucurron Sicard* (figure 6) by Deaf artist Jerome-Martin Langlois were ordered for the celebration. Biographical sketches of these artists can be found in the online de l'Épée library guide at http:// infoguides.rit.edu/content.php?pid=300927&sid=2513431.

The significance of de l'Épée's work lies in his recognition of the value of sign language in Deaf children's education, which is exemplified in toasts signed at the Deaf-Mute banquets with this common theme: "Before him, we were nothing; we were pariahs, plunged into chaos and ignorance, marginal and ignored; now we exist; we have been restored to society."[11]

FIGURE 6. Abbé Roch-Ambroise Cucurron Sicard *by Deaf artist Jerome-Martin Langlois (Deaf teacher Massieu is in the back with his hand on the board).*

FIGURE 7. *From the Deaf Studies Archives, a de l'Épée platter that was designed by a De'VIA artist, Ellen Mansfield, was on display for the celebration of de l'Épée's birth.*

Sidebars

The following quotes are by Pierre Desloges, the first Deaf author to write in defense of sign language—in 1779. These quotes were translated by Lisanne Houkes from the Dutch DVD script for *The Man, the City, and the Book:*[12]

> Sign language is visual. Your hands paint feelings in the sky, like fine brush strokes of a pencil, soft colors or big movements, with clear speaking colors.

> The things that reach our mind through the ear have to reach the Deaf through the eye. What cannot go through a door has to go through a window.

Notes

1. Hedberg and Gates, "No History, No Future," 92.
2. Holycross (1913).
3. "Literature, Dramatic Characters in," 161.
4. Mirzoeff, "Signs and Citizens: Sign Language and Visual Sign in the French Revolution," 281–82.
5. "Scene from the Drama of 'The Abbé de l'Épée,' " 74–75.
6. "Literature, Dramatic Characters in," 162.

7. *St. Mary's School for the Deaf: de l'Épée Memorial Statue.*
8. Bragg, *NAD on the History of the Abbé de l'Épée Statue.*
9. "Literature, Dramatic Characters in," 161.
10. Mottez, "Deaf-Mute Banquet and the Birth of the Deaf Movement," 31.
11. Ibid., 36.
12. *De Man, de Stad, en het Boek: Een Monoloog Voor Drie Mannen.*

Bibliography

Acbard, J., and B. Privat. Photograph of characters (students and de l'Épée) in the film *L'Enfant du Secret.* January 2007. Accessed September 2, 2012, http://ph.bourdais.pagesperso-orange.fr/.

Bernard, Y. "Silent Artists." In *Looking Back: A Reader on the History of Deaf Communities and Their Sign Languages,* edited by R. Fischer and H. Lane, 75–87. Vol. 20, *International Studies on Sign Language and Communication of the Deaf.* Hamburg: Signum, 1993.

Bragg, B. *NAD and the History of the Abbé de l'Épée Statue.* Gallaudet University Deaf Collections and Archives, Washington, DC, 1950.

De Man, de Stad, en het Boek: Een Monoloog Voor Drie Mannen. Directed by M. Julien. Amsterdam: Handtheater, 1997.

Hedberg, U., and D. Gates. "No History, No Future: Preserving and Archiving History." In *No History, No Future: Proceedings of the Seventh DHI Conference, Stockholm, 2009,* edited by Tomas Hedberg, 92–97. Örebro: Swedish Deaf History Society, 2011.

Holycross, E. I. *The Abbé de l'Épée, Charles-Michel de l'Épée, Founder of the Manual Instruction of the Deaf, and Other Early Teachers of the Deaf.* Columbus, OH: Holycross, 1913.

"Literature, Dramatic Characters in." In *Gallaudet Encyclopedia of Deaf People and Deafness,* edited by J. V. Van Cleve, 161–62. Vol. 2. New York: McGraw-Hill Professional, 1987.

Mirzoeff, N. "Signs and Citizens." In *Silent Poetry: Deafness, Sign, and Visual Culture in Modern France,* 48–89. Princeton, NJ: Princeton University Press, 1995.

———. "Signs and Citizens: Sign Language and Visual Sign in the French Revolution." In *The Consumption of Culture 1600–1800: Image, Object, Text,* edited by Ann Bermingham and John Brewer, 281–93. New York: Routledge, 1995.

Mottez, B. "The Deaf-Mute Banquet and the Birth of the Deaf Movement." In *Deaf History Unveiled: Interpretations from the New Scholarship,* edited by J. V. Van Cleve, 27–39. Washington, DC: Gallaudet University Press, 1993.

"Scene from the Drama of 'The Abbé de l'Épée.' " *American Annals of the Deaf* 2, no. 2 (1849): 74–77. Accessed September 2, 2012, http://dspace.wrlc.org/doc/bitstream/2041/59632/AADDvol02no2display.pdf#page=10.

St. Mary's School for the Deaf: de l'Épée Memorial Statue. Photograph. Gallaudet University Historical Photograph Collection. September 18, 2009. Accessed September 2, 2012, http://dspace.wrlc.org/view/ImgViewer?img=2&url=http://dspace.wrlc.org/doc/manifest/2041/72566.

CONTRIBUTORS

Melissa Anderson
Freelance Auslan Consultant/Deaf
  Educator
Aurora School Early Intervention—
  West
Melbourne, Victoria, Australia

Marc-André Bernier
Librarian
Bibliothèque Le Prévost
Ville de Montréal, Québec, Canada

Veronica Bickle
Author
Toronto, Ontario, Canada

Clifton F. Carbin
Deaf Freelance Researcher and
  Writer
Burlington, Ontario, Canada

Breda Carty
Conjoint Lecturer

RIDBC Renwick Centre
University of Newcastle
Sydney, NSW, Australia

Julie Chateauvert
PhD Études et Pratiques des Arts
Montréal, Québec, Canada

Tatiana Davidenko
Moscow Centre for Deaf Studies
  and Bilingual Education
Moscow, Russia

Newby Ely
Freelance Historian
Oreland, PA

Albert J. Hlibok
Freelance Writer, Researcher,
  and Historian
New York, NY

Peter Jackson
Chief Executive Officer

British Deaf History Society
Warrington, England, United
  Kingdom

Christopher A. N. Kurz
Associate Professor
Master of Science in Secondary
  Education
National Technical Institute for
  the Deaf at Rochester Institute
  of Technology Rochester, NY

Harry Lang
Professor Emeritus
National Institute for the Deaf
Rochester Institute of Technology
Rochester, NY

Jannelle Legg
Digital History Fellow
Department of History and Art
  History
George Mason University
Fairfax, VA

Patricia Levitzke-Gray
Independent Scholar
Perth, WA, Australia

Susannah Macready
Independent Scholar
Sydney, Australia

Tony L. McGregor
Artist
Austin, TX

Diana Moore
Librarian (retired)
Gallaudet University
Washington, DC

Joseph J. Murray
ASL and Deaf Studies
  Department

Gallaudet University
Washington, DC

Joan Naturale
Reference Librarian
National Institute for the Deaf
Rochester Institute of Technology
Rochester, NY

Victor Palenny
Historian
Department of Social Policy
  and Rehabilitation
All-Russian Society of the Deaf
Moscow, Russia

Bob Paul
Professor
Languages Department
Harper College
Palatine, IL

Jennifer Paul
Author
Palatine, IL

Drew Robarge
Museum Technician
Department of Medicine and Science
National Museum of American
  History
Smithsonian Institution
Washington, DC

Kim A. Silva
Coordinator, Amistad Tours for The
  Farmington Historical Society
Board Member, Connecticut
  Freedom Trail
Hartford, CT

Anita Small
Founder
small Language Connections
Ontario, Canada

Kristin Snoddon
Assistant Professor
School of Linguistics and Language
  Studies
Carleton University
Ottawa, ON, Canada

Akio Suemori
Chief Researcher
National Institute of Advanced
  Industrial Science and Technology
  (AIST)
Tsukuba, Japan

Tomasz Świderski
President

Historical Institute of the Deaf
  "Surdus Historicus"
Warsaw, Poland

Ulla-Bell Thorin
Author
Lindome, Sweden

Darlene Thornton
Freelance Auslan Consultant
Sydney, Australia

Theara Yim
Secondary Teacher, Lucien-Pagé
  High School
Montréal, Québec, Canada

INDEX

Figures and illustrations are indicated by italicized page numbers, and tables are indicated by "t" following page numbers.

3